THE WEDDING PRESENT

For Dave, Seanin, Nick
and Catherine who always says
'Everything is precious to me.'

The Wedding Present
Domestic Life Beyond Consumption

161101

LOUISE PURBRICK
University of Brighton, UK

ASHGATE

Published by
Ashgate Publishing Limited
Gower House
Croft Road
Aldershot
Hampshire GU11 3HR
England

Ashgate Publishing Company
Suite 420
101 Cherry Street
Burlington, VT 05401-4405
USA

Ashgate website: http://www.ashgate.com

British Library Cataloguing in Publication Data
Purbrick, Louise
    The wedding present : domestic life beyond consumption
    1. Marriage customs and rites - Great Britain - History -
    20th century ? Gifts - Great Britain - History - 20th
    century. 3. Consumption (Economics) - Social aspects - Great
    Britain
    I. Title
    392.5'0941'09045

Library of Congress Cataloging-in-Publication Data
Purbrick, Louise.
    The wedding present : domestic life beyond consumption / by Louise Purbrick.
      p. cm.
    Includes bibliographical references and index.
    ISBN-13: 978-0-7546-4472-9
    ISBN-10: 0-7546-4472-3
  1. Marriage customs and rites--Great Britain. 2. Gifts--Economic aspects--Great Britain. 3. Economic anthropology--Great Britain. 4. Households--Great Britain. 5. Consumption (Economics)--Great Britain. 6. Great Britain--Economic conditions. 7. Great Britain--Social life and customs. I. Title.

    GT2743.P87 2006
    392.5--dc22

    2006013185

ISBN-13: 978-0-7546-4472-9
ISBN-10: 0-7546-4472-3

Printed and bound in Great Britain by Antony Rowe Ltd, Chippenham, Wiltshire.

Contents

List of Figures

Acknowledgements

I would like to acknowledge the support of the Arts and Humanities Research Council. A Research Leave Scheme Award in the academic year 2002–2003 enabled me to complete this book. My work on marriage gifts and everyday domesticity began some five years earlier while I was working Manchester Metropolitan University and I am very grateful for the support received from the History of Art and Design Department Research Committee and for the encouragement of my colleagues, especially, Jim Aulich, Fionna Barber, Diana Donald, Simon Faulkner, John Hewitt and John Taylor. I would also like to thank Marica Pointon, who invited me to give a paper at Anglo-German Feminist Art Historians symposia devoted to ideas of 'home', which helped, at an early stage of the project, develop my thinking about the gift as a material representation of social relationships.

Over the last seven or so years, I have discussed the possession of wedding presents with many people, formally in seminars and conferences but also in an everyday way, in snatched conversations along corridors, standing in office doorways and by the photocopier. Those I have worked with in the School of Historical Studies and Faculty of Arts and Architecture at the University of Brighton deserve many thanks. I have benefited greatly from discussions with Gill Scott, Sarah Cheang, David Green, with Paul Jobling, Lou Taylor and students on the MA Design History and Material Culture. The Gender and Built Space research group, coordinated by Elizabeth Darling and Lesley Whitworth provided an important forum for work such as mine. Lesley, as an editor of the 'Anxious Homes' Special Issue of *Journal of Design History* 16.3, gave me an opportunity to publish an formative account of marriage gifts and domestic consumption. The generous comments of the readers and reviewers of that article and, later, the proposal for a book helped sharpen my focus. I am especially grateful to Judy Attfield for her sustained, critical interest in my work.

I must thank Jill Seddon for her careful reading of early chapters on giving as an act of approval and on the practice of making lists as well as Jonathan Woodham and Paddy Maguire for their support as this research finally developed into a book. Monica Brewis' help has been invaluable. She painstakingly proof-read the whole work and guided my selection of images. Very kindly, Ray Leaning turned my jpegs into publishable images. Mel Searle, Donna Robson, Mike Hill and Amira Driscoll have patiently provided much needed technical support.

This book is based on a Mass-Observation 'directive' of Autumn 1998, entitled Giving and Receiving Presents. All this material is copyright ©The Trustees of the Mass-Observation Archive and is reproduced with permission of the Trustees of the

The Wedding Present

Mass-Observation Archive. I would like to thank them and especially those who work in the Archive. I am indebted to Dorothy Sheridan, Director of the Contemporary Mass-Observation Project, for taking up an investigation of gift exchanges upon marriage within the Contemporary Mass-Observation Project as well as for expertise of Joy Entwhistle and Judy Pickering who managed the material generated by the Giving and Receiving Presents directive over the many years I was reading and re-reading it. Sandra Koa-Wing, Simon Homer and Karen Watson have been of great help in final stages of preparing Mass-Observation material for publication. Above all, I would like to thank the Mass-Observation correspondents who replied to the directive and generously shared the details of their wedding presents and everyday lives as they did so.

Introduction

Making Homes and Worlds: Marriage and Consumption from 1945 to Today

'The world, in truth, is a wedding' (Erving Goffman, 1959).[1]

Introduction

The Wedding Present is a study of exchange relationships and acts of possession. It traces the transaction of domestic objects, examining how women and men accept and create material and social worlds. A recurring set of practices make and maintain domestic environments: buying, giving, using and keeping objects. The deployment of these practices in Britain since 1945 is the specific subject of this book. It offers an account of domestic consumption.

The home is the key site of consumption in capitalist culture. It is also a social space, the place where the most enduring relationships are routinely enacted. It is the destination of almost all commodities because it is where most people live and thus the place where their possessions are stored, preserved, displayed and used. But home is not simply the place where consumption happens to occur. Homes are created through consumption, as Stevi Jackson and Shaun Moores point out:

> Practices of consumption are one of the key ways in which home is culturally produced and sustained. Houses and apartments, whether owned or rented, are transformed into homes and made habitable largely via an appropriation and display of consumer goods.[2]

In other words, the meanings of home are created, sustained or changed through consumption. The concentrated materiality that characterizes homes has routinely powerful effects. Homes can envelop their regular or transitory inhabitants so that they become reluctant to leave or can make either feel so ill at ease that the cold

---

1   Erving Goffman, *The Presentation of Self in Everyday Life* (London: Penguin, 1990) p. 45.

2   Stevi Jackson and Shaun Moores, 'Introduction,' *The Politics of Domestic Consumption: Critical Readings,* ed. Stevi Jackson and Shaun Moores (London: Harvester Wheatsheaf 1995) p. 13. See also Suzanne Reimer and Deborah Leslie, 'Identity, Consumption and the Home,' *Homes Cultures* 1. 2 (2004) p. 192 and for an overview of the meanings of home, see Peter Corrigan, *The Sociology of Consumption* (London: Sage, 1997) pp. 96–114.

of outside air of the street is a real relief. The forms of a home, the objects placed in the foreground or put in the background, the things that are displayed or stored, their constituent material, their surface pattern, their age and the details of their arrangement, all present particular versions of how everyday life should be lived. Homes embody ideas and are our everyday realities.[3]

As Jackson and Moores point out, every home, whether single person dwelling or multiple occupancy, is a site of consumption. This book, however, examines the dominant idea and embodiment of home: the family household. The composition of the family household has never been constant. The size of families and the types of relationships that constitute them vary across time as well as within communities at any one time.[4] It is not uncommon to belong to two families at the same time and to establish two or more families over one lifetime. Whatever the variations, the involvement of the family in consumption has remained remarkably constant. As Christine Delphy rather wearily pointed out in 1984:

> If there is one universally recognised function of the family, it is 'consumption'. It would be tedious to list all the books and articles which mention this, because there is no sociologist, and more generally, no author dealing with the family, who does not at least allude to it.[5]

The Wedding Present examines the moment when many homes and families are established. Of those practices used to make and maintain family homes, it focuses upon gift exchanges, detailing the rituals of giving and receiving objects upon marriage in Britain between 1945 and the first few years of the twenty-first century. Getting married is the most significant stage in the process of setting up home over this period as a whole. Even since the mid-1970s when families are frequently established without marriage and co-habitation (at least its dominant heterosexual form) has become a widely accepted practice, marriage remains popular. Cohabitation tends to be the 'prelude' to marriage rather than its replacement.[6] Marriage is now

---

3 Tim Putnam, 'Introduction: Design, Consumption and Domestic Ideals,' *Household Choices,* ed. Tim Putnam and Charles Newton (Futures Publications and Middlesex Polytechnic, 1990) p. 7.

4 Leonore Davidoff et al, *The Family Story: Blood, Contract and Intimacy 1830–1960* (London: Longman, 1999) pp. 101–143 and pp. 185–220; Jane Lewis, *Women in Britain since 1945: Women, Family, Work and the State in the Post-War Years* (Oxford: Blackwell, 1992) pp. 11–39.

5 Christine Delphy, *Close to Home: A Materialist Analysis of Women's Oppression* (London: Hutchinson, 1984) p. 40.

6 Kathleen E. Kiernan and Valerie Estaugh, *Cohabitation: Extra-marital Childbearing and Social Policy*, (London: Family Policy Studies Centre, 1993) p. 5; Carol Smart and Pippa Stevens, *Cohabitation Breakdown* (London: Family Policy Studies Centre for the Joseph Rowntree Foundation, 2000) pp. 15–18. Although marriage is usually held up as the dominant tradition against which being single and cohabiting is considered the newer alternative, Susan McRae in *Cohabiting Mothers: Changing Marriage and Motherhood?* (London: Policy Studies Institute, 1993) argues 'it may be the single-earner, high fertility family of the 1950s – against which both lone parents and cohabiting couples are often measured and found wanting – which is at odds with history' p. 8.

an affirmation of the permanence of a family household as well as an announcement of the existence of a significant sexual, social and economic relationship and the establishment of its legal status. Thus, long-term cohabitation is relatively rare. John Ermisch and Marco Francesconi's 1998 study based on the General Household Survey has found that cohabiting unions 'last only a short time before being converted into marriage or dissolving: their median length is about 2 years.'[7] Patricia Morgan also emphasizes the 'fragile and transitory state' of cohabitations but observes that they have become 'less likely to lead to marriage – and thus more likely to be a prelude to separation.'[8] Furthermore, the statistical trend emerging from the 2002 General Household Survey is of increased cohabiting by single, non-married and divorced women aged between 18 and 49.[9] Thus *The Wedding Present* is a study of married household as the dominant ideal of the permanent home written at a moment when homes are becoming more temporary. Homes premised upon cohabitation, marriage, a mix of both over time, are being continually created and, it seems, increasingly frequently dismantled and then re-created in, usually, a very similar form.

Marriage and its alternatives are a long established focus of sociological and historical enquiry.[10] Interest in the wedding itself, the preparations for the day of getting married and the performances of that day, is a recent addition to scholarship on the meanings of marriage, prompted by the global expansion of the wedding industry. Works by Sharon Boden, Chrys Ingraham, Cele Otnes and Elizabeth Pleck all examine, albeit in quite different ways, the cultivation of desire for the perfect wedding day and the bride, in particular, as a consumer of wedding images and objects.[11] I hope that my book will make some contribution to the analysis of the wedding within its larger project of investigating domestic consumption. The continued popularity of getting married when marriage is regarded as old-fashioned

---

7   John Ermisch and Marco Francesconi, *Cohabitation in Great Britain: Not for Long, but Here to Stay* (Colchester: Institute for Social and Economic Research, University of Essex, 1998).

8   Patricia Morgan, *Marriage-Lite: The Rise of Cohabitation and its Consequences* (London: Institute for the Study of Civil Society, 2000) p. 14.

9   Office for National Statistics, *Living in Britain: 2002 General Household* (London: The Stationary Office, 2004) <http://www.statistics.gov.uk/cci/nugget.asp?id=824>.

10   Diana Leonard Barker and Sheila Allen, ed. *Dependence and Exploitation in Work and Marriage* (London: Longman, 1976); John R. Gillis, *For Better, For Worse: British Marriages, 1600 to the Present* (Oxford: Oxford University Press, 1985); Aafke Komter 'Hidden Power in Marriage' *Self and Society*, ed. Ann Branaman (Malden, MA: Blackwell, 2001) pp. 359–380; Penny Mansfield and Jean Collard, *The Beginning of the Rest of Your Life* (Basingstoke: Macmillan, 1988); Patricia Morgan, *Farewell to the Family? Public Policy and Family Breakdown in Britain and the USA* (London: The IEA Health and Welfare Unit, 1995); Lawrence Stone, *Road to Divorce. England 1530–1987* (Oxford: Oxford University Press, 1990).

11   Sharon Boden, *Consumerism, Romance and the Wedding Experience* (Basingstoke: Palgrave Macmillan, 2003); Chrys Ingraham, *White Weddings: Romancing Heterosexuality in Popular Culture* (London: Routledge, 1999); Cele Otnes and Elizabeth H. Pleck, *Cinderella Dreams: The Allure of the Lavish Wedding* (Berkeley: University of California Press, 2003).

and cohabitation is equally as socially acceptable ought to make it an interesting case study in the practice of consumption. To get married is knowingly to perform a tradition. The study of marriage and consumption can therefore demonstrate the intersections, the connections and conflicts between the practices of everyday life, the rituals that punctuate and dramatize it, and the dynamics of consumer capitalism.

An Archive of Everyday Life

The exchanges that occur within the domestic sphere are harder to trace than other consumption transactions such as the act of purchase, which is usually a computerized operation, automatically recorded for use within the retailing industry (and then analysed sometime later by academics). Selling and buying is the only moment in the consumption of an object about which information is systematically stored while those who seek to interpret practices such as giving and using are also often involved in the processes of recording them. This is the case here.

My investigation of wedding presents is based upon responses to a Mass-Observation 'directive' entitled Giving and Receiving Presents collected in Autumn 1998.[12] Mass-Observation was founded in 1937; its name summarizes the social commitment of its founders, Tom Harrisson, Charles Madge and Humphrey Jennings to the investigation of what would now be called everyday life in modern industrial society. Indeed, Ben Highmore locates Mass-Observation within the study of everyday life.[13] The name Mass-Observation also implies a particular methodology. Two versions of participant observation were used in this initial inter war period: 'observers' were recruited, 'briefly' trained and sent out to record the behaviour of other people and a 'panel' of volunteer writers established.[14] At the time Mass-Observation was founded its mission was formulated in a number of ways: a 'people's ethnography', an anthropology of ourselves' and an anthropology 'at home.'[15] It has more recently been called 'part history project, part anthropology, part auto/biography, part social commentary.'[16] The Mass-Observation Archive, held at the University of Sussex, houses the documents relating to the initial phase and the writing, such as that generated by the Giving and Receiving Presents directive, which is part of the Contemporary Mass Observation Project. The Contemporary Project dates from 1981 and is a re-launch of Mass-Observation instigated by David Pocock using the most participatory of the early social research methods: a panel

---

12 See Appendix 1.

13 Ben Highmore, *Everyday Life and Cultural Theory: An Introduction* (London: Routledge, 2002) pp. 75–112. Highmore sees a productive instability in the Mass-Observation project since it lies on the 'fault-line between science and art.' p. 77.

14 Dorothy Sheridan, Brain Street, David Bloome, *Writing Ourselves: Mass-Observation and Literacy Practices* (Cresskill, N. J.: Hampton Press, 2000) pp. 83–4.

15 Sheridan, Street and Bloome, p. 82. For an account and analysis of Mass-Observation's founding moment see also pp. 21–38.

16 Sheridan, Street and Bloome, p. 12.

of volunteer writers responding freely to suggested themes, to 'directives.'[17] Nearly three thousand people, recruited through the local and national media, have taken part in the Project with around three and five hundred on the panel at any one time.[18]

The 1998 Giving and Receiving Presents directive asked about gift giving generally with one section solely devoted to wedding presents, which I co-wrote with Dorothy Sheridan, Director of the Contemporary Mass-Observation Project and the Archivist of the Mass-Observation Archive. Correspondents were invited to 'be as detailed as possible' about the objects they received when they married, who gave them, when they were given, whether they were requested, where they have been kept, how they have been used and if they held any memories. The Giving and Receiving Presents directive also asked about bought and collected objects used to set up a home and contained one question that sought to establish whether gifts held special significance: 'Were these things different from your gifts?'[19] This was the only moment in the directive when correspondents were encouraged to comment upon the status of objects rather than describe them, yet commentary and not description characterizes their responses. This particular question was often ignored and correspondents used the directive to raise and write about their own concerns. For example, they often compared what they were given when they married with current expectations about marriage gifts and the material plenty of domestic life. When I planned the 'Wedding Presents' section of the Giving and Receiving Presents directive, I intended to find out about actual marriage gifts and correspondents provided an enormous amount of information about these objects, but they also directed my attention beyond them. They explained why they received particular objects and what those objects meant.

I have been reading, re-reading and thinking about the responses to the Giving and Receiving Presents directive since it was collected in late 1998 and archived in early 1999, about seven years. I have read the same accounts many times but each time with a new set of questions. At different moments in my research I have been interested in why some objects are repeatedly deemed appropriate marriage gifts, the different ways in which they are requested or offered, how their receipt might give expression to ideal identities, how their use might sustain or reject traditional ideas of the family, the extent to which practices of using such objects are collective and conformist, why particular objects are preserved as the repositories for memories and others abandoned, whether there are significant differences between useful and decorative objects in the economy of preservation in domestic life, what are the rules of such domestic hierarchies and how all these things, which make up a domestic

---

17 Sheridan, Street and Bloome, pp. 95–103. For an examples of David Pocock's use and interpretation of the material generated by through the Mass-Observation re-launch see David Pocock 'Introduction,' *Movable Feasts: Changes in English Eating Habits*, ed. Arnold Palmer, (Oxford: Oxford University Press, 1984) pp. xi–xxxiv.

18 The Mass-Observation Archive, 'The Mass-Observation Project: Recording Everyday Life in the 1980s and 1990s' (Brighton: University of Sussex, n.d)

19 See Appendix 1.

material culture, might change. Eventually, these issues developed into this book. The effect of this seven year long period of reading and re-reading is that I feel as if I have been engaged in a dialogue with Mass-Observation correspondents. It has certainly not been a straightforward information gathering exercise, not least because the responses to the Giving and Receiving Presents directive contain reflections upon practices of giving as well as descriptions of gifts. Analysis is not the exclusive preserve of academics and Mass-Observation correspondents, like most people, have their own ideas. I realize that many correspondents may not immediately recognise their ways of giving and receiving objects as a form of exchange or as a consumption practice although I have used these terms, I hope, with some thought and care, in my interpretation of gifts. It is often only levels of material possession that are understood as an issue of consumption (often the only noteworthy issue) and many of the directive responses do present a view of the amount of objects it is appropriate to acquire upon marriage. Over-consumption is the most visible form of consumption but the definition that anthropologists use, and sociologists, historians and others have adopted, is more all-encompassing: it could include the transfer of any number of objects, large or small, in an attempt to communicate meaning.[20] Following this now orthodox academic interpretation of exchange, I understand that giving and receiving objects upon marriage as an exchange ritual despite some correspondents explicitly rejecting the suggestion that any traditions governed their forms of wedding present giving. [21] Our dissimilar terms express different perceptions of the meaning of things and what emerges from the Mass-Observation Archive is a disjunction between academic and everyday understandings of the significance of the exchange of objects and this too is a theme of this book. Chapter 1, in particular, considers some of the discrepancies between academic and popular definitions of the gift.

There were 254 responses to the Giving and Receiving Presents directive and the accounts of wedding presents within them were substantial. At least two pages of

---

20 The starting point of a number of definitions of consumption is usually a reference to Mary Douglas and Baron Isherwood, *The World of Goods: Towards an Anthropology of Consumption* (London: Allen Lane, 1979). See, for example, Corrigan, p. 17. As well as sociology directed towards an analysis of culture, an anthropological interpretation of consumption has influenced studies in consumer behaviour: Russell W. Belk, Melanie Wallendorf, John F. Sherry, 'The Sacred and the Profane in Consumer Behaviour: Theodicy on the Odyssey,' *Journal of Consumer Research* 6 (June 1989) pp. 1–38; Dennis W. Rook, 'The Ritual Dimension of Consumer Behaviour,' *Journal of Consumer Research* 12 (December 1985) pp. 251–264.

21 See responses to the Autumn 1998 Giving and Receiving Presents directive from Mass-Observation correspondents C1939, M1395 and R1025 for denials about drawing upon traditions. The writing of Mass-Observation correspondents is identified and catalogued by one letter and three or four numbers to preserve their anonymity. Mass-Observation numbers will be inserted in brackets into the text rather than footnoted and will always refer to their response to the Giving and Receiving Presents directive except in Chapter 3 and Chapter 6 that draws on other Mass-Observation material.

handwritten or typed script were typical, with many correspondents writing at much greater length. For example, an 'ex-sales assistant' from Bingley, near Bradford, who had worked in an office before her marriage in 1958, hand wrote ten pages on her wedding presents. Her account introduces many of the issues that recur within the directive responses as a whole: it indicates the way in which familial and work relationships are embodied in gifts, what kind of gifts constitute an appropriate domestic collection and outlines some of the proprieties surrounding their receipt and display. It reveals that the preservation of objects is an important domestic practice that plays a part in sustaining memories but it also suggests that attachments to objects are shaped by prevailing ideas of good taste and it illustrates how men and women are allocated different domestic responsibilities. It is therefore worth quoting at length:

We received *72* wedding presents, and I kept all the gift tags that were on them, along with the wedding day cards – I have just taken them out of the Box they are stored in, to count them. I have quite a large cardboard Box, where all special occasion cards are kept in bundles. My parents and my husbands parents bought us, or gave us big presents. My parents bought us an oven (gas oven) and a small 'hoover' washer, which in 1958 had rollers that you wrung the clothes through. They also provided us with cleaning materials and other bits and pieces. My husbands parents gave us a Walnut Bedroom Suite, and a green Spode Tea service, also various bits and pieces. My mother's Brother, his wife, and their daughter and Son-In-Law bought us a Combination Dinner/Tea Service, fruit set etc – from the most expensive china shop in Bradford. I was invited to go with them and to choose one out of three designs. It was Royal Doulton, 'Frost Pine', it was lovely, and I still have the large meat platter, 3 Tureens (2 with lids) and the gravy boat and stand, and they are in very good condition. I worked at the old Bingley Building Society, Head office (now it is the large Bradford and Bingley B. Soc) and each month, all staff contributed money to the Staff Association funds, which paid for presents for the staff to cover weddings and leaving presents. I was told to go out and choose a present to a certain value and then hand it over to them – I choose a fancy table lamp, this <u>had</u> been suggested by them and we wanted one. It was gorgeous at the time, but very 'Naff' now. It was cream wrought iron base and stand, quite delicate, with a leaf and flower design running up the stem, I choose a pink shade and we used it in the bedroom. The afternoon before my wedding, they presented me with this on behalf of the Staff Association. The girls in my department bought me a pair of pink Blankets, and a pair of pink flannelette sheets as a separate present from them, even though they had contributed to the lamp. The other presents we received from relatives, friends, friends of both sets of parents, and neighbours, included everything under the sun. I don't remember having a wedding list, in those days you did not, but some people did ask us what we wanted…. My cousin, her parents and brother 'clubbed up' to buy some weighing scales, I was amazed at the time, that they only cost £1-2-3d, and that was between four people. We had colour schemes in the kitchen and bedroom, so that anybody who did ask, had some idea of colours, but generally speaking the presents were a very random collection of things. We were inundated with pairs of towels, but no matching Bath Towels to go with them…. We received egg cups, a rolling pin and wooden spoon set, Pans and several casserole dishes, in the latest modern designs – I still have two casseroles from then, that I use all the time, although the lids are missing. My best friend bought us a pair of wood and ceramic salad servers, very pretty ceramic handles, which we still use. An elderly lady on our side of the family, who had 'been in service' and knew about etiquette, bought us a metal swan brand teapot, telling me that I would be able to entertain anybody to tea, having a decent teapot, not to be used for kitchen tea drinking, but for the tea table in the front room or dining room. My husbands mother got us a matching teapot to use with the green spode teaset that she had given us, and she knitted a tea cosy in green and pink to be used with it, which only got done in recent years... We even received gifts from people we hardly knew, and I wrote all our thank you letters as the gifts arrived, I wrote to my husbands relatives and friends because he did not care for letter writing. By the time the wedding was over, there were only last minute presents to say thank you for – they started arriving at both houses, around two weeks before the wedding, and I do not remember being given any at the actual wedding, as people tend to do now. On the day of the wedding, all the presents were assembled at my parents house, and most guests came back afterwards to see them, that was a traditional thing that people did, in those days (W571)[22] (see Figures 0.1 and 0.2).

Importantly, detail characterized both long and short responses to the Giving and Receiving Presents directive. For many correspondents, marriage gifts had been part of their routines and rituals over many years. Their knowledge of about these objects was intimate and for a researcher almost overwhelming. A librarian from Middlesex remembers the dates when her Habitat glasses and earthenware casserole broke: 1977 and 1982, respectively (G2640). A housewife from Durham gives an account of what happened to her gifts and reveals how the destiny of these domestic objects are inseparable from the history of her family:

All the wedding presents, because they were for the house, have been in use during the years. Even the ghastly fruit bowl I have always hated and I didn't have the sense to break 'accidentally'. The Hoover gave up the ghost a few years ago, the ironing-board was replaced, the iron blew up the duvet cover wore out and the duvet was replaced, the bed went, the airing rack got used as a pirate's ladder once too often. The motor on the food mixer blew out and the coffee machine was replaced and then given to my daughter when she moved in with her boyfriend. Plates get broken, though we are still using some of the originals, saucepans wear out though we still have two from the Swan set. The toaster couldn't cope – I bought an industrial sized one last year, Big Blue, so it can deal with a family Saturday supper. A family of five wears out, breaks or demolishes everything eventually. My Hitchhiker's Guide tapes are still around, very worn and crackly and one of them is screwed up, but I keep them to remember a lost friend by (M1201).

Extensive detail is more often provided by female Mass-Observation writers than male ones. The narratives that the directive generated from some female correspondents read like stories waiting to be told. Words spill out. Women have more to say about wedding presents than men. Also, proportionately more women replied to the directive than men. At the time the directive was sent out female correspondents outnumbered male ones by 5 to 2. Following the usual procedures

---

22 The bracketed number and letters refer to the Mass-Observation correspondent's number. See footnote above.

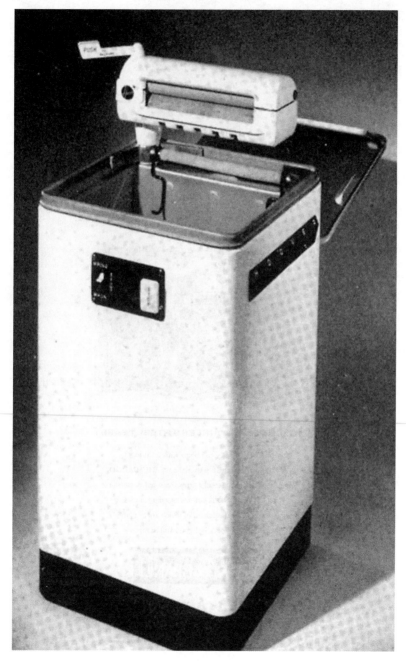

Figure 0.1 'A hoover washer, which in 1958 had rollers that you wrung the clothes through' (W571)

Figure 0.2 'A decent teapot' (W571)

of the Contemporary Mass-Observation Project, the Giving and Receiving Presents directive was sent to all Mass-Observation correspondents, which in Autumn 1998 numbered 354. Of these 252 were women and 102 were men. The 254 responses which were generated from the directive and which form the basis of this study extended the gender bias. 194 women (74 per cent) and 60 men (56 per cent) replied. This discrepancy in response statistics occurs because writing itself is gendered. Men and women tend to engage in different kinds of writing and when they are involved in the same writing project (such as replying to a Mass-Observation directive), it is possible to discern differences of content and form. As the 'ex-sales assistant' from Bingley remarked about her husband: 'he did not care for letter writing' (W571). A male Mass-Observation correspondent also states letter writing was not his choice: 'I was put hard to work writing letters of thanks' (B1509). Thus the unequal quantities of writing that the Giving and Receiving Presents directive elicited from men and women can be explained by the predictability of gender roles. Nevertheless, the fact that fewer men replied, and wrote less when they did, can be interpreted as a kind of silence. Silence upon domestic matters confirms the patterns of men's memory identified by oral and other historians: having not regarded domestic detail as significant, as not constituting anything like a defining moment in their life, men do not remember much about it.[23] 'I have been married twice, in 1948 and 1974, church and civil wedding respectively – have no recollection of wedding gifts on either occasion', writes an engineer from Gloucester (L2669). 'We had quite a lot of presents from relatives on both side', begins a shipping company manager, 'My wife remembers them all, and who gave them, but I am afraid I do not' (W2117). Many male correspondents apologize for being unable to remember much and some compile or at least complete their responses to the wedding present section of the Giving and Receiving Presents directive with their wife's help, adding details of gifts and givers after discussing it with her.[24] However, a typesetter from Woking, married in 1948, insists that his lack of memory is historically accurate. 'I have been trying to remember some of our presents and it is not my age that is making me fail as at the time I took little interest in this operation.' He lists the gifts he does remember. There are four:

> The things I recall are, clockwork alarm clock, wall mirror, meat safe (a necessity then) and a meat mincer. The meat mincer was zinc plate cast iron and was manually operated by a nine inch crank handle and had an Archimedes type screw to cut the meat and force it from the open funnel at one end through different interchangeable diameter holes at the other end (H1806).

Although insisting that he lacks memories, he in fact sets out substantial detail about a particular object: a useful, mechanical and safely masculine thing. A denial followed

---

23 Michael Peplar, *Family Matters: A History of Ideas about Family since 1945* (Harlow: Pearson Education Limited, 2002) pp. 100–119.

24 See also the responses to the Giving and Receiving Presents directive from Mass-Observation correspondents S2662 and B1426.

by detail is found in other responses from male correspondents. An engineer, whose marriage took place in 1965, writes:

> Oh dear, such a long time ago, and very difficult to remember…it was all very conventional …. What's left? Out of the usual sheets, towels, pillowcases, cutlery, china, glass, saucepans, a clock, ornaments and money, I have to say not much. We still look at the clock on the mantelpiece and use the cutlery daily, also there might be the odd blanket about but that's about it. Oh yes, I forgot the ironing board, a good strong metal one from the Scottish Co-op, it's still going strong (R 1719).

Overall, the responses to the Giving and Receiving Presents directive confirm the existence of a traditional familial division of labour: wedding gifts are nominally jointly received by brides and grooms but quickly become the preserve of only the wife. 'We received gifts from everybody and believe me – I don't know what they were,' as one male correspondent stated (T2469). However, inconsistencies about an inability to remember and what is actually recalled suggest that the responses were also shaped by what it is possible to say. Mass-Observation writing, like other biographical forms, negotiates ideas about ideal masculine and feminine behaviour as well as relates what actually happened.[25]

Some correspondents did not discuss actual objects and a small number claimed no knowledge of marriage gifts. A single-female student based in East Sussex explained: 'I am not married and neither was my Mum and Dad, so I don't know much about wedding presents' (H2829). The Wedding Presents section of the Giving and Receiving Presents directive was prefaced by the announcement that most of it 'applied to people who have got married' but encouraged the unmarried to 'comment on the questions in relation to the experiences of your friends and relations.'[26] Many single and cohabiting correspondents did discuss the established practice of giving to friends and family members and the objects assumed to be appropriate to give those about to marry. For example, an unemployed correspondent from York begins by saying that 'I've never been married myself but I've been to so many weddings over the past few years that I consider myself a bit of an expert!' (A2801). Others distanced themselves from the theme of the directive. A London-based local government officer, who describes her marital status as 'single but with male partner and children' wrote that she 'had never experienced the Wedding Present syndrome myself.' 'Also', she explains, 'perhaps because of my age and the attitudes of my peer group, I have been to remarkably few weddings.' Of those 'one was so utterly informal and frankly weird that it doesn't provide any information to relate to the question.' However, her own experience of cohabiting did in fact relate to the directive:

---

25 Monica Brewis, '"The Garden that I Love": Middle-Class Identity, Gender and the English Domestic Garden, 1880–1914', unpublished Ph.D thesis (University of Brighton, 2004) pp. 181–217.

26 See Appendix 1.

As far as my partner and I are concerned, we received an un-wedding present from our common outlaws (his sister and her husband). These were a beautiful mahogany Victorian chest of drawers and an Edwardian brass and iron bed. We have them to this day and will doubtless pass them on to our children if they want them (B2728).

Comments about gift giving and cohabitation were very interesting but limited in number as would be expected in response to questions about wedding presents. In order to reflect upon different material culture of cohabitation and thus the specificity of that of marriage, I contacted those correspondents who had discussed non-married unions, following up their responses with additional specific questions.[27] These replies are discussed as part of my concluding Chapter 6.

At the same time as I re-contacted Mass-Observation writers who were unmarried at the time they replied to the Giving and Receiving Presents directive, I also wrote to those who, in 1998, were recently married. With these correspondents I was trying to follow-up why in some cases attitudes towards objects received upon marriage had remained very much the same and in others seem to change over time.[28] Within material culture studies, one of the most influential works, *The Social Life of Things* (1986) edited by Arun Appadurai, is concerned with the effect of changing contexts upon object categories.[29] Some Mass-Observation correspondents' writing, however, draws attention to the way that meanings of things seem to alter whilst they remain in the possession of the same person and even in the same domestic space. How things change is the subject of Chapter 3, which also draws upon responses to another Mass-Observation directive, entitled Objects about the House that were collected in the Summer of 1988.[30] Even in this chapter where the 1998 Giving and Receiving Presents is compared to Mass-Observation writing produced at different times, it remains the key source and is the main one throughout this book.

Many of those who replied to my follow-up letters concluded or prefaced their accounts by stating, 'I hope this is of some use to you' (B2728) or 'Hope this has been helpful' (R1227). When writing in response to regular directives Mass-Observation correspondents also occasionally remark upon the value of their testimony for future researchers. Writing for the Mass-Observation Archive is a voluntary act, and compared to other kinds of writing, such as writing for publication, it is un-prestigious and altruistic. Publishing a book, even an academic one such as this, can bring individual rewards, especially status within the community who might read it. By contrast, Mass-Observation writers are anonymous (their names held by the Archive but not released to researchers to help ensure openness through confidentiality) and their writing is completely un-commercial, ultimately motivated by the desire to be part of a collective process of recording everyday life. Mass-

---

27 See Appendix 4.

28 See Appendix 3. A total of 23 follow-up letters were sent out eliciting 11 replies, of which 5 related to cohabitation and 6 to changed attitudes towards marriage gifts.

29 Arun Appadurai, ed. *The Social Life of Things* (Cambridge: Cambridge University Press, 1986).

30 See Appendix 2.

Observation writers describe themselves as 'ordinary people.' Dorothy Sheridan, Brian Street and David Bloome in their analysis of Mass-Observation correspondents as literary subjects, *Writing Ourselves* (2000), have identified how the description 'ordinary' is used to evoke both a common experience of just being part of an everyday world and shared a position outside institutions of cultural and political influence, particularly the professional media. 'I'm fairly ordinary', states one Mass-Observation correspondent, 'I think ordinary really, you think of yourself as someone who hasn't perhaps achieved fame, or great success; just live a normal, everyday life, going to work and with your family' (M1498).[31] Mass-Observation writing is thus the 'ordinary voice' of 'the person who wouldn't have a voice otherwise' (B1106).[32] Sheridan, Street and Bloome note that 'the everyday literacy practices of ordinary people are nearly invisible' and 'frequently not even considered to be writing.' The legitimacy of writing depends upon the location of the writer, as they point out:

> Novelists, journalists, academics, government officials, poets and a small number of others are viewed as legitimate writers; their writing carried authority. The power of their writing – its ability to define reality, to set before the public the questions for debate, to inscribe emotions and morality in narrative, to make law and order – derives in part from their connections with institutions of power (for example, mass media, universities, government, business)[33]

By contrast, ordinary people's writing takes place at home. Indeed, Mass-Observation writing as a unpaid but purposeful domestic activity has the same status as other kinds of tasks that are not quite labour nor exactly leisure that are often viewed as an extension of housework. It is no surprise, then, that the Archive contains the writing of so many women. Mass-Observation writing thus requires its reader to consider the institutional and arbitrary ways in which some forms of writing achieve authority while other forms and the kinds of knowledge they contain do not, or do not usually, receive such validation.

The Wedding Present draws upon, is indeed indebted to, Sheridan, Street and Bloome's analysis of Mass-Observation writing, its place within everyday life and the way it functions as knowledge of that life. As well as following their interpretation of ordinary people's writing, I use their definition of Mass-Observation

---

31 Dorothy Sheridan, '"Damned Anecdotes and Dangerous Confabulations": Mass Observation as Life History,' *Mass-Observation Archive Occasional Paper*, No. 7 (Brighton: University of Sussex Library, 1996) p. 10.

32 Sheridan, Street and Bloome, p. 215. Interestingly, Marianne Gullestad notes that 'the young urban working class families' that she worked with in Bergen, Norway, used the expression 'ordinary people' (*vanlige folk*) as a designation for themselves. Marianne Gullestad, *The Art of Social Relations: Essays on Culture, Social Action, and Everyday Life in Modern Norway* (Oslo: Scandinavian University Press, 1992) p. 68.

33 Sheridan, Street and Bloome, p 7. For an analysis of Mass-Observation writing as a discourse see Valerie M. Swales, 'Making Yourself at Home: a Study in Discourse,' *Household Choices*, ed. Tim Putnam and Charles Newton (Futures Publications and Middlesex Polytechnic, 1990) pp. 103–118.

as a case study. I discuss the case study as a methodology of studies in consumption alongside others, such as surveys, in Chapter 5. Those interested in the relationship between the method and content of research, the issue of how a phenomenon such as consumption is studied affects what can be concluded about it, may want to read that chapter first. Others may not want to enter into what probably seems a rather technical discussion quite so quickly (if at all). Although I have attempted to locate *The Wedding Present* as a study of domestic material culture that has some implications for how consumption should be understood to operate, the book can be read as just a case of gift giving upon marriage and the establishment of ideas and realities of home. Chapter 2 explores the strategies of preservation deployed within domestic domains directed at wedding presents, and wedding china, in particular and Chapter 4 examines the practice, specific to marriage, of requesting gifts through a list. But even for those who want to skip the discussion of methodology for the details of married domesticity, I must make one methodological point now: Mass-Observation as case study is not a simple illustration. The role of case studies within anthropology, particularly as set out by J. Clyde Mitchell, has informed Sheridan, Street, Bloome's (and my) understanding of the relevance of Mass-Observation. Mitchell argues that 'case material' is better put to 'analytical rather than illustrative purposes.' He states:

> What the anthropologist using a case study to support an argument does is to show how general principles deriving from some theoretical orientation manifest themselves in some given set of particular circumstances. A good case study, therefore, enables the analyst to establish theoretically valid connections between events and phenomena which previously were ineluctable. From this point of view, the search for a 'typical' case for analytical exposition is likely to be less fruitful than the search for a 'telling case' in which the particular circumstances surrounding the case, serve to make previously obscure theoretical relationships suddenly apparent.[34]

Put probably too simply, his distinction between a 'typical case' and a 'telling case' is that between an instance that is representative of the patterns cultural formation and one that is revealing of its underlying principles. Sheridan, Street, Bloome suggest that Mass-Observation writing 'can be seen as providing telling accounts of specific aspects of the culture that they both inhabit and observe.'[35]

As must be clear already, *The Wedding Present* has been shaped by both the ideas about everyday life, domesticity and consumption contained in Mass-Observation writing and those presented in academic writing, especially anthropological writing. However, I am an historian just trying to 'think with' anthropology theory. I often call myself a cultural historian and my training was in art and design history. Thus *The Wedding Present* combines different disciplinary practices. The 254 responses to the

---

34 J. Clyde Mitchell, 'Case Studies,' *Ethnographic Research: A Guide to General Conduct*, ed. R. Ellen, (London: Academic Press, 1984) pp. 238–239. See also Sheridan, Street and Bloome, pp. 14–15.

35 Sheridan, Street and Bloome, p. 107.

Giving and Receiving Present directive are a case study and I have also treated each as an historical document, as a 'work' in the art historical sense that both deliberately and unintentionally contains meanings and requires interpretative attention.

Production and Consumption

The Wedding Present provides evidence of domestic consumption, identifying exactly which objects were, and are, used to establish family households, tracing their meanings as they circulate or are stored within domestic space. As well as describing the actual practices of consumption that take place within the home, the book reassesses the relationship between home and consumption. The recent positioning of consumption within arts and humanities disciplines as an undervalued creative act is shaped by the understanding of home as a place of respite from work and freedom from the marketplace.[36] In fact it is possible to trace how preoccupation with consumption, especially within the disciplines of history and sociology, grew out of the study of the significance of home within industrializing societies. Prompted or informed by late twentieth century feminism, the home became a site of investigation as a source of inequality between men and women. A sustained examination of the causes of women's secondary status as economic and political subjects by feminist historians in particular found that assumptions about the affinity between women and a private sphere affected their ability to participate on the same terms as men outside it.[37] The ideology of separate spheres, the moral order associated with the industrial bourgeoisie in the late eighteenth and early nineteenth century, cast the public and the private spaces of home and of work, as dependent and unequal opposites. Activities that characterized the public sphere (the operations of the market and the state) have been privileged over those of the private (the familial and emotional). For example, the definition of work with the market has shaped the idea of work itself. There was, and is, a tendency to 'equate work with employment'[38] and thus the labour that took place in the home, which was once described by feminists as well as Marxists as 'the labour of reproduction,' did not count as real work because it was not paid and

---

36 Jackson and Moores, p. 1; Hugh MacKay, 'Introduction,' *Consumption and Everyday Life,* ed. Hugh Mackay (London: Sage, 1997) pp. 1–12; J. Scanlon, ed. *The Gender and Consumer Culture Reader* (New York: New York University, 2000) especially pp. 13–99.

37 Sandra Burman, ed. *Fit Work for Women* (London: Croom Helm, 1979); Leonore Davidoff and Catherine Hall, *Family Fortunes, Men and Women of the English Middle Class 1780–1850,* rev ed. (London: Hutchinson, 2002) pp. xiii–l; Leonore Davidoff, *Worlds Between: Historical Perspectives on Gender and Class* (Cambridge: Polity, 1995); Catherine Hall, *White, Male and Middle-Class* (Cambridge: Polity Press, 1992).

38 R. E. Pahl, 'Editor's introduction: Historical aspects of Work, Employment, Unemployment and the Sexual Division of Labour,' *On Work: Historical, Comparative and Theoretical Approaches,* ed. R.E. Pahl (Oxford, Blackwell, 1988) p. 15.

ultimately it appeared as consumption.[39] Thus the opposition between public and private appears also as an opposition between home and work, consumption and production.

Although the public/private opposition is an important explanatory framework for feminist historians, they have also been the scholars most concerned to point out the partial, incomplete and uneven separation of home and work. Sonya Rose noted some twenty years ago that 'We now know that variations in the transformation of the processes of production did not have a uniform effect either on the location of waged work or the timing of women's various contributions to their families.'[40] While it has been assumed that a separation was completely established by the mid-nineteenth century, there was always a difference between the ideal of separate spheres and the actual separation of home and work. From the establishment of the 'male breadwinner norm' around that mid-nineteenth century point to its demise today and the emergence of the notion of a 'working family,' single and poorer women have always worked for money outside the home. The apparent moral benefits of different masculine and feminine domains and the supposed propriety of organizing family life in this way was, and is, a powerful idea even when it was not, or could not, be consistently or completely put into effect. 'Even if the experience of domesticity was far from universal,' note Leonore Davidoff et al, 'the ideology of separate spheres was certainly influential.'[41] Where it has been most influential is over spatial separation of home and work. Public and private are represented as fixed opposites through the layout and location of home, specifically the suburban home. By the third quarter of the nineteenth century, the successful and respectable middle class family had removed itself from the sites of wealth creation and from the signs of industrial work (dirt and poverty) that had become associated with dense, urban development.[42] But even within the archetypal late-nineteenth century middle class family or indeed within those successive groups (other factions of the middle class and later the affluent white collar working class) that sought to appropriate the suburban dream, there was still, of course, an economic connection between work and home. The ideology of separate spheres, the belief that it is preferable and possible for masculine and feminine endeavour in the fields of production and consumption to have autonomous existence in their own isolated domains, is only actually realised spatially. Furthermore, complete spatial separation is a physical illusion; the

---

39 Rosemary Pringle, 'Women and Consumer Capitalism,' *Defining Women: Social Institutions and Gender Divisions*, ed. Linda McDowell and Rosemary Pringle (Cambridge: Polity Press, 1992) pp. 148–152.

40 Sonya O. Rose, '"Gender at work': Sex, Class and Industrial Capitalism,' *History Workshop Journal* 21 (Spring 1986) p. 113.

41 Leonore Davidoff et al, *The Family Story* (London: Longman, 1999) p. 27.

42 F. M. L. Thompson, 'Introduction: The Rise of Suburbia,' *The Rise of Suburbia*, ed. F. M. L. Thompson (Leicester: Leicester University Press, 1982) pp. 1–26; Simon Gunn, 'The Middle Class, Modernity and the Provincial City: Manchester c1840–1880,' *Gender, Civic Culture and Consumerism*, ed. Alan Kidd and David Nicholls (Manchester: Manchester University Press, 1999) pp. 112–127.

geographical distances that appear between home and work are a reassuring denial of the constant economic trafficking between them. Regular profits or wages can create and maintain homes only when the income is carefully managed, transformed into the stable forms of respectability, such as enough nutritious food and appropriate forms of decoration. The traditional family division of labour, masculine involvement in paid employment and feminine organization of consumption, upon which the spatial separation of home and work rests thus presupposes a single economic unit. No matter where home and work are located, production and consumption are inextricably linked in the family. Production never disappears; it is disavowed. In fact, rather than production and consumption becoming more detached in the western world of the late-twentieth and early twenty-first century, as is often suggested,[43] it is possible to argue that the relationship between home and work is closer than ever, especially in countries such as Britain where home ownership has increased, ensuring that the lifestyle of the majority who do not have an inherited income is underpinned by borrowing against a regular income. [44]

Thus, consumption and production are only theoretically separate. They are in fact simply categories in a theoretical model used to analyze economic relationships. The terms production and consumption acquired explanatory force in the early investigations into the operations of industrial capitalism. In the opening sentence of *Wealth of Nations*, (1766), Adam Smith distinguishes one from other:

> The annual labour of every nation is the fund which originally supplies it with all the necessaries and conveniences of life which it annually consumes, and which consists either in the immediate produce of that labour, or in what is purchased with that produce from other nations.[45]

The separation of production from consumption, labour from the 'necessities and conveniences of life', is made within a large system over a long period, within a national economy. Although the terms have been incorporated into the analysis of consumer or material culture, they are not here descriptions of individual actions or the relatively small-scale collective activities that can characterise culture as it is lived everyday. Production and consumption were broad categories, rubrics under which the messy, related practices of everyday life (making, exchanging and re-

---

43 Alan Aldridge, *Consumption* (Cambridge: Polity Press, 2003) pp. 1–9. The experience of home and work as separated spaces and the negotiation of the boundaries between them is the subject of Christina E. Nippert-Eng, *Home and Work* (Chicago: Chicago University Press, 1995).

44 Irene Cieraad has pointed out that 'Despite the myth of two worlds apart, home life and life chances came to depend more and more on public systems, including those of education and occupation.' Irene Cieraad, 'Anthropology at Home,' *At Home: An Anthropology of Domestic Space* ed. Irene Cieraad (New York: Syracuse University Press, 1999) p. 10. Her comments relate to Tim Putman's essay '"Postmodern" Home Life' in the same volume, pp. 114–152.

45 Adam Smith, *Wealth of Nations I–III*, 1776 (London: Penguin Books, 1986) p. 104.

making) were retrospectively separated. Adam Smith, like other political economists and enlightenment philosophers, created an historical idealization, a projection not a description of society. Production and consumption were never identified as separate areas of life for an actual person as either an individual or member of a community but as functioning parts of a system that in fact are not recognized by the participants in that system, but discernible only to observers. The truth of economics is based on the notion that an informed but disinterested outsider detects patterns that those who are working, recovering from work and getting ready for more work, are too busy to see.[46] Production and consumption are abstractions, long-term patterns of accumulation and dispersal visible only as representations, much like statistics, but imposed upon the complexities of existence under capitalism. To argue that economics is an abstraction is not new; it is now almost a set piece of cultural theory. Most criticism has been heaped upon the rational subject of economic relations: economics relies upon assumptions about the subject that makes rational choices based upon immediate considerations of loss or gain, need and want. No history, culture or social circumstance influences the decisions of such a blank sheet. The 1979 account of the limiting effect of reducing consumption to decisions about use offered by Mary Douglas and Baron Isherwood in the *World of Goods* has been incorporated into the academic analysis of culture.[47] Economic behaviour cannot, of course, be separated from cultural formations: women do not shop for food because they are better at averaging the totals of multiple items as they push a shopping trolley but because they belong to a gendered culture in which historically they have been responsible for household provision and well-being. While most cultural theorists do not believe that a domain of pure economics actually exists, abstract economic categories have been transposed onto specific lived experiences without much critical reflection. Abstraction has become a description. Categories of accumulation and dispersal that exist within large scale, long-term economic models have been given a historical reality. There has been a slippage between the idea of production and consumption and the existence of producers and consumers: explanatory categories have provided historical subjectivities obscuring the connections in everyday life between work and home.[48]

---

46 John Barrell, 'Visualising the division of labour: William Pyne's "Microcosm"', *The Arts, Literature and Society*, ed. Arthur Marwick (London: Routledge, 1990) pp. 95–132.

47 Douglas and Isherwood, pp. 3–10.

48 For example, Celia Lury assumes that consumer identity is a given. Celia Lury, *Consumer Culture* (London: Polity Press, 1996). Of course, some people at particular historical moments have identified themselves as consumers and the emergence of this a political identity is traced within Gill Scott, *Feminism and the Politics of Working Women: the Women's Co-operative Guild, 1880s to the Second World War* (London: UCL Press, 1998) and Lawrence Black, *The Political Culture of the Left in Affluent Britain, 1951–64: Old Labour, New Britain?* (Basingstoke: Palgrave, 2003). The discrepancy between the abstractions of consumption and lived experience has, of course, been pointed out before. Christopher Breward's work has sought to 'question those explanations which conflate such theoretical processes with the day-to-day activities of women and men.' Christopher Breward, *The Hidden*

So, if production and consumption are only theoretically separate, pulled apart in the process of economic analysis, how are they actually related? Is going to work actually understood as participating in production? What is the real relationship between home and work? And when is home life equated with consumption? I have used the word consumption to describe the transactions and use of objects within a domestic setting because the term its part of an analytical vocabulary that I share with historians, anthropologists, sociologists and others. But I have tried to use it sparingly and, rather than continually group the specific practices of home-making under the heading consumption, I have employed more blandly descriptive but, I think, more accurate terms, such as, giving, using, keeping. What I want to tentatively suggest is that consumption may not be always be the most accurate descriptive or analytical term for domestic life.

Identity in Context: Gifts and Marriage

Studies of consumption carried out within a variety of academic disciplines have fairly frequently demonstrated how selecting and using objects is a process of self-definition.[49] In *The Wedding Present*, however, a disjunction between material possession and self-expression is identified and it is suggested that it is not ultimately possible to assert a straightforward relationship between what has been identified as acts of consumption and the creation of individual identity. I suggest that the material relationships of a domestic realm may be part of a culture of conformity that curtails individualist versions of self-hood and in doing so swing behind the observations and arguments already made by Marianne Gullestad and Daniel Miller in particular.[50] My interpretation of the material practices of domesticity is also, importantly, the

---

Consumer: Masculinities, Fashion and City 1860–1914 (Manchester: Manchester University Press, 1999) p. 2. Victor Buchli, Alison Clarke and Dell Upton's 'Editorial' in the first issue of *Home Cultures* 1: 1 (2004) also asserts the discursive significance of separation of spheres. They state that 'the problem of boundaries is where we delineate the so-called domestic apart form the public, and whether we can segregate these two at all, calls into question categories of public and private, self and social', p.2.

49 This relationship between consumption and individual identity has run through work over the last twenty-five years. For just a few examples see: Russell W. Belk, *Collecting in a Consumer Society*, (London: Routledge, 1995); Grant McCracken, *Culture and Consumption: New Approaches to the Symbolic Character of Consumer Goods and Activities*, (Bloomington: Indiana University Press, 1988); Lury, pp. 239–242. Lury's text illustrates the way Anthony Giddens' ideas of identity formation in late modernity are mapped onto the supposed subjectivity of the individual consumer, in particular his work with Beck and Lash. Ulrich Beck, Anthony Giddens, Scott Lash, *Reflexive Modernization* (Cambridge: Cambridge University Press, 1994).

50 Marianne Gullestad, *The Art of Social Relations: Essays on Culture, Social Action and Everyday Life in Modern Norway* (Oslo: Scandinavian University Press, 1992) pp. 61–91; Daniel Miller, 'Consumption as the Vanguard of History,' *Acknowledging Consumption*, ed. Daniel Miller (London: Routledge, 1995) pp. 1–57. See also Suzanne Reimer and Deborah Leslie, 'Identity, Consumption and the Home,' *Homes Cultures* 1.2 (2004) p. 187 and pp. 204–205.

outcome of my reading of Mass-Observation material. Their writings about wedding presents sent in response to the 1998 Giving and Receiving Presents directive form a collective account of the creation of the domestic environment and how little of it is subject to individual control. The content of the responses varied: some people received numerous gifts, others only a few, some were kept, some used until they wore out, some were given away and, occasionally, thrown away. Whatever the variations, correspondents explain how the objects that become their belongings are always bound up with their wider social realities. For example, a school secretary from Hemel Hempstead, who wed in 1949, writes:

> We didn't want – and couldn't afford a big "do". Our parents and a friend of mine attended. Travel was difficult and friends and family were scattered in different parts of the country.... My husband recently demobilised had just started work after failing to obtain a grant to continue his higher education full-time. Although I had a well-paid job, living away from home left very little spare cash. We didn't have a "proper" home until January 1957 when we moved into this New Town (R2136).

Her wedding presents, of which the 'most expensive' was an 'Ekco Model A104 radio' and the others were mostly 'plain' tableware, represent the efforts of working women to achieve the ideal of the respectable in 'furnished rooms' (R2136). Another correspondent, a housewife from Staines, who married a year later in 1950, received similar gifts, including a 'radio and china.' Such similarities are the obvious effects of being in the same situation, which is to say that material culture of marriage is, or at least their marriages were, shaped by set of social conditions, wealth and property relations to be precise. The Staines housewife, who had 'a civil wedding, but in a very pleasant room,' explains, 'I was 19' and 'We were hard up and non-religious so it suited us.' She points out that she and her husband 'couldn't have many presents as we were starting life in furnished rooms' and concludes by saying that it 'was not until we were buying our own home, about 2 years later that we bought furniture, on Hire Purchase mainly' (B2605). Restrictions imposed by wealth seem obviously apparent in the modesty of objects, however, correspondents married in a much more affluent time than the period of post-war austerity also received gifts that could be described as the material effects of social conditions. A correspondent from Banbury, who describes herself as 'Mother/Art student/Graduate,' married in 1985 when she was 22 and four months pregnant. 'I never wanted to get married and would have thought that a soppy thing to do at the time,' she writes. The wedding was a quick decision as was the request for wedding presents. 'It is so cringey to us now but I think we hastily grabbed the Argos catalogue and made a quick list of basics – oooh dear – wish I didn't have to admit to that one!!' (E2538). The wedding presents received by a museum assistant from Cleveland whose marriage took place in 1990 were much more carefully planned and were mainly single purpose objects that could be defined as domestic luxuries, items such as a cocktail shaker, champagne flutes, soufflé dishes and ramekins (Figure 0.3). This correspondent also had a list 'mostly drawn up by myself but with some help from fiancé.' She states that she 'mostly didn't specify designs etc, except for the tableware which was to expand the set we already had. However, I did indicate preferred colours and said what I did not want' (B2832). At last there is an assertion of individual preference but her marriage gifts, even those that completed her 'poppy design' dinner service, are not simply individual choices. They are effects of the variation of household composition, which by the end of the twentieth century included a greater number of single person homes and homes based on cohabitation. The museum assistant already had a particular pattern of china because her married home was not her first.

Figure 0.3   The single purpose object as wedding present

Mass-Observation writing, which had already alerted me to the differences between academic and everyday concepts of consumption, also frequently demonstrated how those who inhabit domestic worlds and fill them with objects could only accept and amend rather actually create their meaning. It could, of course, be argued that because the practice of giving objects is central to the analysis of consumption that I offer in *The Wedding Present*, the book inevitably illustrates a lack of individual control over objects. Gifts, according to anthropological orthodoxy, are obligatory. This is the first fundamental characteristic of the gift identified by Marcel Mauss in his 1925 essay of the same name.[51] Gifts are not freely given nor necessarily willingly accepted but are impossible to reject without jeopardising the relationship to the person who offers the gift. Thus they are objects that express social ties.[52] That the purpose of the exchange overrides the content of the given object is contemporary

---

51 Marcel Mauss, *The Gift: the Form and Reason for Exchange in Archaic Societies*, 1925 (London: Routledge, 1990).

52 The continuing sociability of the gift is emphasized by David Cheal in particular. David Cheal, *The Gift Economy* (London: Routledge, 1988) p. 19.

everyday knowledge. It is never considered appropriate for the recipient of the gift to openly express their dislike for it.

Although gifts, unlike bought things, do not always allow their eventual owners to decide whether they want to possess them, never mind whether they like the details of their design, they are not unusual objects. Gifts are the most significant category of objects exchanged outside the market in economies where the market dominates.[53] Gift transactions dominate in domestic life. The practice of giving and receiving objects is the means through which objects circulate within the domestic environments. Not all gifts are wrapped up and ceremoniously offered. The provision of food and clothing within a family are intergenerational gift transactions repeatedly performed by adult females in their role as wives and mothers.[54] Thus the association of consumption with individuality is either an ideological assumption or at least unrepresentative of everyday forms of consumption practice.

Like the focus upon the gift, my investigation of marriage as a context of consumption, leads me to conclude that the exchange of objects and the act of their possession is about relationships between people rather than self-expression and individual identity. Since people marry in order to establish or secure a family home, the definitions of a family household as a site of consumption also hold for marriage. In fact, in the same way as it is argued that marriage provides legal recognition of family relationships by enforcing the customary familial responsibility for the provision physical and financial, or in other words, material support for family members; it can also been seen to authorize and even institutionalize domestic consumption practices.[55]

The collected responses to the Giving and Receiving Presents directive contain accounts of marriages that took place over a 60 year period, from the late 1930s to the late 1990s. The earliest wedding described was in 1939 (Y2498) and the latest in 1998 (L1504). *The Wedding Present* has a slightly different periodization, it offers an account of married domesticity in Britain between 1945 and the present day. Because so many more Mass-Observation correspondents who replied to the directive were married in the post-war austerity period than during war-time, it seemed logical to begin there. Also, the replies to my follow-up enquiries provided details of marriage and cohabitation up until 2003, indeed, one long-term cohabitee got married in that year (B2728). A significant proportion of weddings recorded within responses to the Giving and Receiving Presents directive took place in the first twenty years of the period, between 1945 and the mid 1970s, reflecting the popularity of marriage in this period and the dominant age group of Mass-Observers at the time the directive was sent out, but there is also substantial writing relating to marriages, including second

---

53 C. A. Gregory, *Gifts and Commodities* (London: Academic Press, 1982) p. 71; James G. Carrier, *Gifts and Commodities: Exchange and Western Capitalism since 1700* (London: Routledge, 1995) pp. 18–38.

54 Peter Corrigan, 'Gender and the Gift: the Case of the Family Clothing Economy,' *Sociology* 23.4 (1989) pp. 513–34.

55 Morgan, p. 88.

marriages, that took place in the last quarter of the twentieth century and into the first years of the twenty-first.

Civil marriage ceremonies are common, especially immediately post-war and again from the 1980s, if not before. In both instances, they are regarded as a no-fuss, practical way to get married and as an explicit alternative to tradition. Thus, as we would expect, most correspondents who wed in the middle years of the period of this study did so in a church of some kind.[56] But the religious aspect of wedding rituals features very little in the accounts of marriages across the period as a whole. Church represents an idea of tradition rather than importance of Christian theology. Performing a wedding in a church or chapel or one of the various Christian denominations referred to within the responses to the Giving and Receiving Presents directive, was more indicative of belonging to a particular community than holding a set of beliefs. While it is important not to conflate affiliation with churches or chapels with exclusively 'white' British communities, the family histories and sense of place contained within Mass-Observation writing on marriage does not suggest that, for example, it represents a 'black' British or immigrant experience. We should note, then, that to claim the identity 'ordinary' in the way that Mass-Observation correspondents call themselves 'ordinary people' recognises their marginal position in relation to official institutions at the same time as it places them securely and centrally within the 'mainstream' culture of everyday life. Having said this, it must be emphasized that for Mass-Observation correspondents neither Christian beliefs nor the cultural identities associated with church or chapel define their weddings. The indicative phrases used by correspondents to discriminate between types of weddings are the small or the posh do, the quiet or the big affair. Thus regardless of whether it took place in a church or registry office, a wedding is defined by its sociability, by the number of people who were there and the ways in which they endorsed the match.

That a wedding is first and foremost a social occasion is probably no surprise since to be married is to occupy a particular social position. Marriage is often understood as a public declaration of the permanence of a sexual relationship but more importantly, it is an event that transforms familial relationships, altering the position and primary allegiances of the bride and groom within their respective families. A son and daughter become a husband and wife. Marriage is a rite of passage to adulthood[57] conferring higher status upon the married couple even if they remain living in one of their parental homes for the first few years of their marriages, as was fairly common in earlier part of the period that *The Wedding Present* covers. It has always been possible to achieve adulthood by other means, such as entry into appropriate kinds of paid work, a proper job or profession, and the importance of

---

56 Marriages recorded within the responses to the Giving and Receiving Presents directive were performed in Anglican, Church of Scotland, Catholic, Methodist, Presbyterian, Baptist churches or chapels. Two ceremonies took place in Synagogues. After weddings in Anglican churches, civil ceremonies were the most common form.

57 Leonard, p. 256.

marriage in becoming an adult has declined but not disappeared entirely. At the same time, the ultimate aim to establish an independent and permanent home has become its immediate goal. Marriage and home making have, if anything, become more closely aligned.

With almost no exceptions, whatever the type of wedding, civil or religious, large or small, and whenever it occurred, in the mid-twentieth century or in the early twenty-first, there was a gift.[58] Even in the most discreet weddings, presents are offered and accepted. For example, one Mass-Observation correspondent, a female fire brigade control worker from Somerset who married in 1985 after cohabiting for 17 years stated, 'we had a very small, quiet affair, in fact we only told one close friend who acted as a witness' adding 'We obviously didn't expect any wedding presents and had owned our own home about 12 years.' They received two gifts of money (with which she bought a food processor and washing machine), towels and bed linen, rose plants and goblet wine glasses (W1918). 'We got married very quietly' explains another correspondent, a Glasgow housewife. 'Just 2 witnesses who were warned not to buy us anything. (They did – 2 crystal glasses)' (M1171). Gifts are an integral part of the wedding ritual. Getting married is inevitably and inseparably a social and a material affair.

---

58   There are only two Mass-Observation accounts of weddings without gifts and only one within the Giving and Receiving Presents directive (W1835). The other (B2728) is contained in her reply to my 2003 follow-up letter.

Chapter 1

Objects of Approval

'Whatever the wisdom of ordinary people may turn out to be, it would seem to be worth listening to them' (David Cheal, 1988).[1]

Defining Gifts

A Mass-Observation correspondent, an unemployed woman from York, describes how giving a gift upon marriage is the forced fulfillment of a duty and desire of her own. She begins:

> I always feel embarrassed about the quality of my presents – I'm on a very low income. I usually have to buy something very ordinary like an ovenware dish, but sometimes I've gone for "unique" and given the happy couple a piece of my own artwork. Very time-consuming, but at least no-one else will have bought the same thing. When my sister got married in 1997, I spent six months planning and creating a pastels picture to hang in her bedroom. I was very proud of it at the finish, but it was an incredibly arduous task and I was drained by the time I'd completed it. I'd wanted to give her a present which no-one else would give her, something special. In the end, by the time I'd bought the art materials and paid for it to be framed, it was considerably more expensive than the present I would have purchased. Still, they both loved it, which was my main objective (A2801)

Gift giving, as it is described here, is both an obligatory and a voluntary act. This Mass-Observation correspondent had to give when her sister married and she wanted to. Or, perhaps more precisely, since she had to participate in a sibling's wedding rituals she wanted to give the right kind of gift, 'something special.' Giving was an obligation that she wanted to fulfil and do so in the right way. Marcel Mauss, in his famous 1925 essay, defined gifts as 'in reality' obligatory against the prevailing assumption that they are freely offered and accepted.[2] Mauss appears to overturn the meaning of giving as a free and therefore virtuous form of exchange, but in fact he keeps the virtue of the gift intact and recasts the meaning of obligatory. It is 'the

---

1   David Cheal, *The Gift Economy* (London: Routledge, 1988) p. 57.

2   Marcel Mauss, *The Gift: The Form and Reason for Exchange in Archaic Societies,* 1925, (London: Routledge, 1990) p. 3. One Mass-Observation correspondent explicitly describes his family's wedding present transactions as obligatory: 'my parents tell me that very few of their wedding presents were either meaningful or useful, however well-intentioned – the presents demonstrated a remarkable instinct among their own families to buy out of obligation' (M2826).

Figure 1.1   An ordinary gift

obligation, on the one hand, to give presents, and on the other, to receive them[3] that makes giving a social and even communitarian act. Compulsory presentation and acceptance of objects is initiated by a governing obligation 'to reciprocate presents received.'[4] That gifts must be returned creates cycles of exchanges fuelled by continual indebtedness between people who have exchanged gifts, eventually establishing permanent relationships. Importantly, this social, and indeed sociable, character of the gift is an effect of a process of embodiment. Given objects, according to Mauss, 'still possess something of the giver.'[5] It is not difficult to see how a gift carries a trace of the person who gave it. For example, the pastel colours of a picture demonstrate the decisions and efforts of a sister; they are signs of her agency, if you like, which ensure that she is present in the picture that hangs on the bedroom of a newly wedded couple. Gifts function as constant reminders of the givers. Thus a gift is inevitably a social thing. What is at stake in every gift exchange is a relationship between people since the object is understood to carry some part of a person with it.

To give is to be in a social relationship, to recognize and reinforce it. The pastel picture affirmed an old family relationship at the moment when a new one was about to begin. To neglect or even refuse to give would have the opposite effect, announcing the end of a relationship or at least bringing its existence into question. If one sister did not give to another upon marriage their connection could be broken.

---

3   Mauss, p. 13.
4   Mauss, p. 13.
5   Mauss, p. 12.

Receiving carries the same social responsibility as giving. Accepting your sister's picture into your married household honours the seseurial relationship in exactly the same way as offering the picture in the first place. Furthermore, for Mauss, as an object is accepted as a gift it calls upon its recipient to acknowledge the giver by giving in return. To take the case of the pastel picture once again, the sister who gave it might expect to follow it into her sister's married household and be offered a place at the dinner table on special occasions at the very least.

The social solidarities enforced through gift systems appear as the obvious opposite to the alienation of the capitalist market wherein an exchange can actually be concluded. Exchange through selling and buying ends with the freedom to use the exchanged object in any way, including throwing it away. Every market transaction therefore reproduces the condition of alienation under capitalism: to be without obligation, free but alone and consoled only by exclusive, individual rights in objects. Mauss's essay has been used to provide anthropological, sociological and philosophical authority for an opposition between gift and commodity.[6] A comparative analysis of gifts and commodities is not the subject of the essay but its historical trajectory is certainly the erosion of gift-giving societies and moralities through the extension of the market.[7]

A simplistic dualism, which positions gift giving culture as the mirror image of commodity capitalism is one of the many criticisms of Maussian interpretation of the gift. Annette Weiner, in her book *Inalienable Possessions* (1992), has pointed out that to assume that reciprocity that drives gift exchanges is to invest them with the principles that were ideally supposed to operate within western European market systems.[8] Reciprocity underpins, or so it was argued in the first writings of political economy, the natural 'propensity' to 'truck, barter and exchange one thing for another' that ultimately balances out and brings benefits to society as a whole.[9] Giving and receiving that generates further giving and receiving is an innocent version of commodity exchange and appears as both a prehistory of capitalism and as an always endangered surviving form of exchange within it. According to Weiner, the principle and motivation of giving is in fact its opposite, keeping. She argues that some things are given in order to keep others out of all spheres of exchange. Kept objects, 'inalienable possessions', are highly valued because they promise to

---

6   James G. Carrier, *Gifts and Commodities: Exchange and Western Capitalism since 1700* (London: Routledge, 1995); C. A. Gregory, *Gifts and Commodities* (London: Academic Press, 1982); Mark Osteen, 'Gift or commodity?' *The Question of the Gift: Essays across Disciplines* ed. Mark Osteen, (London: Routledge, 2002) pp. 229–247.

7   Mauss was also concerned with the increasing power of the state but less attention is paid to this threat to the gift in more recent studies of the gift that have been written at a time when free market capitalism is the more powerful global force.

8   Annette Weiner, *Inalienable Possessions: The Paradox of Keeping-While-Giving* (Berkeley: University of California Press, 1992) p. 2. Her comments are directed at Bronislaw Malinowski's 'norm of reciprocity' more than Mauss's comments upon the gift, which to some extent she redeems from her criticism of eurocentrism.

9   Adam Smith, *Wealth of Nations I–III*, 1776, (London: Penguin Books, 1986) p. 117.

guard against the losses of time. Weiner states 'an inalienable possession acts as a stabilizing force against change because its presence authenticates cosmological origins, kinship, and political histories.'[10] Thus gift-exchanges are not explained by gift-exchanges but by stepping outside the virtuous circle of giving (or exchanging since that is the model of giving) to see how they are premised upon the imperative to maintain possession of the most precious forms of material culture.

Maurice Goldier's re-thinking of anthropological theories of the gift, *The Enigma of the Gift* (1999), which was, he states, inspired by Weiner's *Inalienable Possessions* (1992), also questions, among other orthodoxies of gift theory, the capacity of reciprocity premised upon embodiment to explain the initiation of a gift exchange. 'Now even if the existence of an in-dwelling spirit in things may seem to explain the obligation to return gifts, it does not', he states, 'account for the obligation to give them.'[11] Thus, he suggests, 'in analyzing a gift, whatever it may be, one needs to consider the relationship that existed between the giver and the receiver *before* the former made a gift to the latter.'[12] Their relationship might be one of equality but is more likely a hierarchy of some kind and 'if this hierarchy already exists, then the gift expresses and legitimizes it.'[13]

Aafke Komter, who holds onto the notion of reciprocity, also locates gift exchanges within unequal power relationship. Studies of gift giving in contemporary western capitalist cultures demonstrate that women are the 'greatest givers' and this creates an 'alternating asymmetry' of reciprocity.[14] As she reminds us, to be obliged to reciprocate a gift is far from a sign of equivalence between receiver and giver.[15] Indeed, the failure to return an equal gift, to offer something of lesser of higher worth is the social dynamic of gift exchange. A gift positions and characterizes people in relation to one another. Whenever gift giving is practiced or avoided it defines and re-defines strong or failed friendships, large, small or close families, bad mothers, good mothers, dutiful or uncaring children, forgetful, cruel or responsible fathers. Komter's particular concern is how women's gift giving positions them in relation to men. Women may give much only to receive little in return and, furthermore, all gift transactions may also be assigned less value than market ones, such as payment for work performed by men. Alternatively, women's gift giving may underpin female social networks and familial, and even matrilineal, authority from which men are excluded. Within the Giving and Receiving Presents directive, there is a wealth of evidence relating to gendered patterns of giving. For example, a railway clerk from

---

10 Weiner, p. 9.

11 Maurice Godlier, *The Enigma of the Gift* (Cambridge: Polity Press, 1999) p. 11.

12 Godlier, p. 13.

13 Godlier, p. 12.

14 Aafke E. Komter, 'Women, Gifts and Power,' *The Gift: An Interdisciplinary Perspective,* ed. Aafke E. Komter (Amsterdam: Amsterdam University Press, 1996), p. 121 and pp. 127–130. Komter notes her debt to Marilyn Strathern, *The Gender of the Gift: Problems with Women and Problems with Society in Melanesia* (Berkeley: University of California, 1988).

15 Komter, p. 125.

Birkenhead who stated when he married in 1947 'we received gifts from everybody and believe me – I don't know what they were' also explained 'I have never shown any ability in the choosing of gifts for friends and relatives and it is a fact that I have left that particular part of everyday affairs to my wife' (T2459). Another male correspondent, a heavy goods vehicle driver based in Basildon stated, that 'my wife did all the present giving and picking.' However, he does know the 'household goods' that he and she received when they married in 1958 and remembers their givers. He writes that the 'set of Prestige stainless steel kitchen tools and carving knife from my mother-in-law are still in regular daily use' (R470). Men, in this case husbands, who claim no part in any gift giving may do so because their position within the domestic realm is secured without their direct involvement in work within the sphere of domestic exchange. Women, particularly wives, are therefore able to exert unfettered control of the material culture of the home. A fragment of the HGV driver's writing is a small record of his respect for his wife's decisions about which gifts were allowed to circulate within their domestic space:

> While clearing out after my wife's death I found some towels we were given. My wife would never use them because they were white. They were in the back of the airing cupboard, yellow and grey on the fold. They washed up alright so I donated them to a charity (R470).

While Komter suggests that gift giving is embedded in the unequal share of power and advantage between the market and home and within the home itself, her notion of 'alternating asymmetry' suggests that relationships between women and men will be differently negotiated as their gift relationships are played out. Or in Komter's words, 'It is not clear before hand which genders benefits most from women's generosity.'[16]

It would take another book to detail the critiques of Maussian ideas of the gift and that book has already been written several times.[17] All I have been able to indicate here is some of the current revisions of the gift theories most relevant to this study of domestic consumption. Of course, the role and remit of consumption in the creation of domesticity has also been subject to some revision. In particular, work that has asserted the potential of commodities to be revalued and recreated as the meaningful objects of everyday life has an important bearing on the idea of the gift. Living with objects after they have been bought, that is, making domestic culture, or any other kind of material culture, out of commodities, has been widely interpreted, albeit with

---

16 Komter, p. 130.

17 Godlier, p. 1999; Jacques T. Godbout with Alain Caille, *The World of the Gift*, (Montreal: McGill-Queens University Press, 1998); Mark Osteen, 'Introduction: Questions of the Gift,' *The Question of the Gift: Essays Across Disciplines,* ed. Mark Osteen, (London: Routledge, 2002) pp. 1–42.

differing emphases, as an act of appropriation,[18] as a process of singularization[19] or personalization[20] or even as sign of individuality pitched against the authority of the market.[21] If commodities can achieve such significance, a gift does not seem quite so special. I do appreciate the routine importance of altering commodities into the essential objects of everyday life (not least because, like everyone else, I initiate this kind of material transformation everyday) and I understand that the characterization of the commodity and the gift are to some extent dependent upon each other so that once the meanings of commodities shift and re-shape then those gift also becomes less stable. However, as Mark Osteen, succinctly points out, 'people *do* give.'[22]

Rather than attempt to refine the category of the gift in anthropological, sociological, political or philosophical theory what this first chapter of *The Wedding Present* tries to do is set out some of the meanings of gifts contained in the responses to the 1998 Giving and Receiving Presents directive. It should be noted first of all that within Mass-Observation writing gifts are not a single category of object. For example, the unemployed correspondent from York, identified gifts of different types: the 'ordinary' and the 'unique'. She gives an affordable 'oven dish' as an example of the former and a 'piece of my own artwork' as the latter (A2801) (Figure 1.1). Such a distinction between ordinary and unique gifts falls either side of the commodity/gift opposition.[23] In theory, all gifts should be unique because they have a human imprint and all commodities ordinary because they have been reduced to just an object, their connections to people severed through their sale. An ordinary gift seems to be one that cannot be made to overcome its commodity condition. If this is indeed the case, it implies that giving, the act of exchange that is supposed to affirm a relationship between those who are party to the exchange and thereby transform the meaning of the exchanged object, did not entirely manage to lift the thing out of its market context.

---

18 Daniel Miller 'Consumption and its Consequences,'*Consumption and Everyday Life*, ed. Hugh Mackay (London: Sage Publications, 1997) p. 14, and Daniel Miller, 'Appropriating the State on the Council Estate,' *Man* 23 (1988) pp. 352–72.

19 Igor Kopytoff, 'The Cultural Biography of Things: Commoditization as Process,' *The Social Life of Things*, Ed. Arun Appadurai, (Cambridge: Cambridge University Press, 1986) pp. 65–91.

20 Mihaly Csikszentmihalyi and Eugene Rochberg-Halton, *The Meaning of Things: Domestic Symbols and the Self* (Cambridge: Cambridge University Press, 1981).

21 Dick Hebdige, *Hiding in the Light: On Images and Things* (London: Routledge, 1988).

22 Osteen, p. 16.

23 The difference between commodity and gift has also been interpreted as one between a gift-object and a gift-article, see Clive Dilnot, 'The Gift,' *Design Issues* IX.2 (1993) p. 63. For Daniel Miller, such a dualism is a formulation of the myth of modern superficiality, Miller, 1997, pp. 21–25. Godlier's remarks that 'gift objects and valuables are caught ... between two principles: between the inalienability of sacred objects and the alienability of commercial objects' (Godlier, p. 94) offers a way of re-thinking the place of the gift.

One of the ways in which Mass-Observation writers responded to the Giving and Receiving Presents directive was to engage in a discussion about what counts as a gift; they reflected upon which of the objects they received when they wed were their wedding presents. Their writing suggests that not all given things are gifts. Their definitions of gifts do not entirely rest upon giving as a type of exchange, on the fact that giving is not selling, but on the intentions of the object. Those given to keep appear within Mass-Observation writing as proper presents. But this is not, I would hasten to add, a rule of giving a gift but one of its recognized forms. Money was a frequent and much appreciated wedding present and it was given to be spent and spent quite quickly, early on in marriage when it was most needed. Wedding presents are invested with particular purposes, the most striking of which is approval. So many of Mass-Observation correspondents indicate, imply or more explicitly state that the gifts they received upon marriage were materializations of social approval that I want to offer this as the most important but not the only definition of gift received upon marriage. Many of these approving objects were kept and their continued possession is recounted with some pleasure and pride. However, these things could not be described as preferences for they were not objects of choice. Mass-Observation correspondents explain gifts as the effects of a range of existing or emergent social relationships and are rarely presented as subject to any kind of individual control.

Giving without Gifts

To argue that there are different kinds of gifts is to do no more than point out that dominant material values, like hierarchy of hand-made over mass produced or expensive over cheap, which prevail in institutional contexts such as markets and museums also can be evident in domestic gift giving practices. The differential value of gifts before they are given is an everyday knowledge. Some objects are more or less appropriate to be given to some people. Finding the right thing for a particular ritual or relationship is always considered a real social success. To take the examples offered by the unemployed York Mass-Observation correspondent once again: the ordinary oven dish and the unique artwork. The sister was not given an oven dish because it would not be enough on the occasion of her marriage. A close family relationship ought to be expressed though an intimate or expensive object, a unique one occupying the highest gift slot. On the other hand, an oven dish would be entirely appropriate wedding present for a more distant member of the family, a colleague or member of the same social circle. Indeed, in these more remote relationships a gift of an artwork could be interpreted as a social intrusion based on a false claim to know the recipient of the object.

Although ordinary and unique gifts bear different values, this Mass-Observation correspondent still regarded both as gifts by virtue of their being given, according to other correspondents, however, not all given things achieve the status of the gift, even that of an ordinary one. Correspondents describe how newly-weds moving into unfurnished rooms or homes were given pieces of furniture from family members but these things are not considered gifts. A social worker from Hertfordshire states:

> I was married in 1947, already pregnant so in those days weddings were quietly and hastily arranged ... My parents and my in laws gave us furniture, etc, to start us off, but these things didn't feel like presents. They just did what they had to do to help us (B1533).

When a Durham housewife married in 1982, she had no furniture for a newly bought house except 'a strip of carpet 18' by 4' feet long and two borrowed deck chairs.' She writes:

> We bought, secondhand, or were given things that were necessary, a bed, a cooker, a twin-tub washing machine (which I wish I still had, it was much better than the blasted automatic that I've got now) and a three piece suite. But these things weren't Wedding Presents, they were the things that get passed around to anyone starting out, and then when other things are acquired, most of them get passed on again to the next couple starting out (M1201).

Continually passing around furniture between newly married couples could easily be interpreted as evidence of a micro Maussian gift society in contemporary domestic culture. First, these transactions are obligatory. Since the marrying couple did not have the objects necessary to create the bare minimum of domestic respectability nor means of getting them themselves, they had to be given them. Second, these gifts are reciprocated, 'passed on' again. They are not, of course, returned directly to their givers but in all likelihood to younger members of that family line, perhaps to a sister or sister-in-law who got married the following year. However, both the Hertfordshire social worker and the Durham housewife are clear that these objects were not gifts. This may be a case of the all important difference between what people say and what they do but equally it should not be assumed that these correspondents are mistaken just because their ideas do not fit in with established theoretical frameworks. Their writing suggests that giving an object is not necessarily a declaration that it is a gift. The given furniture was second-hand rather than new, although this should not make it less of a gift. Newness is a commodity condition, which may welcomed in many gifts, including wedding presents because they may allow the newly married couple to perform the most fashionable housekeeping techniques. But ideas of tradition and the patina of age are also highly valued in gifts. A good gift, one that is intimate or unique, certainly does not have to be new. More important, I would argue, in the Mass-Observation accounts of 'passed around' furniture is that both giver and receiver understand these things were not meant to have a permanent place in the newly married household. All parties to their exchange knew they would be replaced as soon as the married couple found or could afford something better. Given objects, which as one correspondent put it, were 'to start us off' were not gifts because they were never going to be kept. Such giving-for-keeping is not quite the same as Annette Weiner's 'giving-while-keeping' although it does indicate a similar underlying 'paradox' of giving and not giving. A recognized gift is one that when received is then removed from all spheres of exchange.

Giving for Keeping

The imperative to keep a gift could be interpreted as an effect of its embodiment. For Mauss, the idea that givers never completely leave the objects they give was the reason for reciprocation but it can also explain the requirement to keep. If a gift bears a giver with it into its new destination, a newly formed married household for example, to disregard or dispose of the object upon arrival or even some time after would be to disavow the giver's presence, to deny their investment in the receiver's domestic affairs. Making an effort to retain gifts, usually understood as an appropriate act, as the right thing to do, demonstrates respect for the givers and provides permanent recognition of the relationship between giver and receiver along with the households to which they may belong. Of the gifts she received when she married in 1954, a West Sussex sub-postmistress states, 'I'm happy to say we still have many of them and I still associate the giver with the gift when we use them' (M1571). Although few correspondents discussed the reasons why gifts should be kept, successfully keeping them was a central theme of the Giving and Receiving Presents directive.

Both men and women express a degree of pride in continued use and possession of their wedding presents. 'We have kept and used all the items' stated a Surrey health services administrator about gifts from his second marriage in 1947 (R2065). Another male correspondent, a lecturer from Watford who wed in 1977, wrote much the same thing. ' We kept all our presents until they broke or wore out' (S2211). So did a teacher of hairdressing, a female corespondent from Stockport who married in 1971. 'I keep every gift and try to use everything' she explained. 'I had over 20 prs of pillow cases ... I used a few as pram and cot covers when our son was born – every colour you can imagine' (R860). Lifetime commitments to keeping gifts are clearly expressed by a nurse who married in 1963 and now lives in Brighton. 'I am very attached to my remaining wedding presents and if I have to move into a smaller place because of old age I shall do my utmost to take them with me' (L1991).

Giving Money

There is a problem with defining a gift as an object to be kept. Mass-Observation correspondents consistently describe money as a gift. 'I had some money as a gift from work colleagues' remembers the Hertfordshire social worker, 'about £10 I think, but otherwise I didn't have any presents' (B1533). Other correspondents, many of whom wed as she did in the immediate postwar period, recall being given money. A carpenter from Peacehaven, who married in 1945, noted that he and his wife received 'three glass water jugs, a five pound note, cannot remember anything else' (T2741). A female correspondent whose marriage took place in the same year received 'the magnificent sum of £50' from her parents. 'I can only imagine that it was money saved to help me through university, which would not be needed, since I got married instead' she explained. Ten pounds was spent on a 'tin chest full of second-hand household goods, many of them pre-war, which had been advertised in the local paper' but since she and her husband had little savings the 'cheques were most important to us' (P2546). Post-war impoverishment combined with the lack of consumer goods in the shops meant that money as a marriage gift increased in importance at this time but almost every Mass-Observation correspondent received a financial gift of some kind whenever they wed. Money was a significant gift throughout the period of this study. A Shoreham correspondent who lists her occupations as artist, teacher, gardener and hospital worker and had a registry office wedding in 1970 writes that wealthy family friends gave 'a cheque for £12, which was *hundreds*!' (A1706).

These monies were spent, not saved, not kept. The artist-cum-hospital worker's went on a sewing machine. Theoretically, money should not be a gift; it is not exactly a thing but an image, a representation of market value, the most functional commodity. Moreover, it is difficult to see how money, a representation of an abstract value can become embodied. It has so little form. Yet, almost every correspondent recorded money as a marriage gift; they often remembered exactly how much and who gave it, remembering these givers with great respect.[24]

A director of a finance company, a male correspondent from Sevenoaks, was able to marry whilst an indebted law student because his future wife's mother warned against wasting life waiting and gave money she had recently inherited. He writes that 'thanks to my mother-in-law's gift and advice, we did not have to endure a long Victorian type engagement' and adds 'she is still alive, aged 95, and I have always loved and admired her' (C110). Gratitude is reserved for money above all else. 'My wife's parents gave us £60 towards the cost of arranging a wedding and reception' writes a Staffordshire teacher, adding '(apart from this money, which was an immense help and a huge sacrifice for them, we did all the arranging and paying ourselves)' (W2322). Marriage gifts of money have been identified by David Cheal as a transfer of wealth from one generation to another.[25] That given to the law student who became a company director was exactly this and other Mass-Observation accounts indicate that it is parents and the relatives in the parents' generation that give the most money.

Although money's economic value is its most obvious attribute, it is also clear from the responses to the Giving and Receiving Presents directive that it has an

---

24 Jonathan Parry and Maurice Bloch, 'Introduction: Money and the Morality of Exchange,' *Money and the Morality of the Exchange* ed. Jonathan Parry and Maurice Bloch (Cambridge: Cambridge University Press, 1989) pp. 8–12. See also comments in Mary Douglas and Baron Isherwood, *The World of Goods*, 1979, (London: Routledge, 1996) p. 38.

25 Cheal, pp. 92–98; Mary Ann McGarth and Basil Englis, 'Intergenerational Gift Giving in Subcultural Wedding Celebrations: The Ritual as Cash Cow.' *Gift Giving: A Research Anthology*, ed Cele Otnes and Richard F. Beltramini, (Bowling Green State University Popular Press, 1996) pp. 123–141.

Figure 1.2   A sign of approval

important symbolic function. Money is a sign of approval. Large amounts demonstrate approval because they contain an element of trust: they show that the giver values the judgment of the bride or the groom (in both their choice of their partner and ability to use the money well). Smaller amounts may not be able to project faith in the future for a sensible couple but identifies a worthy individual. Marriage as a rite of passage is a moment of evaluation. It provides an opportunity to formally show approval, with a financial gift. 'The only money I received' wrote a typesetter from Woking, married in 1948:

> was from an old bachelor who lived next door. In his youth he was badly injured... all through his life he had been ridiculed because of his crippled bones. He never spoke to many people but from a child I always talked to him when he allowed. He was poor because he was never in work.... The day before I was married he called me over and fished a one pound note from his pocket for me. A week's wages was then about five pounds and he did not earn anything like that (H1806) (Figure 1.2).

Giving Approval

I want to try to argue that money is not exceptional gift and in a way I have to attempt this because money is so regularly given on marriage. It is possible to claim that most wedding presents in varying (and deliberately gauged) degrees show approval of the giver for the receiver. 'Everyone who came to the wedding buffet – at my parents' house – brought a present,' states an infant school teacher from Kendall who married in 1952. This is typical; it is what usually, even always, happens at weddings: guests bring gifts. Those invited to the religious or civil ceremony, to share food or other celebrations, such as dancing, are expected to endorse the marriage with a gift. All these things, whether they are ordinary or unique, intimate, expensive or still in a commodity condition, function within the wedding arrangements as seals or tokens of approval. With money nothing distracts from this function. Money is only an exception because all it does is show approval.

In a number of different ways, Mass-Observation writers relate how approval is part of the definition of a gift, or a wedding present at any rate. Giving, I would suggest, is widely understood as a performance of approval for those marrying even though it may not always be discussed in these terms. Giving as approval is only made starkly clear when gifts are few or absent. 'I got no presents' states a Suffolk housewife, 'because both marriages were not approved by any sets of parents' (W1835). A Bolton secondary school teacher who has 'never been married' herself but is in a lesbian relationship with a divorcee reported that:

> When my partner told me about her wedding in 1975, I was shocked that her parents, who didn't approve of her choice as a penniless student for a husband, gave her twenty pounds and a pair of towels. She feels hurt about that, particularly as it was such a contrast to the way her brother and sister had been treated on their wedding days (O2349).

Approval, therefore, can be withheld with a gift of low value in the same way as it is expressed with one that is appropriately expensive or has other high qualities. A divorced correspondent based in Grimsby describes how in 1986, some five years after she began her long-term lesbian relationship, 'my partner's parents gave a set of silver-plated cutlery, such as her brother had received when he married, which meant a great deal to us both' (L2835). The gift was used to demonstrate the parent's acceptance of equivalence between their daughter's cohabitation and their son's marriage. Eating equipment suitable for family celebrations and made of a substance that is known to last is one of the most conventional wedding presents and was a token of approval of the highest order.

It is second or third marriages, as well as cohabitation based on homosexual or heterosexual unions that expose how giving is an act of approval. They do so because the conventions that are simply followed at first marriages are more open to question making the reasons for giving gifts momentarily more visible. 'I've been married three times' announced a 'counsellor/researcher' from Preston. When she first married in 1964, an uncle and aunt gave her a 'set of cut glass drinks glasses.' The objects became parts in a dance of approval and rejection:

> I took these with me – bar a few broken ones – into my second marriage at which point the same uncle and aunt said that they had given me a wedding present once and since marriages were suppose to be for life that was that and don't expect another present. The third time I was married in 1977, the same uncle and aunt, who had never been married but were brother and sister, decided for some reason, (though again it was a quiet register office occasion and they were not invited) to ask us what we would like. They agreed to give us the money for a chest freezer but when it came my uncle gave us a sort of written contract that the money be returned to them should the marriage fail "within twelve months." It was all so embarrassing to my husband-to-be that I signed, we've survived

over 21 years of marriage, have replaced this chest freezer, but I still have a couple of the now-chipped cut glass tumblers that I use for flowers (G226).

Announcing that you are not giving a wedding present to a niece and giving one conditionally are both acts of disapproval. To assert the right to claim back money until the marriage has lasted beyond a certain point is to withhold any symbolic endorsement that gift can bring while fulfilling the obligation of close family to give. The cut glass tumblers seem to offer the niece some compensation for the harsh judgements of her uncle and aunt. Despite their attempts to manipulate marriage gift giving to register their opposition to re-marriage, their original gift demonstrates its propriety. A vase of flowers is always a sign of a respectable home.

Figure 1.3   A show of presents, 1953 (Mass-Observation correspondent D2589)

Show of Approval

In the earlier part of the period covered by this study, between the immediate post-war period and the mid 1970s, the ritualized receipt of wedding presents could be interpreted as a material display of approval of the marriage. A number of correspondents describe a practice called 'a show of presents,' the deliberate arrangement of wedding gifts at the bride's parents' home or at the reception (Figures 1.3, 1.4, 1.5, 1.6, 1.7, 1.8). Mass-Observation correspondents indicate that

Figure 1.4   A show of presents, 1953 (Mass Observation correspondent D2589)

the practice has been discontinued. They explain that it 'was the custom at the time' (D1697), 'a traditional thing that people did, in those days' (W571), 'as expected in those days' (W633).[26] The last show of presents recorded in response to the 'Giving and Receiving Presents directive took place in 1974 (C119). A very simple form was described by a housewife from Swanley in Kent who listed her paid occupations as clerk, telephonist and shop assistant. She married in 1947. 'I remember having 3 sets of fruit bowls and 3 saucepans but that is all. We received them at the reception and put them on a table for all to see' (B1424). More often, the show of presents was a separate event within the wedding ritual. As a research chemist who wed in 1954 explains:

> Everyone invited to the wedding was expected to give a present, and there was an element of competition here, as there was a 'show of presents' at the bride's home, to which all the bride's family's friends and neighbours would be invited. This meant setting aside a room – usually the dining room – so that the table, sideboard and trolley etc could be a display area for the gifts, with the donor's card sitting on the present (M1395).

---

26 Shows of presents are described in Diana Leonard, *Sex and Generation: A Study of Courtship and Weddings* (London: Tavistock, 1984) p. 235.

Figure 1.5   A show of presents, 1953 (Mass-Observation correspondent D2589)

Spreading out new possessions on all available flat surfaces for those within the nearby social network to see may all initially appear to be a status display, a form of competitive consumption, a parade of position through acquired objects. There are formal similarities between a show of presents and, say, the arrangement of a front room wherein objects are also placed for outsiders to view. But in the latter, the owner's taste, wealth and class appears visible in their objects and this is not the case with the former. The 'element of competition' at the show of presents that the research chemist remarks upon was not just between the bride's family that hosts the display and the neighbours who look on but also between the givers to the bride and groom. 'All the gifts were laid out in one room of my parent's house with cards showing who had sent them' wrote a male correspondent, a pharmacist from Bolton, married in 1957. He added, 'this was a 'Mecca' for various aunties eager to see if they had been upstaged in the gift war' (M1544).[27] The 'setting-on' of donor's cards invites comparisons of generosity. But generosity is also a measure of recipient as well as giver of a gift. Importantly, and unlike the front room, it is the donors (the bride's and groom's family and friends) who are judged in the display of objects not their owners (the bride and groom themselves). For example, a family member may wish to be represented by a small gift when their relationship to the one or other of the couple getting married is quite distant or is close but characterized by dislike. They may use a modest wedding present to indicate they do not wholeheartedly approve of the match. Thus the meaning of each gift indicates the state of familial or friendly relationships and that of the collection as a whole is not quite the sum of its complex parts. Its meanings greatly depend upon on who is looking at it. A well-informed aunt may find family alliances and disputes as well as hierarchies of wealth manifested in each gift but a neighbour might only see economic and social position of a family as a whole.

Those Mass-Observation writers who report that they had shows of presents only really to provide an outline of them, accounting for the practice in general rather the specific conduct of the one they held. They would not, of course, know the reactions their family, friends and neighbours to the collection of objects that would be using to set up their married home. Critical evaluations of objects are rarely relayed to their owners and bland praise dominates such discussions. An assistant personnel officer from Derbyshire, married in 1969, circumvents the difficulty of discussing how her presents might have been judged by suggesting the experience of guest rather than the bride:

> Most of the gifts were given to us the day before the wedding or on the day itself. A custom quite usual in those days was for the presents to be displayed in a bedroom, spread out on the bed, in the windows, on drawer tops etc and all the guests were invited to view the presents. Cars would be lined up to convey whoever wanted to go and quite often the husbands would decline, leaving the wives to go and cast an interested eye over the presents. The quality and expense would give an immediate guide to the bride's family's social standing and affluence. Also it was a golden chance to take a look upstairs. In those days people didn't invite anyone upstairs, it was like a secret and personal part of the house, unbidden to visitors. So to be able to sneak around, looking at how other people

---

27 Shows of presents did not usually taken place in the groom's parent's house but may have been held there because the pharmacist married on the same day as his twin brother.

lived was satisfying some secret longing in some odd way – especially to a young girl who didn't know what it was like to have nice things (H1703).[28]

This account, which so vividly locates a daughter's gifts in a parent's house, lends much weight to the argument that wedding presents reflect the economic and social position of a whole family rather than just an individual. As the assistant personnel officer put it, they were 'an immediate guide to the bride's family's social standing and affluence.' The bride, especially if she lived at home, was if course implicated in this assessment but the gifts she and her groom received were not so much signs of individual status as they were revelations about the social world to which she belonged.

Giving and Receiving without Choosing

An analysis of giving gifts as a way of issuing approval is based on an assumption that the objects involved have been carefully selected to create a predetermined desired effect. Anyone who has to give a gift on occasions of heightened significance, such as weddings, will have performed some work of selection, attempting to resolve the thorny problem of trying to get the right thing, an object that so clearly presents intention it requires no verbal explanation and is therefore readily appreciated at both a symbolic and material level. When Mass-Observation correspondents reflect upon their acts of giving they foreground their own decision-making as selection process but as receivers they draw attention to the factors affecting gift giving that neither givers nor receivers completely control. They suggest that types of objects are related to social circumstance.

   Property and work relationships as well as both short and long-term financial status are offered as explanations for the receipt of particular types of objects. The property relationships regarded as the norm for married people applied to many Mass-Observation correspondents: immediately after their wedding they established themselves in an unfurnished owner-occupied house. This situation produced recognizably typical marriage gifts or what are often referred to in the Giving and Receiving Presents directive as the 'usual things' (P1278, R1719, S2211). When some correspondents married, however, they already owned their own home, some rented and others did not leave a parental home for the first few years. A counsellor living in Norfolk, widowed only a few years after she first wed in 1973, remarried requiring no presents as she had 'a three-bedroomed house full.' She received a small number of ceremonial rather than useful things: 'cut crystal decanters and tumblers and a clock' (K798). Glass, china and utility furniture were given to a shop

---

28 Her claim that shows of presents took place in bedrooms contradicts the correspondent cited earlier (M1395) who stated that they were held dining rooms. These differences must ultimately be a matter of class. Only the larger houses that tend to be afforded and occupied by middle classes have dining rooms. A bed might be the only empty space in the daytime and early evening in a small dwelling.

**Figure 1.6   A show of presents, 1953 (Mass-Observation
                correspondent D2589)**

worker when she married in 1950 as well as 'some gifts of money' that was 'put
towards a 'bedroom' 'suite' for our rooms we rented.' She explained that 'These
two rooms were in my Parents house' (H260). Gifts were matched to homes as a
London civil servant living in East Sussex, who was an art student when he married
in 1976, explains. He reflects upon how housing, the size of his home and the terms
of its joint occupation, shaped his gifts. He states 'we were living in a one bedroom
bedsit we were not really looking for much in the way of material possessions.' He
received a practical and a humorous gift from friends, a carpet and a rolling pin. Plus
the landlord let him off a payment. 'Have this one on me' was written in his rent
book (J2187). Another correspondent, who was also cohabiting on a tenancy when
she married her partner in the early 1970s, recalls that 'my in-laws gave us 6 months
rent on our flat, which was a great help' (A1706).

    The types of gifts that derived from work relationships varied according to the
nature of those relationships and reflected, especially in the 1950s and early 1960s,
the idea of the male breadwinner norm. Some male correspondents report being
presented with a marriage bonus. 'I worked for a private company,' wrote a chartered
surveyor whose first marriage took place in 1956, 'and received a cash payment from
my employers' (B1509). Colleagues, acting collectively, gave both male and female

colleagues marriage gifts. Those given to women were often more substantial than those to men in anticipation that domestic things would end up belonging to the wife. In 1961, an architect's assistant got 'an electric coffee pot which we hardly ever used' from his colleagues while his wife's gave her 'a dinner service...which we chose at Heal's, lovely to look at, but very brittle' (A833). Women also received more objects from work for future use in their married life because these gifts sometimes doubled up as leaving presents. One correspondent, a Bolton housewife with an employment history in various secretarial jobs, received a series of gifts from fellow workers when she married in 1955:

> At the time I was working as a wages clerk in a textile mill and the girls in the winding room gave me a blue table cloth and four napkins to match. The joiner and carpenter who worked at the mill made a tea trolley for me and the storekeeper gave me a plain white tea set. I know I received presents from other departments but can't remember what they were. My colleagues in the office bought me a carpet cleaner – I think it was Bex Bissell. I didn't have an electric vacuum cleaner for many years (F1614).

Mass-Observation correspondents also frequently point out the relative poverty experienced at the moment they married and the late-twentieth century ideas of wealth. The relationship between financial and material wealth seems so obvious it is simply asserted rather than discussed. However, marrying couples who had little money were given large gifts and or large numbers of them because it was perceived that they needed them. This situation is described by an audiotypist from Leighton Buzzard who married in 1956:

> Like most of my contemporaries, I made out a list and people ticked off what they had decided to buy me and my husband, (as a young couple we were not very well off). My parents, who were fairly well off by the standards of the time, bought us a lovely divan-bed and paid for the wedding (except for my dress and the bridemaids' dresses, flowers and photographer for which I paid) (B89).

Another correspondent married in the same year, now divorced and living in Oxford, discusses the differences between the temporary financial insecurity of newlyweds and the established wealth or relative wealth of their families. She and her husband wed when they were both 21 and he was about to start a PhD:

> As we had very little money and were likely to be in the same situation for the following three years, our need was for practical presents and we did send out a modest wedding list to anyone who asked for one, with such items as an iron, coffee pot, clothes airer, pillowcases (H2447).

They received bed and table linen, blankets, a bedspread, embroidered linen tray cloths, china, a coffee pot, a toast rack, a wooden fruit bowl, decorative dishes, jam pots, a silver muffin dish, cloisonné salt and pepper pots' and a tool set. Concerned that this fairly small collection of wedding presents might be misinterpreted, she directly addresses her reader:

You will see that we did not receive large items such as vacuum cleaner, any furniture or kitchen equipment, because although our families were by no means poor, people did not give such expensive wedding gifts as they do now, everything was on a much smaller, more modest scale. Also we were moving into a furnished flat many miles away and I expect large items were thought to be inappropriate as it would cost us quite a lot of money to have such things moved from one part of the country to another (H2447).

The amount of money families may spend on a wedding, the property and work relationships of the marrying couples are thus complexly related to class position. Class is also occasionally offered as an overall explanation for the objects received upon marriage. A shop worker from Brentwood married in 1950 noted that she received money 'but not large amounts, as most people were only average working class' (H260). The Derbyshire assistant personnel officer who married in 1969, prefaced her discussion of what she received by announcing that she and her husband 'were both children of working class families and my family in particular were at the poorer end of the spectrum although all my family including my father was in regular work' (H1703).

Thus signs of class identity, such as occupation, accommodation, and financial position as well as class itself are related to the gift exchanges in a series of mundane but actually quite revealing ways. Given objects are traced to a set of social conditions: the property relationships that the bride and groom were about to enter into, their

Figure 1.7   A show of presents, 1953 (Mass-Observation
                    correspondent C1405)

Figure 1.8   A show of presents, 1953 (Mass-Observation correspondent C1405)

position within the world of work as primary or secondary wage earners, the wealth and the class of their families. A drive to contextualize can be seen the writing of Mass-Observation correspondents; they explain how the things they accepted as gifts have been determined for them and not in the sense that they were chosen by givers. Brides and grooms received a limited set of objects, including china, money, kitchen utensils, bed linen and some furniture, but the specific values, forms and combinations of these gifts varied according to social circumstance.

Gifts are so implicated in the various relationships of everyday life, those of family, neighbourhood and work that we should not wonder that they elude easy or unitary categorization. Nor can they be reduced to just the moment of their exchange important though that moment may be. The ownership of an object changes and, as is evident from Mass-Observation writing, the exchanged object can gain a specific social purpose. Even objects devoted to exchange, like money, become gifts if the giver uses them to issue approval. The show of approval is one of the forms of the gift, which, we should add, cannot be straightforwardly be reciprocated particularly when the approving object is given by a member of an older generation to a younger one. The gift as object for keeping is another of its forms. Giving as a process of embodiment can invest objects with such significance that they must be kept for a lifetime or longer. Keeping gifts honours the giver and continually so, constantly affirming the relationship between giver and receiver, ensuring that their connection stays alive. Keeping seems to fulfill the sociable purpose of the gift just as well as reciprocation (although this may also, of course, take place).

Thus the responses to the Giving and Receiving Presents directive do not neatly fall in with theoretical projections about the gifts. But neither are notions of obligation to give or the sociable nature of the gift simply disproved or overturned as if Mass-Observation writing is scientific discovery that will lead us to a new gift theory. Rather, correspondent's accounts of their wedding presents provides layers of detail about the conduct of gift relationships and the meanings of gifts that incrementally, and quite gently, questions the wisdom of academic theory with their own, sometimes overlapping sometimes differing, understanding of the practical logic of giving a gift.

Chapter 2

China and Pyrex: The Practices of Preservation

'Inalienable possessions are the representation of how social identities are reconstituted through time' (Annette Weiner, 1992).[1]

Introduction

China is consistently given as a wedding present. It is received at weddings across the whole period of this study.[2] Moreover, it is often the most complex gift and the most highly valued, both financially and emotionally. China is a traditional marriage gift that has retained its relevance in contemporary wedding rituals. It appears as an essential item within every commercial gift list service, the first group of objects featured in all of these lists[3] (Figure 2.1), including the most recent on-line services such as confetti.co.uk (Figure 2.2).

The central place of china in the wedding gift giving rituals relates to its historical role in consumption and domesticity. Indeed, the understanding of the formation of a consumer society in Britain turns upon the purchase, use and display of china. To consider the regularity of china as a wedding present in the second half of the twentieth century, we need to reflect, briefly at least, upon this history. Sarah Richards has identified when the ownership of objects we would call china became widespread, replacing older vernacular eating utensils. She writes that: 'fine earthenwares, and principally creamwares … ousted pewter from a significant

---

1   Annette Weiner, *Inalienable Possessions: The Paradox of Keeping-While-Giving* (Berkeley: University of California Press, 1992) p. 11.

2   Other studies confirm the frequency and importance of china as a wedding gift. See, for example, David Cheal, *The Gift Economy* (London: Routledge, 1988) p. 131.

3   China is the first 'gift idea' in Lewis' 1998 'Bridal Gift Service Pack', first in Selfridges and Co. 1998 information for the Selfridges Bride and the opening item of the 1998 'The Wedding List Co. Check List'; it is the initial and most prominent illustration in Debenhams' 1998 'Gift Service' leaflet, the opening suggestion of www.wrapit.co.uk's 2003 leaflet as well as confetti.co.uk's catalogue of the same year and the first image in Marks & Spencers' 2003 'Wedding List Service' brochure. It occupied the number one slot in *The Independent*'s 'The 50 Best' series, justified by Wedding List Services' Verity Pride's remark that the dinner service is 'the core of every wedding list'. 'All Wrapped Up: the 50 Best Wedding Presents' *Independent* 13–19 May 2000 *The Information* supplement: pp. 4–11.

proportion of urban homes in the latter half of the eighteenth century.'[4] 'By the end of the century', she adds, 'attractive if modest ceramic tablewares were accessible even to the labouring classes in many parts of Britain.'[5] Richards is careful not to assume that there is naturally emulative logic driving the desire for china. Its shiny shapes were not necessarily copies of aristocratic heirlooms nor straightforward family silver substitutes. It was an alternative to both coarse ceramic ware and precious metals, an expression of a new form of propriety and civility of the emergent middle class. [6]

Lorna Weatherill, in her study, *Consumer Behaviour and Material Culture in Britain*, (1988), noted that 'eating and drinking were the occasion of valued social contacts'[7] and 'meals were occasions on which people presented themselves to others'.[8] The set of objects she terms 'new decorated tablewares'[9] played a key role in this performance. They represented the members of the household as a collective (a family) to those of similar standing within their circle (neighbours, friends, and social contacts) that they felt equal to eating with. They had a particularly significant expressive function:

> The equipment used at mealtimes had a singular importance in the material culture of middling households in two ways. In the first place, some of the most valuable and attractive items (sometimes displayed on shelves) were associated with meals. Secondly, some of the most visible changes in domestic equipment in the early eighteenth century were associated with eating and drinking[10]

Expensive and innovative, china demonstrated the extent of its possessor's wealth and fashionability. However, since it was deployed and displayed within an internal and limited social world, it was not used to impress outsiders but to establish social standing *within* a social group. We ought then to note, following Richards and Weatherill and others, that consumerism in its early phases was class-specific:[11] it was a phenomenon of the middle classes, or more particularly of their making. The domestic realm, which promised protection and respite from the market place, was

---

4   Sarah Richards, *Eighteenth-Century Ceramics: Products for a Civilised Society* (Manchester: Manchester University Press, 1999) p. 94.

5   Richards, p. 97.

6   Richards' work can be read as a critique of Neil McKendrick's account of emulation as the motor of eighteenth-century consumption (Neil McKendrick, 'Commercialisation and the Economy,' *The Birth of a Consumer Society: the Commercialisation of Eighteenth-Century England*, Neil McKendrick, John Brewer, J. H. Plumb (London: Hutchinson, 1983) 9–194. See especially Richards pp. 89, 110 and 127.

7   Lorna Weatherill, *Consumer Behaviour and Material Culture in Britain 1660–1760*, 1988 (London: Routledge, 1996) p. 137.

8   Weatherill, p. 155.

9   Weatherill, p. 137.

10   Weatherill, p. 155.

11   See, for example, Ben Fine and Ellen Leopold, *The World of Consumption* (London: Routledge, 1993).

Figure 2.1   Marks & Spencer 'Wedding List Service,' 2003

dining collections

Casual Tableware	10-27
Box Sets	28-29
Formal Tableware	30-39
Silverware & Cutlery	40-45
Glassware	46-49

Figure 2.2   Confetti Gift Service, 'Dining Collections,' 2000

the site of their cultural authority[12] and it was created through consumption. Their moral universe, which becomes an ideal even for those whom the maintenance of spatially separate spheres was an economic impossibility, was a particular formation of consumer culture.[13] This is the contradictory and fragile foundation of the idea of home: the objects that distinguished the domestic domain from the market, such as pretty teacups, were of and from the market. The home, like the female family members who occupied it, were separate but dependent upon the world outside and thus at a structural level were not separate at all.

---

12 Leonore Davidoff and Catherine Hall, *Family Fortunes. Men and Women of the English Middle Class, 1750–1850* (London: Hutchinson, 1987).

13 Don Slater, *Consumer Culture and Modernity* (Cambridge: Polity Press, 1997) p. 15.

Historians of eighteenth century consumption have produced precise demographic analysis of material culture, identifying who was consuming which types of objects[14] tracing the development of practices (such as the display and use of china) that are now traditions, naturalized as the way things are or should be done. The display and use of china are unquestioned conventions of a respectable or even 'normal' domesticity. It is important to remember that eighteenth century fine earthenwares or new decorated tablewares (china in other words) did not fill up a pre-existing family home but created it.[15] China, moreover, was a key component in the development of a specific version of domesticity wherein propriety, respectability and morality were staked upon the possession of particular types of things. The patterns and shapes of china are signs of a culture of respectable aspirations, of limited and controlled sociability; they are emblems of family membership and of belief in the family's beneficial effects. These meanings are echoed in reproduction of eighteenth century forms, often labelled traditional or classical styles (Figure 2.3) and are reconfigured, sometimes with their original class politics overturned or reformed, in modern contemporary designs (Figure 2.4).

This chapter focuses upon the meanings of china created and sustained through its exchange, use and preservation rather than its design. Practices of preservation, unlike those of exchange and display, have not been a sustained subject of analysis within studies of consumption. The testimony I present in this chapter, which like the rest of the book draws upon the responses to the 1998 Mass-Observation Giving and Receiving Presents directive, suggests that preservation is an unrecognised, even alternative, but widespread domestic practice within a consumer economy driven by desire to replace objects that have not worn out.[16] I would like to suggest that preservation is the defining practice of domesticity but cannot make such a general claim based on the study of just one type of object. Within this chapter, therefore, there is a comparison between the specific practices of possessing china and those of keeping an object that could be considered its opposite: Pyrex. Thus, some of the differences between decorative and functional domestic objects are also identified here as I try to think about why some things are more valued than others. While in this book, and indeed all my work in the field of material culture, I have followed Mary Douglas and Baron Isherwood's instructions that all objects are meaningful and not merely useful,[17] some do seem more meaningful, or at least are more highly prized.

---

14 Maxine Berg, 'New Commodities, Luxuries and their Consumers in Eighteenth-century England' *Consumers and Luxury: Consumer Culture and Europe 1650–1850*, ed. Maxine Berg and Helen Clifford (Manchester: Manchester University Press, 1999) pp. 63–85; John Brewer and Roy Porter, ed. *Consumption and the World of Goods* (London: Routledge, 1994).

15 Suzanne Reimer and Deborah Leslie, 'Identity, Consumption and the Home,' *Home Cultures* 1.2 (2004) p. 193 draw on a series of arguments about how home is created through its interior artefacts rather than exterior structures.

16 Victor J. Papenek, *Design for the Real World: Human Ecology and Social Change* (St Albans: Paladin. 1974) pp. 73–85.

17 Mary Douglas and Baron Isherwood, *The World of Goods: Towards an Anthropology of Consumption*, 1979 (London and New York: Routledge, 1996) p. 38.

China: Rarely Used

Wedding china does not refer to all the ceramic objects that a bride and groom might receive upon their marriage. Vases and storage jars, for example, are not included. Wedding china is always tableware. Plates of varying sizes, desert bowls, perhaps soup bowls and serving dishes as well as the cups, saucers, tea and coffee pots are the components of dinner services and tea sets constitute wedding china. These objects have a very special place within the whole assembly of wedding presents. A gift of china is a cultural universal: it is an object of exchange at weddings in communities that occupy different times and spaces. However, how and when they can be used is tightly prescribed, based upon an unwritten but closely followed set of rules. Their use is ritualized, in other words. These objects, most regularly given upon marriage, are rarely used. Eating and drinking from forms designed for that purpose is restricted to 'calendrical rites',[18] such as Christmas, or moments of highly significant social exchange whose purpose is to establish new relationships. Furthermore, wedding china is also frequently displayed and preserved.

Acts of display have been interpreted as attempts to demarcate status, especially class status.[19] There can be no doubt that an economic and social hierarchical order can be established through the demonstration of ownership of more or less prestigious varieties of china.[20] Beryl, Denby, Eternal Beau, Midwinter, Minton, Poole, Rochester, Royal Doulton, Spode, Susie Cooper, Washington, Wedgwood, Worcester are the makes of china that Mass-Observation correspondents report they received. It is, of course, possible to rank wedding china according to its ability to confer status by association with its dominant or normative market meanings. Wedgwood reproduces traditional forms that it once innovated; its expense and effortless historical design is safely prestigious (Figure 2.3 and Figure 2.4).[21] The same goes for Royal Doulton (Figure 2.5), except that the firm's reputation for 'art manufactures,'[22] in particular its sale of figurines, could make its wedding china more or less appealing to Wedgwood end of the market. For those who may wish to assert their preference for decorated objects Royal Doulton would be a good choice but not for others who associate decoration with lack of sophistication. Midwinter, on the other hand, was a modern rather than traditional

---

18 Cheal, p. 148.

19 Thorstein Veblen, *The Theory of the Leisure Class*, 1889 (Dover Publications, New York, 1994).

20 Douglas and Isherwood, p. 44, argue that 'Food is a medium for discriminating values, and the more numerous the discriminated ranks, the more varieties of food would be needed.' Since food is regularly served on china, it would also be part of this discriminating process.

21 See Robin Reilly, *Wedgwood: The New Illustrated Dictionary* (Woodbridge, Suffolk: Antique Collectors Club, 1995).

22 Paul Atterbury and Louise Irvine, *The Doulton Story* (Victoria and Albert Museum, 1979); Desmond Eyles, *Royal Doulton 1815–1965: The Rise and Expansion of the Royal Doulton Potteries* (London: Hutchinson, 1965); Stoke-on-Trent Museum and Art Gallery, *The Legacy of Henry Doulton: 120 Years of Royal Doulton in Burslem, 1877–1997* (Stoke-on-Trent Museum and Art Gallery, 1997).

Figure 2.3   Opening images of Wedgwood's 1997 catalogue

gift when it was received in the 1950s (W640). It now commands relatively high prices in secondhand markets as a sought after example of retro kitsch (Figure 2.6). Eternal Beau is kitsch of a different order; its contemporary popular forms do not hold any nostalgia for the mass-produced (Figure 2.7). This list could go on. But most Mass-Observation correspondents did not name the manufacturer of china that they received when they wed despite being asked in the Giving and Receiving Presents directive to give details of the make, if they had that information.[23] This makes any attempt to draw up a typology of the taste politics of wedding china fairly pointless. The problem is not insufficient information within the responses to the directive since it cannot be regarded as a statistical survey anyway, but that Mass-Observation correspondents have obviously considered that details about the manufacturers are not important enough to remember and include. Two things are consistently noted down in relation to the receipt of a dinner service or tea set. Mass-Observation correspondents always identify the plates, bowls, cups and saucers by the material of which they were made (china or bone china) and they describe how they have succeeded, or not succeeded, in preserving them. The preservation of china is, therefore, the focus of this chapter.

---

23 See Appendix 1. After the opening question 'What gifts did you receive?' Mass-Observation correspondents were encouraged to offer as much information as they could, specifically: 'Please be as detailed as possible – if you can recall not only the items, but also the make and design of objects, that would be appreciated.'

Figure 2.4   'Colosseum,' Wedgwood's 1997 catalogue

Many Mass-Observation writers state that the frequent use of wedding china is prohibited. For example, a civil servant from Orpington whose wedding took place in 1948 began his account of the gifts he and his wife received by claiming, as other male correspondents did, that 'I do not recall much about our wedding presents.' However, this is what he did remember:

> There was a hand-painted tea service from my wife's parents. It was a 'second' because that was all that could be bought legally at the time, the perfect products being reserved for export. We still have it and like it very much. It is rarely used because we do prize it (K1515).

The guarded use that can guarantee long-term possession is also presented with some pride, as success story of married life, by a housewife from Bolton whom had worked in a variety of service sector jobs before becoming a mature student. She received two tea sets when she married in 1955. 'A friend bought us a bone china tea set and my husband's cousin also bought us a bone china tea set.' She also seemed pleased to report that 'We still have both of these sets as they have been kept for display rather than for use' (F1614). Nor are such restrictions upon the use of china an outdated post-war practice. Another female correspondent married in 1984, but now separated and living in Shetland, describes how she removed particular objects from the bustle of family life in order to protect them. 'Most things have been in everyday use, but the more delicate things have been put out of reach of the

Figure 2.5   Royal Doulton, 'Arden,' 1965

children.' She explains why. 'My mum had my Grandmother's wedding china. Her china was in use on special occasions. She didn't tell us it was her wedding china until my brother broke some (C411).

Since damage to wedding china is serious enough to be remembered even its restricted use must be balanced with the need to protect and preserve it. Identifying those moments, the 'special occasions', when wedding china comes out onto the table is a recurring theme of the Giving and Receiving Presents directive. One correspondent, a laboratory technician from Stockport who married in 1969, wrote how she unexpectedly received china that was 'too good to use':

The Royal Doulton China was the most surprising present – at a time when Royal Doulton was very prestigious and out of our class. It was sent by post from a London store by a friend who had admired me but had never been a boy friend – he wasn't even invited to the wedding. Anyway, it ensured that he was never forgotten! At the time it was too good to use other than, say, at Christmas and even now I still keep it stored away for safety. I still like the design and think it looks good – I really should use it more. I got it out recently when my daughter brought home a 'posh' boy friend and she asked where the china was from, she didn't remember seeing it – it was very embarrassing – I was trying to give the impression that we always eat off Royal Doulton! (J931)

To be given wedding china as a farewell gesture, a gift from a friend now never to be a lover who cleverly played upon its meaning to ambiguous effect is unusual. The friend demonstrates his acceptance of her decision to marry someone else while indicating what might have been. However, the subsequent severely restricted use of a given dinner service is typical enough and her account of the problems its use poses is very revealing. Only rarely serving meals on china that Mass-Observation correspondents believe is special, and variously describe as 'pretty and delicate' (H260), 'beautiful' (J1407) or 'prestigious' (J931) implies that the setting for eating is usually rougher, uglier, unimpressive, ordinary. Therefore no mater how prestigious the rarely used china is, it is not very effective as a status marker. Much like the awkward fit of best clothes, rarely used china draws attention to the difference between the realities of everyday life and appearances on special occasions. When members of the same household mark a special occasion or participate in a festival, they may enjoy collectively performing a dream of domestic existence that they do not normally have the resources of time and money to sustain but an outsider, an invited honoured guest, such as a '"posh" boy friend,' can observe that this is an exception to the rule of normal domesticity. The china is ranked higher than the family that occasionally use it. Despite the contradictions of keeping wedding china

Figure 2.6   Midwinter, 'Starburst,' 1957

Figure 2.7   'Eternal Beau,' c1984

for special occasions, it is a popular practice. 'It is used on High days only' remarked a chemist from Felixstowe about a twelve-piece china tea set he and his wife received from her mother when they wed in 1950 (W1893). Another correspondent, a nurse from Sutton Coldfield married in 1959, described how she and her groom planned to receive china that they would rarely use: 'we had a list of 2 sorts best and everyday'

(G1148). A forensic consultant who wed thirty years later in 1989 used the same term for her special occasion wedding china: 'The Eternal Beau dinner set we added to over time and we still use it for best' (J2830).

Best is the everyday name for china that is reserved for rituals that is also often permanently displayed. Strikingly similar descriptions of this practice are contained in a number of responses to the Giving and Receiving Presents directive that were otherwise quite different. A male correspondent from Chelmsford, Essex, an architect's assistant married in 1961, delivers a brief factual account of 'Four Delft blue and white plates circa 1920s in our glass fronted Victorian china cabinet, we don't use them but good to look at' (A883). A young single female correspondent, who tried to remember enough information about her parent's wedding presents to write a response to the Wedding Presents section of the directive, recalled:

> I knew they had a tiny coffee service because it is kept in our china cabinet and never used. They said they'd use it on their silver wedding anniversary, but my father died when they had been married only 16 years (G2769).

Poignantly, she contrasts a family diminished by an unexpected death while the wedding china remains intact. Without intending to offer any interpretation of meanings of wedding china, which is perhaps why this account is so powerful, she illustrates how hope for a marriage can become invested in gifts of china and how mundane cups and saucers take on a immaterial, even magical, quality. Somehow her father's death seems to be the fault of the tiny coffee service: its safekeeping did not guarantee the longevity of the marriage or the life of the husband and father. This response, and all those that discussed the restrictions placed upon wedding china, point to the significance that can accumulate upon objects kept in household spaces that need to be unravelled further.

Keeping china in a cabinet might appear to be an obvious practical solution to an issue of domestic management: being kept behind glass prevents contact and the possibility of any kind of damage so that cups, saucers and plates are permanently safe. Ceramic, such as fine earthenware or bone china, has particular properties that lend themselves to such museum style treatment. China is a compelling combination of durability and fragility. It does not deteriorate but is easily broken, a remarkably stable substance, which is also inflexible and therefore brittle. China will last for many, many years beyond the life of an individual or family generation, if treated carefully. The dinner or tea services held by 'ordinary' people, such as Mass-Observation writers, are produced in large quantities from an industrial material but properties of that material belie its reproducibility, encouraging respectful handling and making each cup, saucer, plate or bowl seem precious. Many correspondents specify that the tea sets they faithfully keep and rarely use are made of bone china, a particularly thin and delicate china that was a popular substitute for porcelain.[24]

---

24 Wolf Mankowitz, *Wedgwood* (London: Spring Books, 1966) pp. 133–138.

The nature of the material does not, however, explain why it must be preserved. Preservation is not, of course, a merely practical matter. China, particularly the dinner service given at a wedding, is kept, and kept on display, because it is meaningful and most of these bright brittle objects will have a number of layers of meaning. Moira Vincentelli argues that a cabinet of china is particularly appropriate to convey the respectability of the well-ordered house:

> The display of polished, clean and shining objects are, then, particularly suitable to convey a visible manifestation of the frequently invisible activity of maintaining a clean house; they give satisfaction to what is a relentless or thankless task. The presentation makes a virtue out of necessity, turning a storage problem into aesthetic effect.[25]

China is symbolically, as well as literally, safer on display. Not only does it stay clean but also it avoids the contradictions being set out on a table and in a room that is normally in everyday use, serving only to highlight the ordinariness of such surroundings. The act of putting and keeping china behind glass shows that they are set apart from the everyday and announces the special nature and symbolic power of these objects. Thus the china cabinet stands in for the clean house, demonstrates cleanliness as a value of the house even when that house cannot be kept clean because it is being used.

The china dinner service also, I would argue, represents the family. In technical linguistic terms you could argue that china is a metonym for the house and a metaphor for the family. The size of a given dinner service, the number of its place settings is equivalent to an ideal family size. It would be inappropriate, for example, to offer a bride and groom a dinner service comprised of two place settings even if that was the number within their household at the beginning or end of their marriage. It would be also incorrect to give a bride and groom a set of plastic plates for their dining table. Plastic is too flimsy, too lightweight. The gift of a substantial dinner service composed of a stable material expresses the expectation that the marriage will last and the married household will swell in size, filling all the places settings (often six, sometimes eight or as many as twelve). To protect such china maintains respect for the large or extended family as an ideal, as the right number to celebrate a special occasion, despite the decreasing household sizes. To preserve it demonstrates the importance attached to the continuity of family, honouring previous owners and expecting new ones.[26] Wedding china represents the family as a connected and

---

25 Moira Vincentelli, *Women and Ceramics: Gendered Vessels* (Manchester: Manchester University Press, 2000) p. 124. She also asserts that a china cabinet constitutes an appropriate display of status. 'The display of apparently functional goods offers a neat balance between the conspicuous consumption of expensive, non-functional objects and the middle-class desire not to be seen as overly extravagant and frivolous' (p. 124). Respectability certainly began as middle class cultural formation but the extent to which it always retains this class character is a moot point.

26 Plates are the tenth category of 'most cherished things in the home' in Mihaly Csikszentmihaly and Eugene Rochberg-Halton, *The Meaning of Things: Domestic Symbols*

bounded collective and projects a family line. It can put up a sustained display of the fundamental purpose of family life because it is removed from its realities. Locking away the best china pieces is an act of sacrifice, a denial that takes these things out of an ordinary realm wherein the regular routines, such as mundane meals, sustains life.[27] Bone china, so-called because the ash of bones are mixed with clay to produce a hard thin form, already has an otherworldly sound and feel. But all special occasion china, regardless of the exact composition of it as fine earthenware, is separated from life in order to become its representation; it sits above the everyday details of the household to represent the meaning of the family.

One response to the Wedding Presents section of the Giving and Receiving Presents directive from a Portsmouth-based lecturer is more or less completely taken up an account of wedding china and its place with her family history. It is worth citing in its entirety:

> I first married in 1960 and although divorced have not actually remarried although I have been with my second partner for over 20 years. Relating to the first marriage, I was very young and some of the gifts given were practical e.g. a wardrobe and a cot (yes there was a baby) from my mother in law, a cooker and a three piece suite (second hand all of it) from my auntie. We had the usual modest type of gifts like wine glasses and a lovely hand painted antique bone china teaset from my mother in law which I still have. I did not have many presents however but this was normal then. We did not have formal lists or anything like that. Some people bought washing up bowls, and other kitchenware and that sort of thing which of course I have not kept all this time.

> I would not part with the bone china teaset as it holds quite dear memories of the old couple who are now dead. They were very kind to me in the early days of marriage and although not sentimental in any way provided many useful items for our life together, including bedding for the cot, baby clothes, a television (the old 1950s bakelite type) a radiogram, and so on. My father in law was a dustman and lived in Harrow where the kinds of things people threw out has life left in them, and that is where the teaset came from too. They were poor but their home was beautifully furnished with antiques and lovely china and linen and it all came from the dustcart!! Both of them were 'in service' when young and came from a rural part of Norfolk. However, they had the tastes and manners of people not of their class and they fascinated me. Tea was always served on white linen tablecloths and she gave me some (which I did not use with a family of three boys eventually!) The teaset was beautifully hand painted. Jam was home made, as was chutney with fruit from the garden. Grace was always said at the start of a meal. Manners were everything and my little eldest son was very impressed by having tea there and obeyed all the rules of the table (which he did not do when at home) My mother in law took in children to foster as a living when she moved to Harrow (I don't know why they moved). They were old (in their late fifties) when I met them and my first husband was their adopted son. She had

---

and the Self (Cambridge: Cambridge University Press, 1981) pp. 82–83. They suggest that preservation is a more generalized celebration of human existence and longevity. 'Thus a china cup preserved over a generation is a victory of human purpose over chaos' p. 83.

27 See, for example Susan M. Pearce, *On Collecting: An Investigation into Collecting in the European Tradition* (London: Routledge, 1995) p. 24.

very strong views in child rearing and passed these on to me in no uncertain terms but in a kindly way. That teaset conjures up all these memories. My eldest son who knew them best was devoted to them and has named his first daughter Emily Martha after her (she was called Martha). In fact he used to call me Martha too sometimes. He was very upset when she died and I think his ideal model for a mother was her (not me!) Children and their needs were her forte, but she was not liberal but very practical. My first husband was not as impressed with her as his own son and felt she was too firm in her handling of him. Father in law was more earthy and often could be seen pinching the old girls bottom as she bent over the oven! (S1383)

The hand-painted china tea set introduces and inter-cuts a description of domestic economy (the use of second-hand things and home-grown produce in a working class culture of respectability that is based on neither wealth nor economic status) and matriarchal family relationships (the authority of her husband's mother only momentarily overturned by his father in the last sentence). An account of the mother-in-law's relationship with her son and grandson take precedence over insights into this correspondent's own experiences within the family, begging a series of compelling questions that go beyond the scope of this study. Did she resent the dominance of the mother in law who had never had children of her own? Where was her mother? Why did she divorce? All she explicitly expresses is gratitude to her first husband's parents, welcoming gifts as acts of kindness and, I would suggest, as signs of their acceptance and approval of her. The 'practical' wedding presents (the cot and bedding) and the 'modest' ceremonial objects such as the wine glasses and china, enabled her to reproduce the codes of conduct of her husband's family and thus be included within their world. Of all the gifts, it is the teaset that is the most significant, the one she 'would not part with'. She has already kept it through years of cohabitation, for longer than the life of married household for which it was intended. Her attachment to it is not, we can safely surmise, because she needs it to uphold the culture of respectability that she describes as a now distant observer. Two sentence fragments explain its value to her. She states that it 'holds quite dear memories of the old couple who are now dead' and that it 'conjures up all these memories.'

The idea that objects generate memories has been remarked upon before now.[28] Calling this process 'conjuring' seems especially significant because it implies that the bone china tea set has a magical power to materialise memories, to give them a presence. 'Hold' is an interesting verb also: it suggests that memories can be stored within or by an object. Perhaps I am staking too much upon the selection of words but it is worth emphasizing that the notion that objects function as storage vessels not only for information about when they were produced but also the experiences of living with them underpins recent initiatives in museum and archaeological

28 Marius Kwint, 'Introduction,' *Material Memories*, ed. Marius Kwint, Chris Breward and Jeremy Aynsley (Oxford: Berg, 1999) pp. 1–16; Susan Stewart, *On Longing: Narratives of the Miniature, the Gigantic, the Souvenir, the Collection* (Durham: Duke University Press, 1996) p. 133.

practice.[29] Recognition that physical structures, objects and others, manifest unrecorded histories, intangible heritage that exists only at the level of individual or collective consciousness has led to the preservation of objects that might not otherwise meet the criteria of 'best example of type.'[30] Undertaking such acts of preservation privileges beliefs and feelings about objects over more conventional judgements about aesthetics, age or rarity. If an object is meaningful enough to an identifiable community that could be justification for guaranteeing its safekeeping forever. Cultural relativism, recognition of the validity of belief systems that differ from the dominant institutions of preservation, such as museums, has become 'best' practice. Thus acceptance that objects are meaningful is relatively widespread but it is probably fair to say that there is less discussion about how they contain and disseminate their meanings, how they can actually hold memories. When their power is analyzed, we can begin to see how it derives from a combination of their place in the past and their durability, their ability to be there then and here now.[31] Thus the materiality of objects has paradoxical properties; it occupies a fixed space in time and overcomes the passage of time, brings the past into the present.

This is demonstrated by a shop assistant from Burgess Hill, East Sussex, who describes how her surviving wedding china carries with it a moment in time. Amongst the plain utilitarian objects that were typical gifts for weddings, which like hers took place in the post-war austerity period, she also received '6 prettily decorated soup and dinner plates and two vegetable dishes, makers Washington Pottery. Hanley, England from father-in-law.' Apologetically, she relates how few of her presents have survived. 'Being packed and unpacked fifteen times, necessitated by as many moves of home have resulted in there being nothing left of these presents other than the six knives and one soup dish, the sole survivor of the dinner service.' She writes:

> That soup dish still holds memories for me, of our first 'home', furnished rooms in Portsmouth, and the delight I had at being a housewife for the first time (how times have changed!) and serving meals for my husband in my own utensils (K310).

Within all the responses to the Giving and Receiving Presents directive there is much evidence of attachments to objects because of the memories that they 'hold'. It is

---

29 See, for example, Simon Knell, (ed.) *Museums and the Future of Collecting* (Aldershot: Ashgate, 1999).

30 See, for example, John Schofield, William Gray Johnston and Colleen. M. Beck, 'Introduction: Materiel Culture in the Modern World,' *Materiel Culture: The Archaeology of Twentieth Century Conflict*, ed. John Schofield, William Gray Johnston and Colleen. M. Beck (London: Routledge, 2002) pp. 1–8.

31 Susan M. Pearce, *Museums, Objects and Collections* (Leicester: Leicester University Press) pp. 197–207. It is worth considering the temporal properties of objects in relation to those of the photograph. Elizabeth Edwards, 'Photography as Objects of Evidence,' *Material Memories*, ed. Marius Kwint, Chris Breward and Jeremy Aynsley (Oxford: Berg, 1999) pp. 221–236.

possible to determine three different memorial functions performed by objects, three separate points of reference. First, china can bring back a moment in which it was once used; it has a pictorial or cinematic effect, evoking a scene that once surrounded it. Secondly, it can refer to itself, its own past existence and, thirdly, it can represent the person who gave it. The first point, I hope, has been sufficiently illustrated by the Burgess Hill shop assistant and so to provide evidence for the second two.

It has been possible for me to argue that china is consistently given upon marriage because the gift is consistently remembered. To be unforgettable is an obvious sign of the significance of one person to another and is no less revealing of relationships between people and things. Some Mass-Observation correspondents express sadness at any loss of wedding china. 'My wife's relatives also gave us wedding presents, including 2 tea sets (now all gone)' noted a male correspondent, an aircraft engineer who wed in 1959 (B1442). A female writer, a radio programme monitor from Ipswich whose marriage took place in 1968 used almost the same phrase. 'We had some Royal Doulton china – all gone now' (C1939). There is also a sense of regret when only fragments of a service survive, even if it is for many years and through one marriage into another. A twice married Norwich teacher describes how at her first wedding in 1959 'relatives gave us small amounts of money which we used to buy a dinner service (Doulton – I've still got a few of the plates) and a tea-set – nothing remains of that but one sugar bowl' (B2258). Here, a past moment is not specified; the attachment is to the objects themselves.

For other correspondents, china's meaning resides within the relationships of giving and receiving. After all, these relationships put these objects in their place. A dinner service and bone china teaset was one of the gifts that a typist from Leighton Buzzard received when she married in 1956. She states:

> 22 years later I was divorced and under the settlement I kept all the contents of our home. By that time much of it was rather worn-out, but even now 43 years later I still have some of the china a few other items … .The remnants of the dinner service and teaset remind of the two aunts, long dead, who gave them to me. They were both very kind to me years ago. Happily I keep in touch with their children (B89).

Her wedding china could be interpreted as a Maussian gift: it always evokes memories of the aunts because they, as the people who gave it, never completely left it. It was the embodied nature of the gift that, for Mauss, compelled its receiver to give back to the giver, generating and maintaining cycles of reciprocity.[32] However, like most marriage gifts, her china is an example of intergenerational giving where a gift is not returned to the giver but to their children.[33] We can safely surmise that 'keeping in touch' with her cousins involves some kind of gift exchange and therefore that

---

32 Marcel Mauss, *The Gift: the Form and Reason for Exchange in Archaic Societies*, 1925 (London: Routledge, 1990) pp. 13–14.

33 Cheal, p. 51 and pp. 57–60; Aafke Komter, 'Women, Gifts and Power,' *The Gift: An Interdisciplinary Perspective*, ed. Aafke Komter (Amsterdam: Amsterdam University Press, 1996) pp. 119–131.

this Mass-Observation correspondent reciprocates by giving to her aunts' children rather than directly to the aunts, even when they were alive. Anthropologists have debated whether such gift cycles can be accommodated within Maussian theory or is evidence that it is not in fact generalizable.[34] Keeping all her gifts, including her china, despite her divorce could also be taken as evidence of gift giving as giving for keeping. But regardless of how the gift-cycle of wedding china is characterized it has a particular power as a domestic possession, that is to say, embodiment is meaningful whether or not it is the cause of future exchange relationships. When an object is offered for inclusion in a house and is accepted, the giver and the giver's relationship to the receiver are recognized. As the object is used or preserved, that is, while it is possessed, the person who gave it makes a contribution to a household where they do not reside. Receiving an object for a household appoints the giver a symbolic place within it. When the giver is a family member, say an aunt or a mother, these given things express connections within a close or extended family, make absent members ever present in another family home; they create the family as 'an imagined community' providing a sense of belonging.[35] Objects exchanged between family members and kept in one of their homes establish continuities between households and between generations. Since such objects usually pass from older to younger generations, they establish continuities between the past and present of a family. If carefully preserved so that they last beyond the life of the giver, they create continuities between the dead and the living. They become sacred.

Inherited Wedding China: Never Used

The final questions of the Giving and Receiving Presents directive were: 'Do you keep any of your parent's wedding presents? Or wedding presents given to other members if your family? When are they used and where are they kept?'[36] When Mass-Observation correspondents replied that did indeed possess such gifts, these objects were, almost without exception, china. Furthermore, it became clear that the strictest prohibitions surround the use of inherited wedding china. It is never used rather than just rarely used. A motor industry parts inspector from Derby and telephone copy taker from Salop, married in 1945 and 1966 respectively, twenty-one years or a generation apart, held the same type of objects in the same way. 'I have got some cups, and saucers that were part of my own parents wedding present.... They are never used,' stated the former (R1468). 'I have what is left of my parents wedding china. There are only three whole cups, saucers and plates and I never use them,' wrote the latter (B1386). Across all directive responses, a correlation between use and significance emerges. The less china is used the more significant it appears to be. Only one Mass-Observation correspondent, a divorced computer programmer

---

34 Weiner, p. 2, pp. 42–3 and 46.

35 Benedict Anderson, *Imagined Communities:Reflections on the Origin and Spread of Nationalism* (London: Verso, 1983).

36 See Appendix 1.

from Chichester, explicitly states that she uses her family china and it is noteworthy that she is unsure of its provenance, not certain who gave it to who, but still felt her disregard for its safekeeping required justification:

> I still have some pieces of china that are reputed to come from a set my grandfather bought my grandmother at the time of their wedding. I have five tea plates, a cup and two saucers. I use these and think if they get broken so be it. I don't like things locked up in cupboards and never used (P2175).

For the most part, however, the plates, bowls, cups or saucers that were once in the possession of a family member rather than bought new to endorse a marriage, are the most carefully preserved. 'My mother married in 1910 and was given a bone china tea service,' begins a divorced secretary:

> A prettier design I have yet to see. It depicts little mauve violets and all the cups, plates, etc are gold edged. The cups are fluted and the set is complete. When we were children it came into use on special occasions. Now it sits in my daughters glass fronted cabinet too precious for daily use (D666).

This testimony confirms that wedding china is only occasionally used when it was a gift and never used once it was inherited. It is now permanently displayed not by this correspondent, but in her daughter's cabinet. Thus she describes with pleasure and pride a set of objects that she is clearly connected with but does not directly possess. Moreover, two other correspondents keep wedding china within their home that they do not claim to own. A shop worker from Brentwood Essex who wed in 1950 stated: 'I have a tea set in my glass cabinet which was my mother's wedding present. It is so pretty and delicate it was never used much' (H260). And, a shorthand typist from the same county who married eleven years earlier wrote: 'I have a teaset that was given to my mother as a wedding gift 86 years ago. I would not part with it' (B36).

These accounts indicate some significant differences between gifts and inheritances. If categorized by its exchange, inherited wedding china is a gift. The original owner received it as a gift, preserved it and gave it away again. The character of all gifts, usually exposed by their comparison with commodities, is that they are not easily forgotten or disposable.[37] A commodity can be used, ignored, disliked, destroyed or even cherished without regard or reference to those involved in its exchange. A gift does not allow such solitary pursuits or pleasures, such complete control. As it materializes a social relationship, the responsibilities of its receipt weigh heavier than a possession gathered through purchase. There are restrictions placed on its use and exchange. In the first place, I would suggest, it ought to be kept. Managing the possession of gifts is a tricky issue for those who live within a capitalist economy saturated with things. The availability of objects through

---

37 James G. Carrier, *Gifts and Commodities: Exchange and Western Capitalism since 1700* (London: Routledge, 1995) pp. 19–21; C. A. Gregory, *Gifts and Commodities* (London: Academic Press, 1982) pp. 10–24.

Figure 2.8   Second-hand china, 2006

purchases in a market means that once gifts are given they are rarely required to re-enter into a further gift exchange. Another new commodity can always supply and sustain the gift economy but gifts are not supposed to return to the market and into a less significant commodity state. Thus, they accumulate. Although, there are certain moments when wedding gifts might be unceremoniously sold, at times of extreme financial hardship, for example.

The use and exchange of inherited objects is more tightly regulated than that of a typical gift. An inheritance is not, then, entirely defined by the act of its exchange, by being given object, because it is usually understood as more than gift or a special kind of gift, at least. Inherited objects circulate within a narrower range of relationships than other types of given objects. Inheritances tend to be restricted to family members and this is certainly the case when the inheritance is a domestic thing. Inherited objects are even more closely binding than gifts. Also, the terms of ownership seem to depend upon whether it was given or inherited. Those Mass-Observation correspondents who had wedding china passed down to them seem to act as its guardians rather than proprietors. It is treated as a borrowed or shared object in which an individual can claim no rights of use. Of the recent anthropological writing on the gift, it is Annette Weiner who makes clearest distinction between gifts and inheritances. She states:

Some things, like most commodities, are easy to give. But there are other possessions that are imbued with intrinsic and ineffable identities of their owners which are not easy to give away. Ideally, these inalienable possessions are kept by their owners from one generation to the next within the closed context of the family, descent group or dynasty.... Inalienable possessions do not just control the dimensions of giving, but their historicities retain for the future, memories, either fabricated or not, of the past. Not always obtainable, keeping some things transcendent and out of circulation in the face of all pressures to give them to others is a burden, a responsibility, and at best, a skilful achievement.[38]

Weiner's analysis of keeping is based on ethnographies of places quite distant from domestic arenas in Britain but much of her account resonates with Mass-Observation writing. Her thesis that keeping drives giving cannot be simply mapped onto the domestic relationships contained within market economies, but the notion that an inalienable possession is a guardian of family history travels well. Differences between rarely and never used china do seem to turn upon a distinction between a gift and an inheritance. To varying extents, depending on whether a gift or an inheritance, china is subjected to strategies of preservation. There is also an expectation that a well-kept gift might become an inheritance. Thus wedding china gathers significance as it is given and kept, given and kept again. However, such a neat transition from valued gift to precious inheritance is not the trajectory of all wedding china. A Mass-Observation correspondent, a Lancashire teacher turned Cambridge housewife recalls being given china that was an inheritance when she wed in 1951:

> An uncle of my husband's died shortly before the wedding and his only son invited us to choose something from his father's supply of china. We chose a complete dinner set (made in the 1880's) – until then never used. It was one of three given to the uncle and aunt as a wedding present. My husband's sister chose a tea set from the same collection of wedding presents – this was one of five tea sets (W2588).

Although held in a family for an appropriately long time, she does not accept the china as an inheritance but only as a gift. She used it when it had not been used before. Just as all given things may not achieve the status of a gift all objects that are passed on may not become inheritances. Perhaps because her wedding china was selected from such a large collection of inherited china the significance of one set could not be distinguished from the eight that had been preserved. Her husband's uncle had simply kept too much for any to be considered particularly precious or meaningful and were thus being given away rather than handed down. The whole exchange between the Lancashire teacher and her husband's uncle's son (her cousin by marriage) may be too unusual to draw any firm conclusions from but it is worth pointing out that those correspondents who valued family wedding china were daughter's who received it from their mothers. A gift relationship between cousins by marriage is, by comparison, a distant one. Any children that inherit a domestic object from a parent's household would have some understanding of its place within a family home and importance to the family members

---

38   Weiner, pp. 6–7.

but daughters who, traditionally, have been required to pay attention to domestic details would be expected to know their full significance.[39] They ought to remember on what occasions wedding china was used, how the table was set and the types of food that were served. Ideas about how to conduct family celebrations and differences between special occasions and everyday life are encoded in these objects. Female family members and mothers in particular are most likely to be responsible for both domestic rituals and routines and it is therefore maternal family practices or even a maternal family line (which can be lost through traditions of renaming upon marriage) that can be maintained through the transfer of domestic objects. An ethnographic study devoted to contemporary material inheritances might resolve the questions of the categorization of inherited objects as gifts and their precise place in a domestic realm that I have only tentatively been able to deal with. This investigation, I hope, has revealed something of the significance of rarely used and never used domestic objects. The possession of china in married households is commonplace and its preservation is 'common sense', undertaken without question; it is what is expected, the right thing to do, the 'done' thing. It is precisely these kinds of apparently 'trivial' practices that Daniel Miller has argued are important to study because they are 'a key unchallenged mechanism of social reproduction and ideological dominance.'[40] The widely performed and least discussed practises are the uncontested aspects of life, indicative of beliefs and values that circulate in everyday realms. Preserved objects are the recipients of attention and labour; they are given space and time, often both in limited supply, within the home. All this is a sign of being very highly valued. What should also be noted is their value is only recognised within the domestic sphere and by a family network. Even the most complete, pristine dinner services carrying the mark of a prestigious manufacturer does not retain anything like its initial market price. The reverence with which it is treated is unrelated to the dominant system of monetary evaluation (Figure 2.8).

Pyrex and the Culture of Materials

Pyrex is reinforced glass used to make a range of oven and table ware: casserole dishes, jugs, mixing bowls, soup bowls, desert dishes, plates, mugs as well as complete dinner services and tea sets. It is the anti-thesis of wedding china: resilient not fragile, used instead of displayed, functional rather than decorative and modern as opposed to traditional. Both Pyrex and china, however, are durable.

Pyrex is not as consistently given as china. No claims about its universality as a marriage gift can be made; it was a popular present at a particular period, between the end of the war and mid-1970s. Nevertheless, across all the responses to the Wedding Presents section of the Giving and Receiving Presents directive Pyrex is the most frequently cited individual product. This is a reflection of Pyrex as a material and, if

---

39 Csikszentmihaly and Rochberg-Halton p. 116, suggests that 'mothers pass on their meaning system to their daughters but not to their sons.'

40 Daniel Miller, 'Why Some Things Matter,' *Material Culture: Why Some Things Matter*, Ed. Daniel Miller (London: University College London Press, 1998) p. 3.

Figure 2.9   **'A Pyrex Glass Casserole,'**
Home and Gardens (February 1926)

you like, as a brand. The name Pyrex stands for reinforced glassware used for cooking and serving. Like Hoover, Granola or Stanley, which are used in place of vacuum cleaner, porridge oats and craft knife, Pyrex is such as successful market version of reinforced glass that its name has replaced the generic non-market term.[41]

An attempt to understand preservation as a domestic practice ought to investigate the extent to which it is a prevalent activity or specialist one, to consider whether it is applied to just a few precious objects or more mundane things. In this respect, a comparison between functional and decorative domestic forms, such as china and Pyrex should be particularly revealing. However, I do recognize that a simple literal comparison of china and Pyrex is problematic: china is a type of object (formal tableware made by a range of companies known and unknown to Mass-Observation correspondents) whereas Pyrex is a single product that takes a variety of forms. Despite these rather obvious differences, I want to run a comparison between china and Pyrex because I hope it will provide some insights into the similarities and differences between objects that are used and those that are reserved for display, into the processes through which different meanings accrue to different materials as well as allow some consideration of the criteria for preservation in domestic contexts.

A shop worker from Surrey who also describes herself as a 'Housewife and Mother' wrote in her response to the Giving and Receiving Presents directive that among the modest domestic utensils that constituted the majority of her gifts when she wed in 1950, she received 'Pyrex dishes, then a very new and exciting product' (R1532). This post-war period was Pyrex's hey day,[42] but it had been manufactured in Britain from the interwar period. In 1921, Ernest Jobling Purser, business manager

---

41 Stuart Evans, 'PYREX Glassware, a Commentary on Sixty Years of Design,' *Pyrex: Sixty Years of Design* (Tyne and Wear County Council Museums, 1983) p. 21 makes this point.

42 Between 1946 and 1958 the production of 'domestic items' increased by 94 per cent. John C. Baker, 'James A Jobling and Co. Ltd., subsequently Corning Ltd., Manufacturer of PYREX Brand Glassware' *Pyrex: Sixty Years of Design* (Tyne and Wear County Council Museums, 1983) 10.

Cook and serve in This Pyrex Casserole

Think of the saving of time through having less dishes to wash! And although you serve in the same dish yet the sparkling clearness of Pyrex harmonises with the daintiest table appointments.

The ultimate economy of Pyrex is brought about by the fact that it does not flake, rust or stain, and withstands oven heat.

Less fuel too is used when cooking with Pyrex because it *absorbs* the heat whereas metal reflects it. For the same reason the food is cooked evenly throughout.

Write for Illustrated List.

PYREX

THE ORIGINAL TRANSPARENT OVENWARE

Keeps its brightness after years of use.

EVERY PIECE GUARANTEED against oven heat breakage for six months from date of purchase.

A four-piece set of PYREX ware consisting of "Utility Dish, Bread or Baking Pan, Casserole and Pudding Dish," all packed in a useful box, is obtainable at **19 6** per set.

If your local dealer cannot supply, please write direct to:—

JAMES A. JOBLING & CO., LTD.,

Wear Flint Glass Works, Sunderland.

Look for this mark on Pyrex Transparent Ovenware, it is a guarantee against substitution.

**Figure 2.10   'Cook and serve in This Pyrex Casserole,'
Homes and Gardens (October 1925)**

and chief technologist at Wear Flint Glass Works, Sunderland, acquired the license to 'manufacture PYREX brand glassware in Britain and her Empire, excluding Canada.'[43] Pyrex was first produced in 1915 at Corning Glass Works, USA, a 'domestic application of borosilicate glass,'[44] a glass with enhanced resistance to heat, corrosion and accidental force, that had been developed for industrial purposes (railway lighting and laboratory vessels).

The archetypal Pyrex ware is the casserole dish, the first product to be made at the Wear Flint Glass Works and the one that most clearly presents the essential character of Pyrex (Figures 2.9 and 2.10). It is a modern object. Function dominates. The dish is symmetrical and unadorned, a standardized shape determined by the demands of industrial production (the easy removal from press moulds)[45] that simply serves its purpose. It was an embodiment of the ideals of industrial and domestic modernity. The use of a strong, durable invented substance in the construction of bowls and dishes was an application of industrial standards in domestic spaces. Pyrex was a rational form that privileged strength of materials over ceremony and efficiency over tradition; it was a labour saving technology. Its early publicity repeats the claim that Pyrex 'saves trouble', 'saves labour' and is 'a real labour saver.'[46] It did so because it could be used for both cooking and serving food. 'Straight from the oven to the table', summarized an *Ideal Home* advertisement from 1925[47] (Figure 2.11). Another in April 1927 insisted that the female readership of this magazine would be proud of their 'pies, baked and roast dishes if you cook in PYREX Ovenware.' Addressing them directly again, it went on:

> You will be prouder still when you see the dish served straight from the oven, adding charm to your table with its glistening transparency amid your silver and glass.

> Food retains its colour cooked in PYREX Ware, and the flavour is enhanced. Your dishes will keep hotter than they did in those unsightly obsolete metal and earthenware dishes. [48]

The narrative of the advertisement develops from the idea that respectability is established through the performance of domestic routines, through rituals that required particular types of artefacts. Wear Flint and Glass Works was alert to the culture of materials (Figure 2.12). The aim of its advert was reassurance that this new product fits with the conventional materials of respectability (glass and silver) as well as announces a break from tradition: the replacement of china dishes and the interchangeability of kitchen dishes and tableware.

---

43 Baker, p. 8.

44 Cindy Shaw and Stuart Evans, 'Technical History,' *Pyrex: Sixty Years of Design* (Tyne and Wear County Council Museums, 1983) p. 13.

45 Shaw and Evans, pp. 14–15.

46 Evans, pp. 22–25.

47 'Never flakes, Never stains, Always bright!' *Ideal Home* X. 5 (Nov 1924) p. 425.

48 Evans, p. 25.

Respectability, and to a great extent morality, was guaranteed in the archetypal proper home through a series of strict spatial separations. As has been noted many times before, the nineteenth century middle class house was divided into masculine and feminine domains, those of adult and child domains as well as front and back.[49] The latter, a distinction between labour and leisure, was exemplified by the difference between oven and table. Pyrex, which belonged to both, was part of a new propriety; it was a material expression of twentieth century ideologies of the good home that modernized, rationalized and to a certain extent a democratized without entirely abandoning, the past ideals of domesticity. The development, sale and use of Pyrex must be read as a sign that spatial separations were less rigidly enforced within homes where they were once upheld. It was recommended for the female inhabitants of the new 'servantless' house whose responsibility for keeping house now included all actual physical tasks.[50] A blurring of labour and leisure came to characterize domestic practices, especially those performed by women, and this persists in the design and daily routines of contemporary dwellings, perhaps best illustrated by the casting of cooking in a stylish kitchen as a creative pleasure of the late-twentieth and early twenty-first century.[51] Re-definitions of domestic labour, denying rather than hiding the work of housekeeping, made respectability slightly easier for working class women to achieve. Cleanliness combined with efficiency define the good home by the early 1950s, if not before, restricting the importance of polished appearances to the front room and special occasions. Pyrex, an embodiment of the more informal propriety of rational domestic management became more popular than the creators of the 1927 *Ideal Home* advertisement could have envisaged but not for the reasons that they suggest. While it had a lighter appearance than metal or common brown earthenware dishes, it was not compatible with silver or glass nor did it replace china. It had no ceremonial qualities; it was not for 'best' but for everyday; it upheld the respectability of the ordinary.[52]

The many Mass-Observation correspondents that were given Pyrex ware as wedding presents often report that they received it in large quantities. The 'Housewife and mother' who explained that Pyrex dishes were 'new and exciting' also writes: 'I believe I received about a dozen of these' (R1532). Similarly, a 'Housewife/

---

49 Leonore Davidoff, 'Class and Gender in Victorian England,' *Sex and Class in Women's History*, ed. Judith. L. Newton, Mary P. Ryan and Judith Walkowitz (London: Routledge and Kegal Paul, 1983) pp. 17–71; Juliet Kitchen, 'Interiors: Nineteenth-century Essays on the 'Masculine' and 'Feminine' Room,' *The Gendered Object* ed. Pat Kirkham (Manchester: Manchester University Press, 1996) pp. 12–29.

50 Leonore Davidoff, 'The Rationalisation of Housework,' *Dependence and Exploitation in Work and Marriage*, ed. Diana Leone Barker and Sheila Allen (London: Longman, 1976) pp. 143–148.

51 See, for example, Jamie Oliver, *The Naked Chef* (London: Penguin, 2001).

52 Although different in important respects (the methods of sale and the politics of material), Pyrex can be usefully compared to Tupperware: it is part of an increasingly informal domestic modernity. Alison J. Clarke, *Tupperware: The Promise of Plastic in 1950s America* (Washington: Smithsonian Institution Press, 1999).

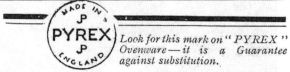

Look for this mark on "PYREX" Ovenware — it is a Guarantee against substitution.

Never flakes! Never stains Always bright!

PYREX Transparent Ovenware *saves* work. You *cook* in a PYREX dish and *serve* in the *same* dish—straight from the oven to the table. Every course is piping hot and infinitely more tempting to the appetite. When the meal is over there is less washing-up—no hard scouring—for each PYREX dish is cleaned easily and quickly.

Ask to see PYREX Ovenware; there are numerous useful shapes and sizes.

Prices now much reduced

PYREX

THE ORIGINAL TRANSPARENT OVENWARE
MADE IN ENGLAND

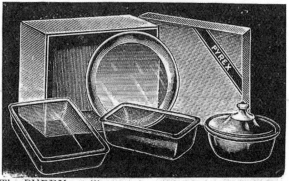

The PYREX set illustrated makes a splendid Wedding or Birthday Gift. It consists of four of the essential PYREX dishes packed in a useful box: "Utility Dish, Bread or Baking Pan, Casserole, and Pudding Dish." They form the basis for a complete range of PYREX Utensils—fit for every cooking need and equal to any occasion. **Reduced price per set 19/6.**

To be obtained of all Stores, China and Glass Dealers Ironmongers, etc. If any difficulty in obtaining locally please write direct to :—

JAS. A. JOBLING & CO., LTD.,
West Flint Glass Works, SUNDERLAND.

Figure 2.11   'Never flakes, Never stains, Always bright!'
                 Ideal Home (November 1924)

"Wasn't that a Dainty Dish!"

How admirably these words of the fairy story descri
a pie cooked *and* served in a Pyrex Transparent I
Dish? You can *see* the pie being cooked and ensu
that it is done to a turn—and though you serve in t
same dish the crystal beauty of Pyrex tends to enhar
the daintiness of the table.

Pyrex Ovenware saves hours of washing-up, does r
stain, flake or rust—you gain in every way by usi
Pyrex. **Write for Illustrated List**

PYREX

THE ORIGINAL TRANSPARENT OVENWARE

Keeps its brightness after years of use.
**EVERY PIECE GUARANTEED against oven he
breakage for six months from date of purchas**
Illustrated above is the Pyrex Pie Dish. Prices:
(Oblong) 1 pt. 3/6, 1½ pt. 4/6, 2⅔ pt. 5/6.

If your local dealer cannot supply, please write direct to :

JAMES A. JOBLING & CO., LTI
Wear Flint Glass Works, Sunderlan

*Look for this mark on the Pyi
Transparent Ovenware, it is
guarantee against substitution.*

**Figure 2.12   'Wasn't that a Dainty Dish!'
Homes and Gardens (February 1926)**

Figure 2.13 **'Happy the bride with Pyrex presents,'**
Ideal Home (March 1951)

Figure 2.14 'Pyrex in the picture,'
          Homes and Gardens (April 1963)

secretary' from Croydon who wed a year later was given '20 separate pieces of Pyrex ware' (M2229). An explanation for such high volume giving in the immediate post-war period is provided by another correspondent, a typesetter from Woking, who married in 1948:

There was not much in the shops for people to buy and it was difficult to find something original. Some factories had been working flat out producing things in the war that either had a demand for in peace time, or they did not need to retool to change to another product, or the raw material was easy to obtain. One of these was the Pyrex oven glass factory and the shops were overstocked with this product for a time. We were overwhelmed with these items and my wife would not give any away as they had been given to us (H1806).

The effect of the wartime economy on Wear Flint Glass Works was that production of Pyrex for industrial purposes increased (radar tubes, glass piping and laboratory wares) and that for domestic purposes was limited to a 'Utility' range.[53] It was this type of dish that would have been given in large quantities to those marrying at the time of post-war austerity. From the end of this period to the end of the twentieth century the forms of Pyrex became more diverse and more conspicuously designed in order to compete directly with china (Figures 2.13 and 2.14). For example, another correspondent who identifies herself as a 'housewife', an audiotypist from Hertfordshire married in 1965 states: 'My husband's boss gave us a super June Roses Pyrex tea service (pieces for which I now pick up in charity shops to keep it going)' (L1290) (Figures 2.15). The modernity of the transparently functional oven to tableware has been compromised in this opaque decorated china tea service copy but nevertheless some essential characteristics remain. Describing Pyrex as super is very telling. Domestic objects that are praised in this way are never those reserved for best but are the things that regularly make a valued contribution to domestic economy, tools that perform well everyday allowing whoever is responsible for the housekeeping to make a consistently good impression. A reliable washing machine, a sharp vegetable knife as well as a useful tea set would be called super.

The usefulness of Pyrex is noted even by those correspondents who received so much of it in the late forties and early fifties. 'So useful – I used the casseroles, etc. for years' remarked the Croydon 'Housewife/secretary' (M2229). Substantial amounts were still being given as wedding presents in the late fifties and through the sixties. 'I was grateful to receive sheets, towels, blankets, Pyrex ware (in abundance)' stated a music teacher from Hebden Bridge whose marriage took place in 1957 (M1381) and a midwife from Shoreham-by-Sea who married two years later wrote: 'I had so many pyrex casseroles that some were stored for years and used much later on' (B2552). They were not the only Mass-Observation correspondents to keep surplus Pyrex until it was needed. Despite distributing a list, a 'housewife' from High Wycombe was given 'a number of Pyrex casserole dishes although they all came in useful eventually' (W1923). In the current culture of marriage exchanges all this Pyrex could be regarded as a problem of duplication, disrupting the symmetry of the wedding presents as the perfect domestic collection. But this is not the case here. While Mass-Observation correspondents married between 1945 and 1975 did not seem to desire Pyrex ware, indeed, many describe the amount they received with a mixture of humour and resignation, keeping all of it was a sign of good housekeeping, of long-term domestic economy, skilful and thrifty planning

---

53 Baker, pp. 8 and 10.

Figure 2.15 'June Rose,'
1960s Pyrex pattern

that involved looking after useful things because there might come a time when they would be needed. One correspondent held onto to Pyrex for 40 years. An Orpington civil servant, whose marriage took place in 1948, reported that 'An old school friend gave us some Pyrex dishes which we still have' (K1515).

Correspondents also proudly relate that their Pyrex has been used continually. One, a bookkeeper from Mirfield, West Yorkshire, explained that at the moment she replied to the Giving and Receiving Presents directive she had 'only just thrown out the last of the pyrex dishes which my sister bought us for our wedding present.' She married in 1973. The dishes had 'served us very well for 25 years', she added (S2581). A social worker from Bristol married a year later, in 1974, declared she had 'a couple of pyrex casseroles – still in use!' (D826) Her dishes must have been twenty-four years old when she replied to the directive and the phrase that she employed to describe such long service is a frequent aside in many other responses. 'Still in use,' sometimes bracketed, follows the listing of durable marriage gifts and Pyrex in particular (Figure 2.16).

The pleasure of the useful and durable object could be considered a culture of consumption counter to the culture of the market, premised upon the necessity of the forever new. I very much doubt, however, that any Mass-Observation correspondent would regard using the same Pyrex dish for twenty-four or forty years as an act of consumption. Careful continual use of a functional domestic vessel is more likely to be understood as its opposite: domestic economy as a defence against the expense of consumption. The activities of good household management, including careful cleaning, attentive handling and safe storage would be defined in a professional context as a practice of preservation. But if, as feminists have argued, we attempt to think outside think outside the conventions of skill and its market value, preservation can be considered an everyday activity at the centre of a domestic economy. Before making any further claims about preservation as a domestic practice, the differences between Pyrex and china ought to be summarised.

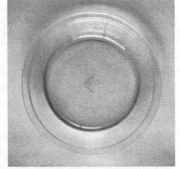

China and Pyrex are consistently differently deployed within the domestic realm. The explanation for this lies in part, and only in part,

Figure 2.16 'Still in use,'
a standard Pyrex form

in their distinctive physical properties, their combinations of attributes. Both are potentially durable but Pyrex's enhanced strength (resistance to high temperatures and knocks) makes it more flexible and intrinsically useful than easily broken china since it can be used for cooking and serving. However, Pyrex's usefulness is less celebrated than china's fragility. Mass-Observation correspondents remembered much of the Pyrex that they received when they wed but devoted far fewer words to it. Functional objects seem to hold less value than the decorative ones reserved for display. Both Pyrex and china are kept for long periods, even lifetimes and longer, but china is protected and revered whereas Pyrex is put to work.

China and Pyrex occupy different places in the system of objects that constitutes domesticity. Both are very stable cultural forms; they stay in their place. Such stability is evident in their similar treatment by different people who must share an understanding of the higher and lower values of useful and decorative things as well as something of the specific historical meanings that have settled upon china and Pyrex. The histories of china and Pyrex, reproduced in their respective classical and modern shapes, have become transformed into their purpose, their self-evident reason for existence. Fine decorated tableware, used to create the space of the proper home has become the essential representation of family life; it carries a more universalizing and powerful idea than Pyrex's modest expression of the respectability of the modern efficient household.

There are just two exceptions to the hierarchy of the decorative object over the useful thing, and the idea of eternal family over that of the modern household. One Mass-Observation correspondent, a Newcastle primary school teacher married in 1952, noted that: 'The wedding presents would all be used and even today I use my large Pyrex bowls or dust my dressing table set, I remember the people who bought them for me' (S2574). The other correspondent still possessed all her wedding presents, a deliberate act of preservation that has included both unused and broken. 'EVERY GIFT I RECEIVED I HAVE KEPT,' wrote a female factory worker from Lowestoft about the presents she accepted when she married in July 1968. She added, 'SOME OF THE PYREX DISHES I HAVE YET TO USE. BUT I STILL KEEP THEM, I WOULDN'T PART WITH THEM FOR THE WORLD' (C2579). Both correspondents seem to regard all gifts as equally significantly, illustrating an instance when the gift exchange has primacy in the process of making meaning. Nevertheless, their Pyrex, embodied and evocative, was used.

Despite divergent physical and historical characteristics between china and Pyrex, their material differences in other words, the practices that surround both point to the prevalence of preservation as domestic way of life. Importantly, preservation is practised with objects at opposite ends of the domestic spectrum: best and everyday, resilient and fragile, used and displayed, china and Pyrex. Heightened security surrounds sacred objects, layers of protection are reserved for inherited things and gifts expected to become inheritances. However, less overtly but more routinely, practices of preservation maintain much, if not all, domestic material culture as it is washed, wiped, dusted, folded, stacked and stored. When homes are cast as sites of consumption, we create a picture of domesticity as a system within which objects constantly circulate that is best illustrated by the economy of perishable food. Another way of thinking about the home is as a storehouse, wherein objects are allocated a place which they occupy for brief spells or for longer periods, sometimes for a lifetime or more.

Chapter 3

Accounting for Change: Forgotten, Neglected and Altered Objects

Change, Stasis and Context in Anthropological Theory

The meanings of objects can appear both fixed and changeable. These two oppositional characteristics are assigned to objects by anthropologists in some of the most influential writings on material culture, works that have shaped the way objects are viewed in art history, cultural studies, design history and sociology. In *The World of Goods* (1979), Mary Douglas and Baron Isherwood urged us to revise the limited interpretation of 'goods' as 'primarily needed for subsistence plus competitive display' and instead 'assume that they are needed for making visible and stable the categories of culture.'[1] The interpretative advice contained in this sentence, which must be the most quoted of the book, has been taken up. Objects are understood to uphold and enforce boundaries by fixing meanings. Douglas and Isherwood enlarge upon this function in a slightly less famous passage:

> The main problem of social life is to pin down meanings so that they stay still for a little time…. As for tribal society, so too for us: rituals serve to contain the drift of meaning. Rituals are conventions set up visible public definitions…. More effective rituals use material things and the costly the ritual trappings, the stronger we can assume the intention to fix meanings to be. Goods, in this perspective are ritual adjuncts; consumption is a ritual process whose primary function is to make sense of the inchoate flux of events.[2]

It is the stabilizing effect of objects that I want to draw attention to here. Objects act to prevent change and wedding presents, the subject of this study, can be seen to have such an effect. Giving and receiving a predictable series of domestic objects upon marriage reproduces dominant ideas of the home and family.

Other writers whose work, like that of Douglas, has developed the field of material culture studies have examined the conditions in which the meanings of objects are destabilized. James Clifford's analysis of the positions that 'exotic' objects have come to occupy in 'Western collecting systems,' which he sets out in *The Predicament of Culture* (1988), is an exploration of the effect of disruptive

---

1   Mary Douglas and Baron Isherwood, *The World of Goods: Towards an Anthropology of Consumption* (London: Routledge, 1979) p. 38.

2   Douglas and Isherwood, p. 43.

movement upon objects.[3] Once removed from their (non-western) location, they enter the "'art-culture system'"[4] and as they do so their 'distinctive histories vanish.'[5] Thus they become mutable. Their meanings altered as they come to occupy different zones of the system and are defined as art, as material culture, as technology or as a curio.[6]

The editor of *The Social Life of Things* (1986), Arun Appadurai, and its first contributor, Igor Kopytoff, are also concerned with the movement of objects, although their destinations are differently defined. They trace movement between spheres of exchange, between two domains often referred to as the moral and the market economy, and are particularly interested in the moments when objects take on or leave behind a commodity-form. Appadurai summarizes: 'things move in *and* out of the commodity state' and 'such movements can be slow or fast, reversible or terminal, normative and deviant'[7] and Kopytoff suggests possible pathways that objects travel in series of starts and stops. Slaves, public lands, special cloth, armbands and bracelets, calabashes, old slippers, beer cans are either regularly or exceptionally commoditized or decommoditized.[8] This mapping of the movement of things by Appadurai and Kopytoff has a quite different purpose to Clifford's exploration of the particular directions in which 'exotic' objects are made to move. They attempt to develop a cross-cultural theory of value that can be applied globally, to both 'small-scale societies' with discrete forms of commodity exchange as well as 'complex' ones shaped through capitalism whereas he is problematizing the cross-cultural encounter. Clifford provides a cultural and political critique of the re-evaluations that occur in what Appadurai and Kopytoff present rather cheerfully as the richly diverse biographies of object. Given these differences the common ground is more significant still: movement, which is the effect of an exchange (a sale, a theft or a gift), causes a transformation of material culture. Re-location disrupts and then re-creates the meaning of things. The movement that accompanies an exchange thus instigates changes to, or in, material culture, but the actual acquisition of meaning is dependent upon context.

An opposition between the fixed meaning of objects and their changeability can be argued away. It is quite possible to suggest that rather than representing two radically different ideas about the nature of material culture, the properties of fixity

---

3   James Clifford, *The Predicament of Culture: Twentieth Century Ethnography, Literature, and Art* (Cambridge, MA: Harvard University Press, 1988) p. 12.

4   Clifford, p. 215.

5   Clifford, p. 5.

6   Clifford, p. 224. The zones Clifford identifies include the art market or museum, the ethnographic museum, the museum of technology or the tourist art market.

7   Arun Appadurai, 'Introduction: Commodities and the Politics of Value,' *Social Life of Things: Commodities in Cultural Perspective*, ed. Arun Appadurai (Cambridge: Cambridge University Press, 1986) p. 13. Emphasis in the original.

8   Igor Kopytoff, 'The Cultural Biography of Things: Commoditization as Process,' *Social Life of Things: Commodities in Cultural Perspective*, ed. Arun Appadurai (Cambridge: Cambridge University Press, 1986) pp. 65, 73–80.

and mutability emerge at different times and places: objects have moments of stasis and moments of transition. Their meanings are known and certain until they are moved and when next at rest new meanings settle upon them. For example, wedding presents that make 'visible and stable' the idea of the home and family and therefore demonstrate Douglas and Isherwood's steadying effect of material forms can also be seen to follow Appadurai and Kopytoff's trajectory of things. The transformation of a high street purchase into a sign of approval or an embodiment of domestic knowledge is a standard wedding present scenario. These assumptions about how objects halt the flow of meanings or how their meanings mutate bear closer investigation for a number of reasons. Recognition of an object's stable or alterable meanings are premised upon the priorities of anthropological inquiry, or in other words, it depends what you are looking for and which cultural moment you have selected for study. This study, *The Wedding Present*, has focused upon the receipt of presents and not upon the moment of transformation of commodity into gift;[9] it has, for the most part, offered an analysis of how objects function within domestic domains, focused upon a moment of stability rather than one of rapid change. It should be no surprise, then, that such a focus has highlighted preservation as a domestic imperative and the maintenance of specific sets of things, like china or Pyrex. However, I have been able to identify moments of change in the way in which marriage gifts are received and displayed, the decline of the 'show' of presents associated with weddings in close communities, for example. Without really intending it, I have implied that the meanings of objects may change as the exchange relationships change and I have also suggested that once safely located within a home their meanings as prized objects have then become settled and stable.

The idea that objects have dual characteristics of fixity and mutability raises questions about the way people relate to things as well as about the nature of things themselves, as creative or passive entities. If the meaning of object stabilizes when it is made still, kept in the same cosy domestic place, does its meaning reside within itself or around it, in its location? If removal strips an object of meaning, does that suggest that meaning is an effect of being seen in a particular place? Is meaning invested only in appearance or is it something more intrinsic to the object that is somehow renegotiated with every minor alteration of its position as well as any big move? Or, are meanings held by people regardless of where their objects end up? Indeed, as the everyday task of tidying up is undertaken either at work or at home it is frequently accompanied by remonstrations that such and such a thing is out place.

This chapter examines the processes of change in the material culture of domestic life. Within the domestic sphere, wedding presents are the objects that are least likely to be subject to change; because they are gifts there is an expectation that they should be respected and retained. I am sure I should be accused of looking for an explanation

---

9   C. A. Gregory, *Gifts and Commodities* (London: Academic Press, 1982); James G. Carrier, *Gifts and Commodities: Exchange and Western Capitalism since 1700* (London: Routledge, 1995).

of change in the wrong place. It is much easier to explain any changes that might occur when objects cross economic and social boundaries or are exchanged between different people. Slight or gradual changes in domestic material culture, the realization that once prized objects are neither used nor missed, or that things that used to please now appear awkward are less obvious defining moments but trying to investigate creeping neglect or growing dislike could be revealing precisely because of this: it could provide some insights into processes of material transformation that are not connected to exchange and its upheavals. Although households and homes are sites of stability, they are not in complete stasis. Families change their composition with generational cycles and as adults make and end sexual relationships. The material environment of household, the physical spaces of the home, will reflect these social changes and are also subject (somehow) to market led fashions in interior decoration. It is now customary to understand the home as expressive, the setting for the carefully managed performance of identities.[10] However, when a householder changes his or her mind about a domestic object this may be a symptom and not cause of change. Rather than assuming that objects are only, or primarily, badges of identity, in this chapter I want to work with and think through the anthropological ideas that objects can stabilize meaning or that their meanings can be altered.

Like many attempts to identify change, this chapter proceeds by comparing moments in time. Responses from Mass-Observation correspondents to the 1998 Giving and Receiving Presents directive are the main sources of this chapter, as they are throughout the rest of the book, but here they are compared to testimony generated by a directive entitled Objects about the House written ten years previously in the Summer of 1988[11] and to replies to a letter sent to a selected number of correspondents sent five years later in 2003.[12] Thus writings about domesticity over a 15 year period from 1988 to 2003 form the basis of this chapter and these writings, like much Mass-Observation testimony, discuss events that extend back beyond this time frame. Changes to an established domestic environment, a home that has been already 'set up', are difficult to plot. The moment of the acquisition of domestic objects has a kind of public record that is traceable in market research. For example, we know a significant number of the homes of couples married at the beginning of the twenty-first century will contain Dualit toasters because it was recorded as a popular wedding present purchase at this time.[13] Also, gift transactions, such as at weddings, are set apart from everyday routine, witnessed and more likely to be

---

10 Marianne Gullestad's chapter 'Home Decoration as Popular Culture' in her book Marianne Gullestad, *The Art of Social Relations: Essays on Culture, Social Action and Everyday Life in Modern Norway* (Oslo: Scandinavian University Press, 1992) pp. 61–91 has been enormously influential in the way homes are understood as an expression of culture. Erving Goffman is a source for the idea of home as the stage for the performance of self. Erving Goffman, *The Presentation of Self in Everyday Life* (London: Penguin, 1990).

11 See Appendix 2.

12 See Appendix 3.

13 Michael Paterson and Laura Borg, 'The Newly Weds with Designs on Luxury,' *Daily Telegraph* 26 May 2000: 3.

remembered. But the subsequent circulation objects in domestic spaces and any change in status that might occur (such as being demoted from the dinning room to the kitchen cupboard) are unobserved. When something falls into disuse it is a gradual process that is not necessarily noticed and its disposal is sometimes quite secret. Tracing change within the domestic sphere is dependent upon remembered details of things that may not have been significant enough to keep and further complicated by the work of memory, which 'composes' rather than simply recalls the past.[14] Thus, although this chapter is an attempt to understand how change might occur in domestic domains some space is taken up with a discussion of memory and the production of testimony. The chapter explores how the shifts, alterations and amendments to domestic collections occur and it is also concerned with how such changes are recorded. Revered, cherished, preserved things, which have been the subject of previous chapters, generated a great deal of writing from Mass-Observation correspondents but neglected and forgotten things do not. Thus, at least in part, this chapter is concerned with the difficulties of discussing both the gradual alterations and the dramatic disruptions of everyday life.

Domestic Hierarchies: Practices of Preservation and Disposal

There is one response to the Giving and Receiving Presents directive, sent from a 'Genealogist and carer' from Aberystwyth who began her working life as a teacher, that is particularly consistent with the idea of the traditional wedding. She married in 1962 in white in a Welsh Wesleyan Methodist chapel. Her mother organized and controlled the gift transactions and the gifts, which were the typical mix of utilitarian domestic objects (including Pyrex) and ceremonial china (such as Royal Doulton). All were displayed in her house the week before her daughter's wedding and on the day of the wedding itself. There were 203 (see Figures 3.1, 3.2, 3.3, 3.4, 3.5, 3.6, 3.7). Since her wedding (a family affair in a small community where given objects were intended to help establish a respectable home) conforms to tradition, or our idea of tradition, we might also expect the ways in which she held and used her gifts to illustrate popular domestic proprieties. That is to say, her testimony may show what, traditionally, ought to happen to wedding presents. The Aberystwyth carer wrote:

> Looking at the list we have either still got them 36 years later or they wore out or have other wise been disposed of. Since we had a number of rayon damask table cloths a lot were re cycled as wedding presents etc. Some of the things I have no memory of at all! No 10 – the canteen of cutlery from my grandfather – a rather splendid set in a light oak box – comes out when we have visitors. My grandfather had been an ironmonger and knew about cutlery so it is a very good set.

---

14 T. G. Ashplant, Graham Dawson, and Michael Roper. 'The Politics of War Memory and Commemoration: Contexts, Structures, Dynamics.' *Commemorating War: The Politics of Memory*, ed. T. G. Ashplant, Graham Dawson and Michael Roper (London: Routledge, 2000) pp. 3–85.

The silver cruet no 16, the minton marmalade and jam pots, the Crown Derby small dish, the silver leaf jug and basin, the pastry tongs and silver sweetmeat dish are all kept in a glass fronted cupboard with other things we have acquired since. They get cleaned once a year and are only used on very rare occasions. The handmade table cloth (no 168) has only been used on the occasion of the christening of both our children....
The wooden bookcase (164) has been invaluable – we have a lot of books.
Some of the vases have been broken and one or two were frankly so hideous that we gave them to charity shops etc.
The pastry slice at no 96 is still in frequent use. Most of the clocks have broken but we still have most of the table mats.
The Royal Albert tea set (No 36) and the Royal Doulton dinner service (18) are both still complete though the other dinner service (159) has completely gone with the exception of the meat plate. The coalport coffee set at No 3 is still with us but is has never been used as the cups are so tiny. Most of the electrical things are not here any more and the fish knives etc were given away as we never used them. They went to swell the building fund for our new church. The kitchen tools (No 70) are giving yeoman service and the red tea trolley and 2 of the anodised aluminium trays – being virtually indestructible are still going strong. Some of the sheets were cotton and needed ironing so we tended to use the polyester cotton ones and 2 pairs of the five cotton ones are still in their wrappers (P1009, 1998).[15]

It should to be noted first of all that the detail of this account is premised upon the preservation of the list itself and this act of preservation is recognition of the importance attached to gift exchanges upon marriage. The receipt of marriage gifts was significant enough for this Mass-Observation correspondent to make and keep a record. In her reflections upon this record, which she makes just after she has written it out for inclusion in her Giving and Receiving Presents directive reply, she identified different kinds of gifts. There are those that are still possessed, those that have been used until they wore out, and those that have been 'disposed of.' Thus she demonstrates the complexity of domesticity as system of preservation and one of the most important hierarchies in domestic material culture: the order of keeping gifts.[16]

The gifts that have been 'disposed of' highlight the fact that not every object, nor indeed every gift, is kept and that domesticity as preservation is only a dominant practice rather than the destination of all domestic objects. However, the things she disposes of are not simply discarded; they are not thrown but given away. The rayon damask tablecloths are 're cycled' as gifts, the 'hideous' vases are donated to a charity shop and 'fishknives etc' are put into the local second-hand fundraising economy of her church. It is worth pointing out that there are differential values even within the lowest categories of domestic object. The importance of objects that are 'disposed of' can be seen to vary according to how long they are kept before they

---

15 In this chapter a date, 1988, 1998 or 2003, follows all Mass-Observation identification numbers. The dates refer to different directives or to the follow-up letter.

16 Annette Weiner, *Inalienable Possessions: The Paradox of Keeping-While-Giving* (Berkeley: University of California Press, 1992).

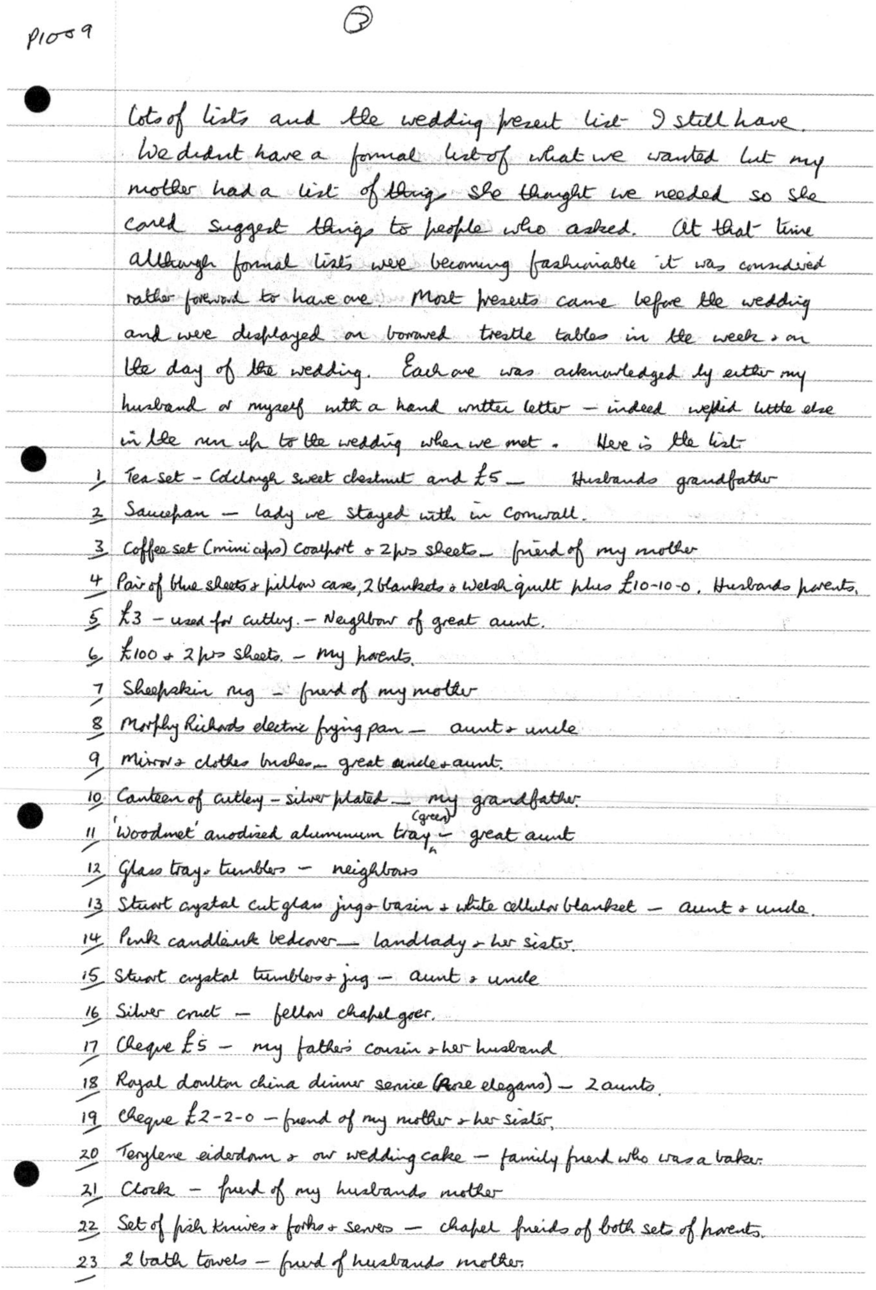

P1009

③

Lots of lists and the wedding present list I still have.
We didn't have a formal list of what we wanted but my
mother had a list of things she thought we needed so she
could suggest things to people who asked. At that time
although formal lists were becoming fashionable it was considered
rather forward to have one. Most presents came before the wedding
and were displayed on borrowed trestle tables in the week + on
the day of the wedding. Each one was acknowledged by either my
husband or myself with a hand written letter — indeed we did little else
in the run up to the wedding when we met. Here is the list

1 Tea set — Coldough sweet chestnut and £5 —   Husbands grandfather
2 Saucepan — lady we stayed with in Cornwall.
3 Coffee set (mini cups) Coalport + 2 prs sheets — friend of my mother
4 Pair of blue sheets + pillow case, 2 blankets + Welsh quilt plus £10-10-0, Husbands parents.
5 £3 — used for cutlery. — Neighbour of great aunt.
6 £100 + 2 prs sheets. — My parents.
7 Sheepskin rug — friend of my mother
8 Morphy Richards electric frying pan — aunt + uncle
9 Mirror + clothes brushes — great uncle + aunt.
10 Canteen of cutlery — silver plated — my grandfather.
11 'Woodmet' anodised aluminium tray — (green) great aunt
12 Glass tray + tumblers — neighbours
13 Stuart crystal cut glass jugs + basin + white cellular blanket — aunt + uncle.
14 Pink candlewick bedcover — landlady + her sister.
15 Stuart crystal tumblers + jug — aunt + uncle
16 Silver cruet — fellow chapel goer.
17 Cheque £5 — my father's cousin + her husband
18 Royal Doulton china dinner service (Rose elegans) — 2 aunts.
19 Cheque £2-2-0 — friend of my mother + her sister.
20 Terylene eiderdown + our wedding cake — family friend who was a baker.
21 Clock — friend of my husbands mother
22 Set of fish knives + forks + servers — chapel friends of both sets of parents.
23 2 bath towels — friend of husbands mother.

Figure 3.1   'The list,' first page (P1009)

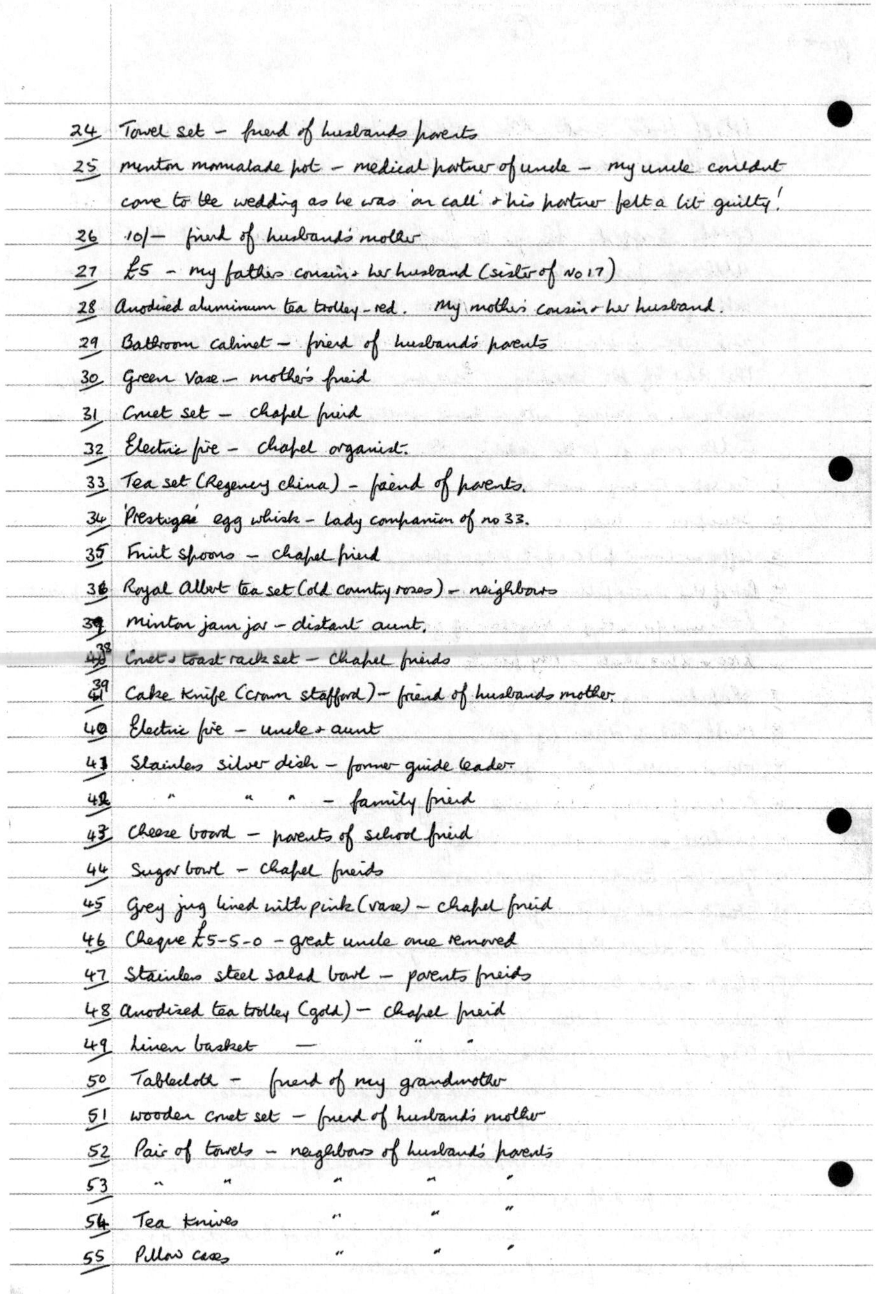

24 Towel set – friend of husbands parents
25 minton marmalade pot – medical partner of uncle – my uncle couldnt come to the wedding as he was 'on call' & his partner felt a bit guilty!
26 10/– friend of husband's mother
27 £5 – my fathers cousin & her husband (sister of No 17)
28 Anodized aluminum tea trolley – red. My mother's cousin & her husband.
29 Bathroom cabinet – friend of husband's parents
30 Green vase – mother's friend
31 Cruet set – chapel friend
32 Electric fire – chapel organist.
33 Tea set (Regency china) – friend of parents.
34 'Prestige' egg whisk – lady companion of no 33.
35 Fruit spoons – chapel friend
36 Royal Albert tea set (old country roses) – neighbours
37 minton jam jar – distant aunt.
38 Cruet & toast rack set – chapel friends
39 Cake Knife (crown stafford) – friend of husbands mother.
40 Electric fire – uncle & aunt
41 Stainless silver dish – former guide leader.
42 "   "   " – family friend
43 Cheese board – parents of school friend
44 Sugar bowl – chapel friends
45 Grey jug lined with pink (vase) – chapel friend
46 Cheque £5-5-0 – great uncle once removed
47 Stainless steel salad bowl – parents friends
48 Anodized tea trolley (gold) – chapel friend
49 Linen basket   "   "
50 Tablecloth – friend of my grandmother
51 wooden cruet set – friend of husband's mother
52 Pair of towels – neighbours of husband's parents
53 "   "   "   "
54 Tea knives   "   "   "
55 Pillow cases   "   "   "

Figure 3.2   'The list,' second page (P1009)

④

56 Electric iron (Morphy Richards) — friend of ~~middle~~ husband's mother
57 Table lamp — chapel friends
58 Coffee percolater — family friends
59 Tablecloth & napkins (rayon) "
60 Tea set (Royal Stafford) — chapel friend
61 Pyrex dish on stand — former minister.
62 Pair of towels — chapel friend
63 £2 — distant relative of husband
64 Set of glass tumblers —
65 Flower stand — friend of husband's mother
66 Pillow cases — "
67 Cups, saucers & plate
68 Silver pastry forks — chapel friends
69 Electric kettle (Hotpoint Hi'Speed) — husband's uncle & aunt
70 Stainless steel kitchen tools — " cousin
71 Wooden stand & 4 egg cups — " "
72 Morphy Richards electric toaster — head & pupils of school where I was teaching.
73 Tea knives — friend of landlady.
74 Egg cups on a plate — parents of pupil at school
75 Anodised aluminium tray (gold) Woodmet. — friend of my mother & former teacher.
76 Companion set (brush, poker & shovel) — husband's friend & usher at wedding
77 Pair of sheets & pillow cases (pink) — parents of 76.
78 Pair of pink & white striped sheet — friend of family.
79 Cruet set — neighbours
80 Italian salad plate & salt & pepper — friend of family
81 Cut glass fruit dishes — former colleague of my father.
82 Stainless steel meat dish & sauce boat — family friend
83 Stainless steel meat & 2 veg dishes — college friend & ~~bridesmaid~~ of my mother
84 Settee set — chapel friend
85 Tablecloth & serviettes — husband's family friend.
86 Tablecloth — chapel friend
87 Pillow cases — relative of husband.
88 Vase — " "

Figure 3.3 'The list,' third page (P1009)

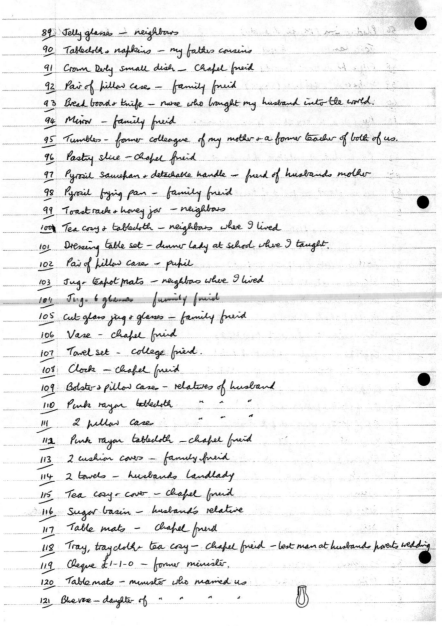

89 Jelly glasses — neighbours
90 Tablecloth & napkins — my father's cousins
91 Crown Derby small dish — Chapel freind
92 Pair of pillow cases — family freind
93 Bread board & knife — nurse who brought my husband into the world.
94 Mirror — family freind
95 Tumblers — former colleague of my mother & a former teacher of both of us.
96 Pastry slice — Chapel freind
97 Pyrosil saucepan & detachable handle — freind of husbands mother
98 Pyrosil frying pan — family freind
99 Toast rack & honey jar — neighbours
100 Tea cosy & tablecloth — neighbours where I lived
101 Dressing table set — dinner lady at school where I taught.
102 Pair of pillow cases — pupil
103 Jug & teapot mats — neighbours where I lived
104 Jug & 6 glasses   family freind
105 Cut glass jug & glasses — family freind
106 Vase — chapel freind
107 Towel set — college freind.
108 Clock — chapel freind
109 Bolster & pillow cases — relatives of husband
110 Pink rayon tablecloth   "   "   "
111 2 pillow cases   "   "   "
112 Pink rayon tablecloth — chapel freind
113 2 cushion covers — family freind
114 2 towels — husbands landlady
115 Tea cosy & cover — chapel freind
116 Sugar basin — husband's relative
117 Table mats — chapel freind
118 Tray, traycloth & tea cosy — chapel freind — best man at husbands parents wedding
119 Cheque £1-1-0 — former minister.
120 Table mats — minister who married us
121 Blue vase — daughter of "   "   "   "

Figure 3.4   'The list', fourth page (P1009)

P1009   ⑤

122 2 Towels — family freid

123 Butter dish — neighbour

124 Coffee table (wood with drop leaves) — family freid

125 Fruit dish with cream inside & green outside - teardrop shape — family friend.

126 Brass magazine rack — chapel freid.

127 Pillow cases — family freid

128 Cheque £1-1-0 - Husbands parents' landlord.

129 Settee set - husbands family friend

130 2 Pillow case   "   "   "

131 £2. - Husband fathers cousin.

132 Crockery holder (plastic covered rack to hold a tea set) - husbands mothers cousin.

133 2 towels - family freid

134 Silver tea pot, jug, milk jug & basin — husbands friend (best man)

135 Cheque £1-1-0 — former colleague of my father

136 6 glasses — son of family friend.

137 Grapefruit spoons - cleaning lady at parents house.

138 Pair of towels — college freind.

139 wooden fruit bowl — friend

140 Irish linen tablecloth - friends former colleague of my mother

141 Pyrex casserole dish — school friend of both of us.

142 Picture of Bedd Gelert (hand painted) - friend of parents who was an artist.

143 'Arcopal' casserole dish — chapel friend

144 Fruit spoons — chapel freid

145 mirror — family freid

146 Divided pyrex dish with stand & heaters — family freid

147 Pyrosil frying pan — friend of husbands mother.

148 Pillow & bolster case - colleague of my father.

149 £2-2-0 - chapel freid

150 Donna towels - chapel freid

151 Rayon tablecloth & napkins - chapel freid

152 £2-2-0 or silver pastry tongs (the most useless thing we had!) - freind of husband's mother.

153 Vacuum flask — neighbour of husbands parents.

154 Tablecloth - husbands relative.

Figure 3.5   'The list', fifth page (P1009)

155   Pillow & bolster set – friend of husband's parents.
156   £2-2-0 – family friend
157   £5 – husbands friend – usher at wedding
158   Table mats – friend of husbands mother.
159   Dinner service (midwinter) – staff of bank where my father was manager.
160   Whishette hand mixer (Phillips) – friends of husbands mother
161   Towels – family friends
162   Hand made tablecloth – husband's second cousin
163   2 pillow cases – parents of 162.
164   Wooden glass fronted bookcase – uncle & aunt
165   Grapefruit spoons & knife – friends of husband's parents.
166   Tablecloth – friend of husband' mother
167   Cheque £1-1-0 – very old family friend
168   Hand made white linen tablecloth with deep surround of exquisite hand
      made lace – chapel friend
169   Cut glass grapefruit dishes – family doctor.
170   3 bath towels – family friend
171   £2-2-0 – family friend.
172   2 pillow cases – friend of husband's mother.
173   Silver sweetmeat dish with pierced rim – close family friend (probably the most
      valuable present financially which we received)
174   Tea towels – friend of mine.
175   Cheque for £4 – used to buy 2 pillows) – a cousin
176   Wooden coal scuttle – family friend.
177   Tea service & matching cake stand (same pattern as No 1) – business contacts
      of my father.
178   Cut glass jug & basin – family friend
179   Tray cloth & 2 serviettes – school friend of both of us
180   Teaspoons – chrome plated – chapel friend
181   Cheque for £5-5-0 – cousin of my husband.
182   Framed mirror – neighbour
183   Bolster & pillow set – former maid & her husband.
184   Pillow cases – neighbour

Figure 3.6   'The list,' sixth page (P1009)

P1009.   ⑥

185	Table cloth & serviettes — husbands parents neighbour
186	£3 — no idea
187	Pair of flannelette blankets — schoolfriend of both of us.
188	Breakfast set — friend of my mother
189	Pillow cases — friend of my husbands mother
190	£2-2-0 — family friend.
191	'Callalite' Combined lamp & alarm clock — friend of my father
192	Grapefruit spoons — friend of my mother (bridesmaid at her wedding)
193	Tea knives — friend of my husband's mother — mother of pearl handles (false)
194	£2-2-0 — former chemistry teacher of both of us
195	Serviette rings — friend of my mother — wooden ones.
196	Electric wall clock — cousin of my husband's mother
197	Breakfast set on a tray — cousin of my father.
198	£3-3-0 — friend of my mother
199	Woodmet anodised aluminium tray (blue) — college friend of mine
200	Crown Derby butter dish & knife — parents of 199.
201	6 glasses — next door neighbours of husbands parents.
202	Silver spoons — Dutch friends of my father
203	£1 — parents of a friend of my husband.

As you can see from that lot we sent a lot of thank you letters — every gift had a hand written letter — printed cards were not considered the thing at all.

You will also see that we ended up with far more trays & glasses than we have ever needed & not enough teaspoons!

Looking at the list we have either still got them 36 years later or they have worn out or have otherwise been disposed of. Since we had a number of rayon damask table cloths a lot were re cycled as wedding presents etc. Some of the things I have no memory of at all!

No 10 — the canteen of cutlery from my grandfather — a rather splendid set in a light oak box — comes out when we have visitors. My grandfather had been an ironmonger & knew about-

Figure 3.7   'The list,' seventh page (P1009)

are given away. For example, the fish knives must have been kept for long enough for the Aberystwyth carer to notice that they were never used whereas the rayon tablecloths were given away almost immediately.

Her used until they 'wore out' category of gifts includes 'Most of the electrical things' and almost all of 'the other dinner service (159).' Checking back through her list reveals that number 159 was Midwinter china given to her by her father's colleagues and she received six gifts of electrical equipment: 'Morphy Richards electric frying pan', 'Electric fire', 'Electric iron (Morphy Richards)', 'Electric kettle (Hotpoint Hispeed)', 'Morphy Richards electric toaster' (Figures 3.8 and 3.9). But in her narrative she provides little information about these objects that she no longer has despite the fact they must have played an important role in her household economy since they were once so regularly used that their constituent material or mechanism gave way. Such absences are indicative of the materiality of memory that is an underlying theme of this chapter.

Gifts that she still possesses, as she informs us after '36 years' of marriage, appear as the most significant objects. I have suggested, in my discussion of china, that there is a correlation between preservation and significance. However,

objects belong to this category of kept things for different, even opposite, reasons. Some objects have remained in her possession because they are continually useful and extraordinarily durable (such as the bookcase, tea trolley, aluminium trays, table mats and kitchen tools in particular) while others are redundant, and because a use has never been found for them they are stored away (for example, the cotton sheets that required ironing and coffee cups that are too

Figure 3.8 Morphy Richards electric iron

small). Gradations of value are also very evident in this 'still got' category and a key distinction must be made between unused objects that are stored and those, like silver or china, which are displayed. The silver cruet, silver leaf jug and basin, pastry tongs and sweetmeat dish, Minton jam pots and Crown Derby dish became the origins of a collection of functional objects transformed into ornaments that are visible and visibly protected ('all kept in a glass fronted cupboard with other things we have acquired since.')[17] Such strategies must be read as signs of their worth as also demonstrated by the ritual of the cleaning and infrequent use ('They get cleaned once a year and are used on very rare occasions'). Amongst these most precious things, a material hierarchy persists. One, a table cloth, described in the reproduced list as 'white linen with a deep surround of exquisite hand made lace' was selected to play a part in the performance of a unique moment in the life of family members; it was used when her children were christened. The qualities of preciousness and rarity are illustrated in this textile form; it is delicate, fragile

---

17 Susan M. Pearce, *Collecting in Contemporary Practice* (London: Sage, 1998) p. 123 for the importance of gifts in initiating collections.

Figure 3.9   Hotpoint Hi-speed electric kettle: 'Most of the electrical things are not here any more' (P1009)

and the detail on its surface demonstrates the devotion of time and labour that created it. When such objects are used to emphasize the importance of a particular ritual it too becomes invested with heightened significance and it is difficult to find another appropriate moment to use it again. A lesser occasion would devalue it.[18]

The different and differentiated values that have settled upon this carer's wedding presents lends some support to the argument made elsewhere in this book that exchange is never the sole determinant of meaning. If it was, the value of objects would directly and simply reflect the value of the gift relationships. Family members do tend to give gifts of the highest cultural or financial value, for example, the Royal Doulton that this Mass-Observation correspondent received was from '2 aunts'. But the giver of the hand made tablecloth is simply referred to as 'chapel friend' and friends plus one 'distant aunt' were the donors of almost all the wedding presents that were subsequently kept in the glass fronted cupboard. Only one, the silver sweetmeat dish, is from a 'close family friend.' These carefully and ritually preserved things have increased in value over time while that of other gifts have decreased, in some cases to the point where they can be disposed of.

The detail in the Aberystwyth carer's account of the difference destinations of her 203 presents allows us to see some of the complexities of domestic material culture. For instance, I have been referring to the meaning of objects as if there was *a* meaning. However, her writing reveals that an object's meaning has at least two different but overlapping components: it has value, which is an assessment of its significance or worth and it is a sign; it expresses ideas such as love, devotion, respectability, wealth. As some objects, the fish knives for example, slip down the hierarchy of domestic things so far that they can be disposed of it is worth asking what exactly has changed. Their significance? Their signification? Both? Furthermore, since they stayed in the same place for 30 years, how did these meanings change? At some point, they become devalued enough to be given away. The fish knives were gifts from 'chapel friends of both sets of parents' (P1009, 1998) and perhaps as time passed this gift relation did not need to be sustained. Increasing acceptability of informal eating may also have contributed to the loss of expressiveness and

---

18 It could be argued that the tablecloth has become contaminated. See Russell W. Belk, Melanie Wallendorf, John F. Sherry, 'The Sacred and Profane in Consumer Behaviour: Theodicy on the Odyssey,' *Journal of Consumer Research* 16 (1989) p. 6. That the most valued wedding present is a piece of cloth is also interesting to note in relation to Annette Weiner's arguments about hierarchies of significance and practices of keeping (Weiner, p. 13).

the decline of the value of these wedding presents.[19] Once they left the house and were inserted into the church sale, the knives were no longer gifts but second-hand commodities. However, we should note, that they had already undergone some alteration in order for the Aberystwyth carer to allow such a transformation to take place. Such small amendments to objects within the domestic domain may seem trivial compared to the cultural upheavals described by James Clifford. But trivial is the stuff of everyday life, commonplace practices routinely performed and removed from controversy. Once the trivial is opened up to scrutiny, it becomes possible to see the organization of everyday life.[20]

Remembering Change

The carer from Aberystwyth was one of the Mass-Observation correspondents who replied to the 1998 Giving and Receiving Presents directives and the one sent out ten years earlier in 1988 entitled Objects about the House. What now follows is a comparison between the directives. Both encouraged Mass-Observation correspondents to describe domestic objects and in some cases elicited similar responses from correspondents: narratives about objects and their place in personal, domestic and social worlds. But the focus of the directives, if not the responses they generated, was not the same. The Giving and Receiving Presents directive asked correspondents to identify particular objects, isolate wedding presents from other domestic things, detail their exchange and use. These questions generated a wealth of information about object types and their role in the creation of a domestic order but correspondents also, without being asked, discussed what the objects they had identified meant to them. The Objects about the House directive explicitly requested this kind of account. The intention of this directive was to make a very particular kind of record of the material culture of domestic life, one that reveals attitudes towards rather than just the existence or appearance of domestic possessions. David Pocock, the then Director of the Mass-Observation Archive, prefaced the Objects about the House directive by suggesting why such a record might be necessary:

> When future generations try to understand how we lived in our homes they will have a great many images to help them, both the glossy images of advertising and family snaps. But neither of these sources will tell them much about what we think and feel about the objects we've gathered round us and how those feelings have changed over time.[21]

---

19 This latter argument about the influence of the market on domestic material culture is the orthodox explanation of change. For a complex account of the way change might be imposed or resisted through the patterns of everyday life see David Chaney, *Cultural Change and Everyday Life* (Basingstoke: Palgrave, 2002).

20 Gullestad, p. 2; Daniel Miller, 'Why Some Things Matter,' *Material Cultures: Why Some Things Matter*, ed. Daniel Miller (London: UCL Press, 1998) p. 19.

21 See Appendix 2.

Objects about the House has already contributed to a more holistic understanding of the home. Tim Putman and Charles Newton drew upon the directive in *Household Choices* (1990). The collection of essays that accompanied the Victoria and Albert Museum exhibition of the same name, which sought to explore the imaginary, social and material practices of home-making.[22] The directive was an important source in this respect, I would suggest, because it contained many insights into the real and idealized relationships embedded in domestic material culture, which structure our everyday lives but are rarely discussed. For example, a cashier from Torquay wrote:

> One of my favourite items in my grandmother's kitchen was a potato peeler, which also shredded runner beans and chipped potatoes and cored apples all in one. When I got married she had a spare one of these in a drawer and gave it to me. It holds memories of my granddad who died when I was eight, because he taught me when I was about four to use this peeler and I have never mastered the art of using a knife. Well somehow my peeler got lost and I've never been able to replace it with one I like (S1238, 1988) (Figure 3.10).

Such an unpretentious thing, a small, cheap object mass produced without consideration for visual effect, which is kept in a kitchen drawer, may not appear to be the repository of cultural or political meanings and thus not worthy of scholarly attention. But details of its exchange and use demonstrate how an individual's and a family's past, present and future are embodied in material objects, how the most mundane things become alienable, unique and irreplaceable and, incidentally, suggests that a fixed periodization of the sexual division of labour is quite problematic. It was the immediate post-war period when this correspondent's grandfather taught her to use a peeler; he was involved in food preparation often enough to become expert in it at the moment when men are assumed to be excluded from domestic labour because

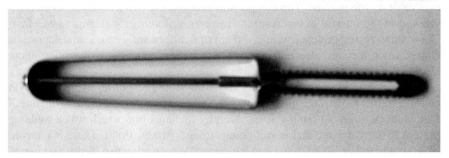

Figure 3.10   A multi-purpose peeler

they adhered to the strict spatial separation of home and work that accompanied the dominance of the male breadwinner norm. This account of a grandfather in the kitchen demonstrates that such spatial divisions are crossed but not overturned: he

---

22 Tim Putnam and Charles Newton, *Household Choices* (Future Publications in association with Middlesex Polytechnic, 1990).

may have prepared food but the kitchen was not his place nor its tools his property. The peeler was the grandmother's to give away.

The cashier from Torquay identifies the peeler as a favourite. 'Favourites' was also a category of domestic object suggested in the Objects about the House directive. David Pocock encouraged Mass-Observation correspondents to think beyond the obvious categories of object with aesthetic value to write about possessions 'which have "stood the test of time,"' 'things of which you are most fond' as well as those 'purchases which we later come to regret' and objects that 'may not have lasted well or don't look the same in today's light.' It is these last two categories of object that may tell the most about changes in domestic life and gathering evidence of change was clearly an aim of the directive. Reading Objects about the House for accounts of objects that have become disliked, have failed in some way and no longer fit within a domestic environment would reveal much about how material culture alters over time and might help us to understand how such changes, however small they may be, came about. The task of this chapter is somewhat different since it retains the focus of the rest of the book on wedding presents although here paying particular attention to those that have become disliked or devalued and forgotten as well as those that are still cherished. Thus, it is an attempt, within the framework of my study of marriage gifts, to examine the forms or stability and processes of transformation of domestic material culture as well as understand the conditions in which either occurs.

As I compared accounts of wedding presents in the Objects about the House and the Giving and Receiving Presents directives, I was particularly interested when the same object was discussed in both or when there was an important absence, such as an object of particular significance in one account not featuring in another. These presences and absences indicated continuities and change over time that can only really be detected over the medium and long-term and therefore are not necessarily noticeable as life is lived. The comparison between the two directives, written ten years apart, was useful in this respect. However, differences within any one Mass-Observation correspondent's writing did not straightforwardly demonstrate domestic change since they are also indicative of the changed conditions of writing about objects.

For example, in her 1988 Objects about the House response, the Aberystwyth carer identifies a marriage gift among the 'things which "stood the test of time."' She wrote 'another old faithful is my Morphy Richards iron which was a wedding present 25 1/2 years ago and is still going strong' (P1009, 1988). There is a record of its receipt in her 1998 Giving and Receiving Presents directive. Entry number 56 on her reproduced wedding list reads 'Electric iron (Morphy Richards) – friend of husband's mother' (P1009, 1998) (Figure. 3.8), but it is not mentioned by name again. Of course, directives do direct the attention of Mass Observation correspondents; their different questions guiding them to discuss the value of any domestic object in 1988 or the meaning of only wedding presents in 1998. Yet this does not entirely explain why a reliable object, once deserving of an affectionate name is forgotten while, for example, the coffee cups that were too small to use are remembered. A relationship between continued material presence and the cultivation of memory plays a bigger part, I would suggest, in the production of different testimonies. At the time of writing the Giving and Receiving Presents directive the coffee cups were still there in the Aberystwyth household but the iron that was 25 years old in 1988 did not last another ten years and belongs to the carer's 'wore out' category of wedding presents for which she provided little information. 'Most of the electrical things are not here any more,' she pointed out (P1009, 1998).

It may be that the value of functional objects is only really evident when they are being used. One correspondent provides a compelling description of interplay of memory and material presence, illustrating the moment of evocation of memory that occurs as an object is inauspiciously put to work, used to carry out everyday domestic tasks. A clerical worker from Leeds lists 'a rather worn wooden spoon with burn marks on the handle' under 'Favourites', a heading in her Objects about the House directive response. The spoon, she states:

> belonged to my mother and must date back to 1920. I still use it when I bake and sometimes I can still "hear" her voice saying "scrape the bowl out well and then you can have the spoon to lick." Only yesterday when we were out shopping my husband wanted to buy a new wooden spoon. He didn't really understand when I said I was quite happy with the one I had. I have used it since my own marriage in 1947 (T540, 1988).

The spoon is not simply being used when she bakes, but re-used in more than one way. Stirring is repetitive, a tightly held spoon moves around the edges of the bowl and through the cake mixture in careful oval movements, each one the same, again and again, until the mixture reaches the correct consistency. As she stirs, she performs exactly the same movements that she watched when she was a child. She traces and retraces her mother's movements, follows the pattern that her mother's hand once made. Her memories are truly embodied in the spoon and it is no wonder that when she uses it, she activates her mother's voice.

She was, as her Objects about the House directive response implies, married twice, for the first time just after the war and the second time in 1975. In her 1998 response to the Giving and Receiving Presents directive, she tried to remember the things she received when she first married in the late forties. 'I suppose we got a few household goods such as towels,' she states, 'but the only thing I can remember and which lasted for a few years was a glass cake stand which I gave to a bring and buy sale a few years ago' (T540, 1998). Although marriage and baking seem inextricably linked in her reply to the Giving and Receiving Presents directive, she did not tell the story of her mother's wooden spoon. Since the spoon was not appointed as a marriage gift, it may have seemed inappropriate to mention and the prompts to write about objects acquired as well as formally given were probably ignored because they did not apply particularly well to her situation. 'I was 19, earning 25 shillings a week and caring for my mother who was ill with arthritis as my father had died of cancer during the war' (T540, 1998). Individual gifts of newly bought things or the transfer of secondhand objects did not seem to make a big impression on her at the time of her marriage because she was not, as were some other young wives, dependent upon them to set up home. Her marriage was the occasion of an overall shift in the control of domestic possessions as she, no longer a daughter but also a wife took over her widowed mother's household. Thus the Leeds clerical worker underwent a form of domestic promotion from supportive child to manager of domestic affairs that involved assuming ownership rather than being given domestic things. As she explained, she simply began using the spoon 'since my own marriage in 1947' (T540, 1998). So the meanings of worn wooden spoon become more dense and its story more complex. The past childhood moment that its use now unlocks, one wherein she received a lesson in domestic management ('scrape the bowl out well') followed by sweet treat ('then you can have the spoon to lick') was a short-lived moment of being treated as a child and not representative of her experience as a teenage carer. Her mother's spoon cultivates selective memories that fix and idealize her relationship to her mother as one where she was recipient of guidance and care.

Between writing a response to the Objects about the House directive and replying to the Giving and Receiving Presents, one correspondent, has successfully suppressed the memory of objects she always disliked. A counsellor from Dartmoor, Devon, who also calls herself a 'housewife', wrote in 1988:

> I don't think there is anything in our house that I really dislike. The only thing I can think of is a willow pattern plate and even that has its use as it is quite decorative if the rest of the colour scheme supported it, only it doesn't. It is the last of what I thought of as a ghastly set of dinner and tea service in clumsy inelegant willow pattern, given as a wedding present by my in laws we were not asked our taste in those days. The vegetable dishes were particularly awful and heavy, I managed to break them in the early days of marriage (C1878, 1988).

She married in 1942, 'which says it all' she remarks wryly. Like many of the weddings, which took place in the immediate post-war period that are cited throughout this study, gifts at this wartime wedding were not the perfect presents. Some Mass-Observation writers have told how they value such utilitarian objects as could be got as signs of the times. In comparison, this correspondent is quite irreverent. In her Giving and Receiving Presents directive response she described her marriage gifts in the following way:

> My parents had promised us a piano "after the war". In lieu we had a set of dressing table brushes, never used. The piano never arrived either. My husband bought a splendid canteen of cutlery, still surprisingly obtainable. I can only remember an item from an aunt, which was a glass container for flower heads, with a nymph holding something or other aloft. It was in green glass and possibly would now be worth a fortune but it went in one of our moves.

> I suppose the relations, many of whom we didn't know nor wanted to, must have given us various useless objects but mercifully I can't remember any of them. It was all a long time ago (C1878, 1998).

Where has the willow pattern china gone? Perhaps the last plate finally got broken and allowed her to forget the entire service that she so disliked. With no reminder, or to put it more forcibly, no material witness to the receipt of a china dinner and tea service from her parents-in-law, she no longer feels compelled to acknowledge any details. The willow pattern plates disappear, subsumed in her category of 'various useless objects' that she 'mercifully can't remember' (C1878, 1998).

Objects that appear in both Objects about the House and the Giving and Receiving Presents directives tend to be those that remained in use. For example, a school secretary from Aylesbury, Buckinghamshire, provided details of a 'set of 3 large aluminium saucepans' in her Objects about the House directive response. She stated in 1988 that they were 'over forty years old and still going strong,'
and that explained that they 'were bought by my mother and father-in-law before their wedding, used by them all their married lives, and taken over by me on my mother-in-laws death' (C1786, 1988). Ten years on she reports that they were the only family presents she possesses. 'I don't think we have anything left which was given to my father-in-law as a wedding present except a couple of very old and heavy saucepans which I still use' (C1786, 1998).

The most striking continuity between the directives occurs in the responses of a research chemist from Cobham, Surrey, who married in 1954 but is now separated. She uses a very similar set of words to describe one set of objects. In 1988, she stated:

> I have the hand-painted 'tea service' which my Aunt, mother's eldest sister, gave her as a wedding present – This is a wild rose spray on 'Minton' china with a gold border – it is lovely, and Mother treasured it. It is kept in the old mahogany display cabinet mother had, and I have only used it once. The same aunt painted a tea-set for my wedding present, but I lost five of the teacups in an accident (M1395, 1988).

By 1998 her own wedding china had 'long gone' but under 'FAMILY WEDDING PRESENTS' she wrote:

> I have the hand painted tea service that my mother's eldest sister decorated as a present to my parents…. I use the china very rarely…. The china is kept in mother's display cabinet (M1395, 1998) 23

Her accounts of her mother's wedding china are so consistent, despite being written ten years apart, because these objects have neither changed not moved. These forms of material culture are guardians of memory. They and their narratives are fixed. The meaning of the tea set as a 'lovely' thing was established by the mother who regarded the gift very highly, 'treasured it' as her daughter explained, and she continues to regard them highly, continues to like them, respecting and following her mother's understanding of their worth. She keeps them as her mother kept them; they are in the same cabinet. Objects that are deliberately kept stationary reflect and sustain a

---

23 She also states that she keeps her mother's tortoiseshell dressing-table set '2 hairbrushes, 2 clothes brushes and a mirror' and they are 'wrapped in tissue in a large shoebox' (M1395, 1998).

determinedly settled understanding of the past. We should expect things that have been preserved, and china especially, to reveal continuities. They are kept in stasis precisely in order to represent lack of change as a virtue, to demonstrate the stability of the family and, in particular, the continuity of maternal presence.

That the meaning of objects, their significance and signification, their value and content, remain intact when they remain in the same place sits quite comfortably with observations that anthropologists have made about the stabilizing function of objects. But drawing conclusions from continuities in material culture is deceptively easy. Presence is always over represented. The long serving saucepans, the much appreciated maternal china are still there waiting for their narratives to be told whereas absent objects cannot call up their stories no matter what those stories may be. Material absences create narrative silences. Once an object is gone, it cannot confront us with its past existence making it easy to forget. Once possessed but no longer preserved objects are not often recalled and therefore rarely discussed by Mass-Observation correspondents, or I would suspect, any other kind of informant. Indeed, such things may have been removed precisely in order that they cannot be remembered. The disappeared object is evidence that change has occurred, that something else existed, but its absence allows the small alterations or larger reorganizations of material environments to be smoothed over. Things that are thrown, given or stored away such as willow pattern plates, fish knives, old irons could be read as signs of a different domestic order at some point in the past but only, of course, if you know these things existed in the first place. Studies in material culture, like this one of wedding presents, can easily overlook changes in the very matter that is being studied. The lack of materiality of the evidence of change, the un-observability of an absent object, places it almost beyond analysis.

Thus the comparison between the Objects about the House and the Giving and Receiving Presents directives raises more questions about the interpretation of change in domestic material culture than it answers. It alerts us to the problem of how material change can be described as well as whether it actually occurred and what such amendments, alterations or transformations of domestic material might mean. The rest of this chapter is taken up with another comparison that between, once again, the 1998 Giving and Receiving Presents directive and replies to a letter sent in 2003 to a selected number of Mass-Observation correspondents. The letter tackled the question of change directly and in so doing tried to redress the dominance of material presences (the currently kept objects) in the accounts of domestic life. Basically, the 2003 letter asked: what is different now?

Asking about Change

In July 2003 I sent nine letters to Mass-Observation correspondents who had replied to the Giving and Receiving Presents directive and had married in, or after, 1988. I asked what had happened to their wedding presents:

Have your feelings changed about any of the gifts you received when you married in [1988–1997]? And, why?
Which gifts, if any, are still used and displayed? Have any been broken, lost, given or thrown away?
Do you still like them? Some? None? [24]

Reading replies to this follow-up letter against the Giving and Receiving Presents directive revealed, like the comparison between that directive and the Objects about the House, the continued presence of some objects in domestic life and the absence of others. But the replies to the follow-up letter contained more insights into the conditions of continuity and for change. Correspondents were explicitly asked about changes that might have occurred between one moment of writing in 1998 and another in 2003. The letter was intended to direct them towards identifying both the wedding presents that they were still surrounded by and those that were now missing; they were asked to report upon the practical matter of what gifts did and did not remain in their households and as well as inviting comments about any shifts in their preferences for their marriage gifts. That is, Mass-Observation correspondents were asked about their feelings. The follow-up letter not only sought a slightly different kind of information to that requested in the Giving and Receiving Presents directive (the questions in the letter were closer to those put by the Objects about the House directive), but it also altered the relationship between myself as the researcher and Mass-Observation correspondents as my informants. Gathering accounts of domestic change from Mass-Observation writers, rather than reading for change through slips, elisions, omissions in their accounts of domestic life gave them more space to act as the interpreters of their own lives. Asking about change directly meant that differences between the past and the present were represented rather than glimpsed and guessed at. Such self-conscious descriptions can, of course, obscure as well as reveal any change and may seem a less accurate way of accounting for change. However, such a view cannot really be sustained since representation is nature of all forms of communication and not just the obviously thought-out accounts. Issues of accuracy are not peculiar to the reflective responses to specific questions. The comparison between Giving and Receiving Presents directive and the 2003 follow-up letter relies upon both Mass-Observation writers' reflections on change and continuity in their everyday domestic lives and my observations upon these reflections. It is, I hope, a more collaborative analysis of change and domestic material culture.

---

24 See Appendix 3. I received six replies and cited all except one: J2830. This correspondent simply stated 'I don't think anything's changed.' She re-reads her Giving and Receiving Presents directive again. It described her 1989 marriage and the different destinies of the objects she was given. She also remarked 'I can tell I was heavily pissed off in the autumn of 1998, but what I said then still holds.'

The Condition of Continuity and Change (1): Securing Meanings

One reply to my 2003 follow-up letter from an administrator from Devon, who married first in 1949 and then in 1998, offers some further evidence of the particular conditions within which the meanings of objects stabilize. Similar to the Surrey research chemist who gave consistent descriptions of her mother's stationary china, this correspondent produces settled descriptions of some his wedding presents. But because the follow-up letter directly asked him directly, he was able to announce that nothing has changed. 'My feelings towards the wedding presents I have received recently and in the past have not altered really, I find them reminders of a past and many of happy thoughts of those who gave' (L1504, 2003). The objects that feature prominently in both his reply to the 2003 follow-up letter and his original Giving and Receiving directive response are a Lloyd Loom chair and linen basket from his first marriage and from his second, a watercolour painting, bone china objects, a decanter, garden roses, shrubs and water feature. It seems that these have been selected within his household and through his writing to represent each marriage. When he wrote his directive response in 1998, he listed a wider range of things, recalling '7 butter dishes', 'plenty of bedding', naming '"Utility" blankets', 'some cutlery and china', 'china teaset' and a 'Dining Room Suite' as well as the Lloyd Loom furniture. But many of these gifts he thought only to be of 'trinket value' even while he was first married and not much now remains. 'Few of the items now exist as my first wife had died and the original home has been disposed of with a few exceptions (including the Lloyd Loom linen basket)' (L1504, 2003). Importantly, deciding upon the destination of his surviving wedding presents was part of the process of establishing a new home with his second wife. The Devon administrator wrote in his reply to the 2003 follow-up letter that 'We also have stored away numerous kitchen items which also arrived as presents at the first wedding.' One of these objects holds memories of a past family life:

> In particular I recall a Poultry Dish which came out a Christmas each year and again was a present from those early days. A dish which often reminds me of Christmas's before, these types of dishes are only required when a large bird and a family to match, surrounded the Dinner Table (L1504, 2003).

In contrast, the objects given upon his second marriage (the watercolour, a decanter, garden shrubs and water feature in particular) evoke 'fresh memories'. 'All present us with a reminder of our day, our friends and relations who shared it with us,' he stated. 'To us they represent something special in our lives if only to remind us of happy days and summer warmth' (L1504, 2003). This reiterates the sentiments he expressed in 1998:

> we have almost everything on display to remind of the kindness of those around us. A more lasting object is a Water Feature in our garden that has been almost paid for by those relatives who could not get down to our ceremony. Again a reminder of a happy day (L1504, 1998).

These things have not yet inserted themselves into a family history, indeed, the Devon administrator's recent marriage, like other late second marriages, does not fit easily into a family history trajectory and remains an always new romance. Thus the second marriage gifts function as souvenirs of the wedding day itself, as objects that represent a moment in time and whose work of representation dominates over any other purpose. Thus they are gifts that are signs of the act and the moment of being given; they recall their own exchange.

The 1949 and 1998 wedding presents are the loci of different memories. They generate separate narratives associated with each of the Devon administrator's marriages and fix their different meanings. The selection of gifts for display in the his home and for commentary in his Mass-Observation writings enables the owner to compose an appropriate account of each marriage, the first that lasted 47 years and the second that took place two years after that one ended. Disposing, storing or showing some gifts and not others is a process of managing memories and presenting life histories. For example, the Lloyd Loom furniture has an antique quality and could be valued just for being old rather for its association with a particular past, making its easier to include in a second married home. Other gifts do not have qualities that distract from their place in an earlier married life. China, such as the large poultry dish, which evoked a family past of shared mealtimes that were almost certainly organized, prepared and cooked by his first wife (and I make this assumption because he gave domestic utensils such short shrift), are stored away.

Continuity of testimony, the consistent identification of the same valued objects, whether they are Lloyd Loom linen baskets, watercolours, water features or china teasets, can be taken as a signs of an unchanging domestic material culture and remarkably settled and stable meanings of familial domestic life. It must be noted, however, that such stability, if not actually a construction, is a desirable representation of happy domestic life. After all, creating a domestic space is often described as 'settling down' and just as frequently having a successful marriage is referred to as being in 'stable relationship.' Such an account of unchanging contentment asserted in writing, like that of the Devon administrator, or in the material arrangements of many homes, are made possible only when significant objects remain in the same place. They may not, of course, stay in the same house but move with the family and thus keep their place in the same household. Continuity of context thus enables continuity of meaning. I do not think it is yet possible to say that domestic context supplies wholesale the meanings of domestic things as is argued is the effect of public institutions upon the meaning of the objects they contain.[25] However, there does seem to be a creative relationship between the place of an object and its meaning.

---

25 See, especially Carol Duncan, *Civilizing Rituals: Inside Public Art Museums* (London: Routledge, 1995) pp. 1–20 and Alfred Gell, 'Vogel's Net: Traps as Artworks and Artworks as Traps,' *Journal of Material Culture* 1.1 (1996) pp. 15–38.

The Conditions of Continuity and Change (2): New Contexts and New Meanings?

A relationship between context and meaning is illustrated by another twice-married Mass-Observation correspondent, a Bristol schoolteacher. Her first marriage took place in 1969 and her second, twenty years later in 1989. Her opening remarks in her reply to the 2003 follow-up letter indicate how the state of a marriage affects the interpretation of marriage gifts: 'I suppose my feelings have changed about presents received for my first wedding because they represent something that turned out to be a failure' (R1227, 1998).

In her 1998 Giving and Receiving Presents directive response, she reflects, with some self-criticism, on her requests and receipt of 'all the "right" things for a late sixties bride': a black basalt Wedgwood coffee service, a Minton tea service, a canteen of cutlery, a crystal glass set, cutlery from her parents, Jonelle towels, sheets and blankets, a Bex Bissell carpet sweeper, Addis kitchen set, wooden salad bowl, Sprong hand mincer, stainless steel carving dish. She wrote:

> I have very few of them now. I hated the coffee set (my husband's choice) and sold it at a car boot sale for £10, after we were divorced. I still have the glass set, because it has never been used much. Ditto the tea service. All the bedding is worn out, but there are still a few vases and ornaments around. Because of the circumstances, I purposely got rid of some of the presents. I think we used everything we were given, apart form a set of 1930's toy building bricks, which I sold this year for £20. I thought it was such a peculiar present (R1227, 1998).

The sale of her wedding presents announces that their emotional effect is over: they are reduced to a monetary sign in the second-hand market place. Disposing of gifts is a way of ending a marriage in the same way as accepting them is a beginning. She kept some, however. The 'only ones which I still have are the tea service, some glassware, wooden salad bowls and a few ornaments' (R1227, 2003). The continued possession of discomforting objects that are connected to an unhappy past is another example of domesticity as a practice of preservation and the importance of keeping particular materials, such as ceramics. There is little other explanation for their continued presence in this Bristol school teacher's household for she does not hang on to her glass, china, ornaments and bowls because, as might be expected over a period of thirty years, they have become part of her domestic life. No, she is detached enough from these objects to make a quite critical assessment of their appearance:

> I don't particularly like any of them, apart from the glass which is Stuart crystal with a corkscrew effect up the stems (I think it was called 'Newtown'). The Minton tea service is far too fussy for my taste now and has barely been used, which is probably why it exists in its entirety. When my small daughter (now aged 30) really let me down by asking "What are those little plates under the mugs, Mummy?" – that tells you we are a mug family. I also think that the presents we asked for and received in 1969 showed a certain amount of pretension – showing that we knew what young marrieds should have (R1227, 2003).

In marked contrast to the gifts she received when she first married, which are cast as objects that belong to another time and another person that existed in that time, gifts from her second marriage are integrated into her domestic life. At a party organized for her and her second husband about a month after their 1989 wedding, they were given: 'an apron, wooden salad bowl, wall plaque, daffodil bulbs, wine, a clematis plants, a Habitat blue and white ceramic bowl, some applique towels, a soap dish in the shape of a bath, tulip bulbs' (R1227, 1998). And, she added, 'All lovely things which we are still using.' Their usefulness affirms that her second marriage is working. Given a place and a function in her current household, they are thus included in her daily reality. The separation of her first marriage gifts from the everyday hustle of domestic routine on the basis that they belong to the 1960s puts that marriage firmly in the past. They appear out of time and therefore out of place. This in-house de-contextualization is not an inevitable process of ageing since, as we have seen in numerous married households, old wedding presents proudly remain in use. These gifts have been marginalized as the marriage has ended and their occupation of permanently redundant domestic position, kept but not used, continuously signals that the previous marriage is over. Marriage is the context in which the meanings of marriage gifts (and, indeed, other domestic objects) are negotiated. A few words about what exactly 'context' is may be useful here.

Context is not always the straightforward equivalent of actual location. Being put into a particular place, unseen at the back of a kitchen cupboard or in the eye-level central spot of a dining room glass cabinet, classifies the object as cherished or unwanted, clearly contributing to its value. Cupboard and cabinet are frames that hold the objects in their place, culturally as well as physically. They position objects within a domestic hierarchy; they categorize them. These frames, which include under the bed, on top of the television, the corners of a room as well as the bounded spaces of cupboards and cabinets that resemble picture frames, exist within the larger framework of the house. The type of household to which the cupboard, the cabinet or other space belongs affects their contents as representations. For example, surviving marriage gifts displayed in glass fronted cabinet in a long established home of a still married couple may be cast as timeless signs of continuity whereas similar things similarly located in a house occupied by a widow or widower become memorials. Or, they might appear as historical mistakes household just set up by a recent second marriage. Context, then, refers to the objects place in a system and the system itself. It is the enclosing frame (cupboard or cabinet) within the larger framework (the new or long-established household). It is also both the house and the home, the material and symbolic environment. Context is, therefore, a temporal and spatial location. A household of newlyweds and one of grandparents who marriage has lasted many decades is a different place, even if the newlyweds just grew up and home and people within it have not changed.

The importance of time as a domestic context is suggested through the Bristol schoolteacher's Mass-Observation writing. She may have kept some of the glass and ceramic gifts from her first marriage but in the new context of her second one they are out of date, from an another time, and therefore out of place. But she is not sure why these things appear so different. I have made a case that her second marriage is a distinct temporal setting in her life and that of her household but she began her reply to the 2003 follow-up letter rather tentatively. 'I *suppose* my feelings have changed,' she wrote (R1227, 2003, my emphasis). She cites her failed first marriage as the main cause of the devaluation these gifts. 'Possibly', she suggests, it is because 'what remains looks decidedly passé.' 'Or', she adds as an afterthought, 'my taste has changed.' Taking my cue from her lack of certainty about the reasons for the altered status of her objects I will continue to investigate the relationship between context and meaning.

The Conditions of Continuity and Change (3): the Persistence of Meaning?

Much of the Mass-Observation writing cited so far illustrates well-established ideas about contextualization as constituent of an object's meaning, especially if the concept of context is broadly defined. Writing from another Mass-Observation correspondent, again a divorcee does the same, but only at first. Her reply to the opening question in the 2003 follow up letter 'Have your feelings changed about the gifts you received when you married' was a definite 'Yes' (B2810, 2003). After ten years of cohabiting, this correspondent, a nurse from Hebden Bridge, married in 1997 and four years later left her long-term partner turned husband. Since she and her husband were cohabitees, as she explained in her 1998 Giving and Receiving Presents directive, when they married 'we didn't need much house stuff.' They received:

> cutlery
> microwave
> Indian drape
> Place mats
> Money for a trip on a gondola (our honeymoon was in Venice)
> Measuring cups, a trendy bottle opener, a few nick nacks, books on the subject of love and cards and flowers (B2810, 1998).

A number of the objects listed here are not the conventional marriage offerings of household things. The flowers, the book about love and gondola trip were romantic tokens. These forms acknowledged and represented their relationship between the nurse and her partner as a romantic affair. The wedding as love match was underpinned by her dress on the day: 'I wore red velvet' she wrote in 1998. Eighteen months after the marriage, the gifts were either being used or were carefully preserved:

> We've kept all the gifts and we use them all or display them all if they are not kitchen type things.
> They remind us of the wedding and the people who gave them to us.
> We kept a list of who gave what and keep it with the cards and a piece of the decoration on the cake etc (B2810, 1998).

These long-term plans for the objects, their preservation and continual shared use, were dramatically disrupted, as the nurse explained in her letter of 2003:

> Our marriage ended 2 years ago because of the pressure caused by my infertility and failed IVF. There were many rows and I was very unhappy. I left the marriage on 17.8.2001. He kept all of the presents. All I have is the Indian material that my aunt and uncle gave us. I also got the cards and glitter confetti angels. Desperate to get out of the marriage without rows over possessions I didn't care, they were only pots, pans, cutlery and a microwave. I received money when we divorced.... I disposed of the cards but kept the icing cats off the wedding cake, they were supposed to be eaten at our "child's" christening. I kept it with the photos of my dead IVF embryos (B2810, 2003).

Objects that are bound up with failed love affairs, especially those that have publicized their hopes for a happy ever after ending with a romantic wedding, can appear ridiculous or, at best, naïve. They evoke the certainty of affection once felt in the past and the projection of future happiness that, in retrospect, seems foolish. The meanings of these things (or more precisely what is signified by them) have been reversed; reminders of high hopes become signs of disappointment, expression of real love its illusion.

Such neat transformations did not occur with every wedding present received by this Mass-Observation correspondent. Her gifts were altered to varying extents, in different ways. She left most when she left her husband and claims no interest in them. 'Desperate to get out of the marriage without rows over possessions I didn't care', as she put it, 'they were only pots, pans, cutlery and a microwave.' Discarding wedding presents is a key process of realizing a divorce in everyday domestic life. Refusing to recognize the symbolic content of an object and reducing it to its use alone is strategy that allows once cherished objects to descend to the category of unwanted. The Hebden Bridge nurse threw away the once preserved wedding cards that reminded her who gave which gifts. But she still remembers the givers of the Indian material, her aunt and uncle, just as she did when she was still married. Moreover, the material is still appreciated and, indeed, prominently displayed. In answer to the more detailed questions in the 2003 follow up letter about what happened to her gifts, whether they were 'still used', 'displayed' or liked, she wrote: 'I like the material very much' and 'It's pretty and it hangs in my living room.' It asserts her taste against her ex-husband's who did not, she thinks, ever like the material ('he took the best of everything, giving me only the things he didn't want'). Keeping it becomes an act of defiance, demonstrating the continuity of her values, gratitude to givers and a preference for pretty things, compared to her ex-husband's disloyalty.

Another exception to the reversal of meanings as a marriage ends is the 'icing cats off the wedding cake'. Although these souvenirs of the wedding day itself are not gifts, they featured among the nurse's collection of preserved objects and these in particular were set aside in order to play a part in the fulfilment of a happily married family life. The iced decorations, kept in anticipation of the birth of a child and his or her naming celebrations, have become something like grave goods. Thus the act of preservation persists in her new situation: divorced, childless and now with a new partner. These objects have not lost their significance, their value remains as high after her divorce as they did when she was married. Meanings have developed rather than drastically altered. The decorations function then as now to give material existence to an embryonic life, an imagined child. They are tokens of a life not lived.

Neither the wedding cake decorations nor the Indian material follow the logic of the notion that as the context changes the meanings of objects follow suit. Their value has not been touched by the Hebden Bridge nurse's new situation as childless divorcee. Daniel Miller, rather uncharacteristically tentatively has opened up a debate about the extent to which the effects of domestic material culture are not completely controllable. Domestic environments have, or seem to have, a power of their own. In an essay in a book he also edited, *Home Possessions*, (2001), he suggests that 'the very longevity of homes and material culture may create a sense that agency lies in these things rather than in the relatively transient persons who occupy them.'[26] This is not an observation about particular sets of domestic objects, such as wedding presents, but rather the whole material order of the house. However, his identification of (and with) a householder's inability to appropriate their immediate surroundings as a 'medium of representation'[27] raises the issue of the location of agency between material and social worlds. Objects are not completely passive. Domestic things can exert some power over their owners, in certain conditions at least.[28] Once they have acquired their meanings (both their value and expressive content, their significance and signification) they do not shift with every move to a new situation or alteration of their surroundings. Thus objects may not always become malleable as they are exchanged nor easily made ready to absorb the meanings of any new context.

The Conditions of Change and Continuity (4): New Meanings in the Same Setting?

While the old meanings of objects may be seen to persist in new contexts, sometimes objects acquire new meanings in the same surroundings. Two replies to the 2003 follow-up letter tell of the shifting status of marriage gifts within very stable households. One is from a secretary from Devizes and another from a London-based film producer or as she puts it 'a freelancer in the animation industry.' They both got married in 1988, both for the first time and both their marriages have lasted. The form of their weddings, however, the way in which they adopted or adapted marriage rituals was quite different. On the one hand, the secretary from Devizes staged the

---

26 Daniel Miller, 'Possessions,' *Home Possessions: Material Culture behind Closed Doors*, ed. Daniel Miller (Oxford: Berg, 2001) p. 119.

27 Miller, 'Possessions' p. 112.

28 Accepting the power of things, or just the appearance of their power, has important implications for the way fetishization is understood. As Miller argues, 'what anthropologists once denigrated in other societies as a primitive cognitive mistake can here be recognised as a sophisticated acknowledgement of the nature of objectification.' Miller, 'Possessions' p. 116.

type of wedding that could be described as the contemporary popular tradition: a big wedding ('150 guests, 7 bridesmaids and 5 page boys') with the bride in a pale dress ('fabulous, fabulous, rose coloured with pink embroidery around the skirt and very along the lines of a 'Diana' wedding dress, bows and pearls, very princessy' and its setting was a church (although 'it wasn't a religious wedding') (P2819, 1998). On the other, the London-based film producer arranged a wedding in the Caribbean in order to escape from the familial and social responsibilities of a large wedding. Their attitudes to the marriage gifts, initial attitudes at least, were as divergent as their weddings. The Devizes secretary in her reply to the 1998 Giving and Receiving Presents directive wrote that she and her husband 'received absolutely loads of presents' and gave details of some thirty or so of them, including a 'Wedgwood tea service in Blue Siam' (Figure 3.11). The film producer also listed some of her presents: a bottle of champagne from her 'boss', a food processor from her father's foreman, an 'expensive coffee cup set' from work colleagues, a 'beautiful bowl,' a 'Zester' from her Mum's friend, a wooden pestle and mortar from her 'cousin in Zimbabwe.' But, she gave few details claiming 'to be honest I don't remember an awful lot about the stuff we received' (D2239, 1998). She explained that conventional marriage gifts were not appropriate in her situation and it is clear that she did not actually want them:

> Because we had already shared a flat together, we had many items that traditionally people give for presents; I do remember getting irritated with my Mother, whose friends, very kindly, wanted to give us presents, and at the time I rather scoffed at this; I felt they didn't know me and in fact they were giving to her in a way, or at least "for" her, and that it was nothing to do with me.... At some point I must have collected all these presents, because my oldest friend was around, and I do remember putting all the presents together, in a piss-taking kind of way, like the end of The Generation Game, when all the stuff that the contestant's have won off the Conveyor Belt is put together, and we took a photograph of it all! (D2239, 1998)

'Our wedding', she added, 'was a very private affair, and none of the presents particularly remind me of the wedding, except for some bizarre reason the coffee cups from work which we never use' (D2239, 1998).

Five years later, in her reply to the 2003 follow up letter, the film producer confessed, 'I actually feel rather ashamed of my attitude towards the wedding presents I received in 1988, well some of them, at any rate' (D2239, 2003). Her detachment from her gifts (and it is detachment that allows people who received objects to dislike them, dispose of them easily and ultimately forget they existed) derives from her unwillingness to participate in the wider family networks that are enforced through a large traditional wedding. She and her husband chose to marry abroad to have a civil ceremony because 'he had been married before and neither of us were religious', moreover, it also:

> saved us from my mother's pressure of wanting us to invite *her* friends and suggesting that we married in ... Town Hall! No, thank you! I was just 27 and I don't think I was mature

enough to put my foot down and tell my mother the kind of wedding I would want, i.e. in London with friends (mine) and only close family. So, to avoid all that we went abroad! (D2239, 2003)

Nor did she want a wedding list, which would allow people from her parent's social networks to participate, albeit it in a tightly prescribed way, in her wedding. As other Mass-Observation correspondents have also stated, she declared that she felt 'uncomfortable' about 'asking/demanding presents from people' (D2239, 2003). Negotiating the act of giving seemed to be much easier with one particular group, however. She wrote:

> The one exception was my workplace. I worked in an animation studio.... My surrogate mum, an older woman who I still see regularly, asked me what I wanted and over the weeks preceding the wedding, in a meandering kind of way we decided maybe some plates/coffee cups and saucers would be o.k. i.e. useful, for all those dinner parties I would give in married life!! So, the studio bought me four dove green with gold edging Apilco plates, and four matching coffee cups and saucers and a wine jug. I don't use the coffee cups or jug – I don't like them anymore, and the plates are just in the general plate store! They are not a first choice, and only get used when most of the other plates are in the dishwasher! (D2239, 2003)

In her 1998 response, she wondered why it was only the coffee cups that reminded her of her wedding and the reason is now clear. Unlike the presents that derived from her parent's social networks, she was prepared to receive them. She accepted the interest and involvement of work friends in her plans to get married. Coffee cups, a modern version of the tea service, seemed eminently suitable for an independent working woman since they embodied a specific knowledge of the forms of sociability of married life: wives give dinner parties. In all likelihood, this gift reminds her of her wedding because it projected an idea about marriage that belonged to the moment that she entered into it. The coffee cups, saucers and plates did not turn out to be the prized possessions that the givers and receivers hoped they would be, and their lowly position ('used when most of the other plates are in the dishwasher') is a register of the difference between expectations and the actualities of marriage. This demotion does not really demonstrate change. It functions as many gifts do, as a reminder of the givers despite the failure to fulfil a purpose. The coffee set was never used as it was intended; it did not fit into the rhythms of her domestic life from the outset.

The objects that have acquired new meanings, or more specifically have been re-valued, are the unwanted gifts from family friends. The film producer retells in her reply to the 2003 follow up letter an incident she mentioned in her 1998 Giving and Receiving Presents directive response. She repeats some phrases, a sign that her memories of her wedding presents have become quite fixed, but she allows herself to recall more details. She prefaces her later description of The Generation Game photograph by stating that it is 'the bit I'm ashamed of':

> My mother's friends wanted to buy me gifts. At the time I was irritated by this. I realise now, of course, they were doing it for her, and actually it was really kind of them. So, I

was sent various things – a wooden bread board, which I left to soak (not domesticated) and it split in half! My father's foreman bought me a Kenwood Chef, my... cousin ... sent me a wooden pestle and mortar from Zimbabwe. The only truly duff present was from mum's friend Ann who embroidered a 'D' on some linen napkins. The 'D' was badly embroidered; but even though we never used them, it was kind of her to put the effort in! I'm straying off the point. My oldest friend ... came to see me, and for a 'laff' we arranged all the presents out like the winning contents of the conveyor belt on The Generation Game, in a horrible piss-taking kind of way. Its that that I am ashamed of! The fact that The Generation Game sprang to mind gives you an idea of the kind of presents we received, and I suppose I wasn't particularly conventional, so they just weren't me, and therefore I felt a bit removed from them I suppose (D2239, 2003).

Thus these objects have been redeemed. Physical re-location plays no part in this process of re-interpretation nor could it because the film producer does not seem to possess many of the things she has now come to value. We can speculate, probably with some accuracy, about why she has recognized the right of her relatives to give to her and her obligation to receive their offerings. Enough time, some fifteen years, has passed since her marriage to allow for reflection upon rather than reaction to the assertion of family connections through gift relationships. What she once understood as interference by her mother is now viewed as something like approval from her mother's network. With two children herself, she now belongs to an older generation and may use gifts in the same complex way as her mother's friends: offering objects that attempt to transfer knowledge from one generation to the next, simultaneously taking up responsibilities for intergenerational giving and using rituals as moments when friendships and relationships within her generation can be endorsed and renewed with a gift.

In the case of the film producer, the reinterpretation of wedding presents is not a matter of taste. Her appreciation of them has not actually altered her dislike of their appearance. But the Devizes secretary who married in fairytale style and valued all her gifts very highly has come to dislike the design of some. Responding directly to the question about whether her 'feelings changed about any of the gifts you received when you married in 1988', she wrote:

Well I'm glad to say I'm still married which I suppose must colour my response, as if I wasn't still married I suppose I wouldn't feel the same way about the gifts we still have. Looking back we had such a lot of gifts, a huge amount and I still feel very grateful for each and every one of them. I suppose I must have wondered at the time whether I might use them all but at various stages I've gone to look for something I've needed and found that one of our gifts have proved to be very useful (P2819).

Despite being overwhelmed with presents, the Devizes secretary deals with them in ways that can be explained by anthropological theories of the gift and the consumed object. She keeps them because as given things they are inalienable and she has formed attachments, established human–object relationships, as she has used (or appropriated) them. However, one set of objects upsets the easy match between theory and lived reality:

If my feelings have changed about any of the gifts its probably about a Wedgwood tea set we were bought. It was a Blue Siam pattern, six cups, saucers, tea plates, a sandwich plate, sugar bowl, teapot and milk jug – very nice and I'm sure we must have chosen the pattern and someone kindly bought it for us. We liked it so much that we collected the dinner service shortly afterwards, right down to the egg cups, but now it just sits in a cupboard and isn't used from one year to the next because I don't really like the pattern now. I suppose it's a measure of how our tastes have changed from when we chose it (P2819, 2003).

Her Blue Siam Wedgwood is another of the gifts that are retained although disliked. As she concludes her reply to the 2003 follow up letter, the Devizes secretary reiterates uncomfortable terms on which she continues to keep her wedding china. 'I don't really like the Blue Siam anymore but because there's so much of it and because it was part wedding present, I'm loathe to get rid of it.' This dilemma, not infrequently faced by many of us who have received gifts that we believe do not suit our image of ourselves, demonstrates that attachments formed through the gift transactions do not always ensure continued pleasure in the given objects. Possession is not always a sign of preference. The Aberystwyth carer cited earlier in this chapter has some insights into why this disjunction between possession and preference might occur: 'attitudes to some things change as one gets older and perhaps better off' (P1009, 1988). Taste is related to generation and to one of the components of class position, wealth. However, it is far from clear that the Devizes secretary's dislike of her wedding china is an effect of either aging or any alteration of class position. She has not changed her mind about all her presents. In fact, she contrasts the awkwardness that now surrounds her preservation of the Wedgwood Blue Siam with her affection for a long serving Panasonic microwave oven about which she remarks that it 'goes without saying that the microwave I love because its saved me so much time.' She also praises 'two sets of pyrex dishes, three different sizes in each set with only one broken glass lid' that are 'so handy for everything' (P2819, 2003).

The obvious explanation for her current dislike of the Wedgwood Blue Siam after choosing it in 1988 and adding to it subsequently is that it is now out of fashion. To put this more precisely, a newer vision of propriety generated in the market and through the media representations that are the interface between the market and everyday life, have effected how she views a domestic possession. This common sense explanation that things become fall out of favour as fashion changes has important implications for an understanding of where meaning resides in material culture. In this case, it is not in the object. The Blue Siam Wedgwood does not have enough meaning of its own; it does not have enough value as a domestic object, enough significance, to generate set of familial significations that can resist the fluctuations of meaning engineered through the market. It is important that the Devizes secretary, who shows all proper respect for the gifts relationships established when she married by keeping her gifts, does not remember the giver of the Blue Siam Wedgwood. 'I'm sure we must have chosen the pattern and someone very kindly bought it for us,' she says (P2819, 2003). Without a known giver, it more difficult for this wedding china to express ideas of family longevity and continuity, which are usually associated with

BLUE SIAM
Traditional Shape

Figure 3.11   'It just sits in a cupboard' (P2819)

such dinner or tea sets. Changes in fashion have much less effect over china as the sign of the past and the future of family, indeed, being dated can become a virtue.

We can sense in the Devizes secretary reply to the 2003 follow up letter that she would actually like to clear the space in her cupboard where the Blue Siam Wedgwood sits but she cannot quite do it. Although devalued, slipped down the hierarchy of domestic material culture, relegated from the dinner table to the cupboard, the richly patterned china still exerts enough power to prevent it being thrown away. It status has changed but not its category; it is still a gift that calls to be kept. It exerts some kind of hold over the owner. It limits her ability to act. Thus in this case, and I would suggest in the many others cited throughout this chapter, the slight alterations or major transformations in domestic material culture, are the result of a balance of forces between the object, its owner and its context.

It is possible, then, to come to some conclusions, albeit quite tentative ones, about when and how shifts in the meanings of material culture can occur. First of all, I should affirm that everyday objects in domestic settings do absorb their context. The simple premise upon which much of this book is based, that there are a set of meanings particular to domestic life, assumes that the space within which objects are placed has some kind of effect. Meanings solidify, ossify almost, in objects that are preserved in one place. But context, both a spatial and a temporal framework, does not always dictate the value or content of an object nor is the destruction of either the inevitable consequence of a change of context. In certain circumstances, objects hold on to the same meanings and the attitude of their owners towards them stays the same. For example, new fashions can be seen as the temporal frameworks within domestic possessions (and almost everything else) are constantly recontextualized. Some things do fall out of favour but others do not. Context is an encompassing force that objects can occasionally overcome. This must mean that they have a power of their own.

Chapter 4

The List: Domesticity, Conformity and Class

'We are forgetting how to give presents' (Theodor Adorno, 1944)[1]

Introduction

'Things weren't as organised in those days,' explains a shop-worker from Hull. 'You didn't ask for anything – just got what you were given' (J1890). Accepting objects that others have decided are appropriate is standard gift giving practice. Upon marriage, however, the practice has changed, states this Mass-Observation writer, since her wedding in 1952. Indeed, as she wrote her reply to the Giving and Receiving Presents directive towards the end of 1998, *Bliss for Brides* was on the newsagents shelves with an article on wedding presents under a headline that repeated the Spice Girls chant: 'Tell them what you want...what you really really want.' The bride no longer waits to receive gifts but requests specific objects. Giving wedding presents had become quite systematic by the turn of the twentieth century, more 'organised' as the correspondent put it. 'You are starting the rest of your life,' ran the *Bliss for Brides* article, 'so the gifts that you receive now must be chosen with the precision of a military operation.'[2]

Bliss, to give the magazine its short title, has a particularly assertive tone throughout, but it is just one of over half a dozen bridal magazines that regularly publish and promote a formula for requesting wedding presents. *Cosmopolitan Bride, Bride and Groom, Brides and Setting up Home, For the Bride, Wedding and Home, Wedding Day* and *You and Your Wedding* all argue that the bride-to-be should use a wedding present list in an attempt to control what objects are put into her married home.[3] In the March/April 1998 issue of *You and Your Wedding*, readers were told that 'Each of your guests will want to buy you a present' – and unless you want to receive gifts that don't suit your taste,

---

1   Theodor Adorno, *Minima Moralia*, 1951. (London: Verso, 1997) p. 42.

2   Lucy Riley and Sally Burns, 'Tell them what you want ... what you really really want,' *Bliss for Brides*, Nov–Jan 1998: 126.

3   All these titles were published between 1998 and 2003. I examined all bridal magazine titles on sale at high street outlets around the time of Giving and Receiving Presents directive (1998) and again when I sent out follow-up letters. For a similar sample taken in 1999, see Sharon Boden, *Consumerism, Romance and the Wedding Experience* (Basingstoke: Palgrave, 2003) p. 59.

you had better think about compiling a list.'[4] It had already claimed in a previous issue that lists were the norm. The repetition of advice, more or less word for word, is typical of bridal magazines' output. 'Each one of your wedding guests will want to buy you a present – and will expect to have a list to choose from.'[5] By the twenty-first century, gift lists were a fact of the wedding. The March/April 2003 issue of *You and Your Wedding* blandly announced an article entitled 'Gift List News' on its contents page.[6] Other bridal magazines offer exactly the same advice: make a list, lists are the expected thing to do these days, lists are a necessary part of wedding preparations.

This chapter examines making gift lists as a material practice and how the content, compilation and distribution of these lists changed between 1945 and today. Change and how it occurs is again the focus as in my previous chapter, however, here I am able to draw upon Mass-Observation correspondents' reports of a change that occurred at the time of their writing. The late 1990s saw an expansion of high street bridal registries. Commentary upon the propriety of making list is therefore read alongside an examination of the role of the bridal industries, and in particular the bridal magazines, in transforming listing practices and, ultimately, gift relationships. Correspondents, who consistently express their disapproval of commercial lists,[7] repeatedly identify differences between wedding present gift lists of the 1950s, 1960s, 1970s (Figures 4.1, 4.2, 4.3) and those of the 1990s. However, it should be noted that despite widely shared assumptions about what are 'traditional' gift giving practices upon marriage, there was no single or uniform practice in the recent past. The type of list that tends to be regarded as traditional is considered here as well as how it differs from the contemporary commercial one. There are continuities, however, between old and new. All lists represent an idealized domesticity and encourage continued conformity to that domestic ideal. The version of domesticity changes with different types of list, but its function as a prescription of appropriate family life remains the same.

The Gift List: Opposition and Use

The Giving and Receiving Presents directive included the question 'Did you have a formal list?'[8] Many Mass-Observation correspondents answered this particular question directly, even repeating some of its words. Of her first marriage in 1958, a teacher form Norwich stated 'We did not have a formal list – never would have thought of such a thing.' (B2258). Others, however, wrote about being asked to select from a list, rather than whether they had one, and used the 'Wedding presents' section of the directive to register their opposition to listing as a practice. One correspondent, who was unemployed and single at the time of writing, explained:

---

4   'The Wedding Organiser,' *You and Your Wedding*, Mar–Apr 1998: 94.

5   'Wedding Planner.' *You and your Wedding,* Nov–Dec 1997: 59.

6   'Gift List News,' *You and Your Wedding* Mar–April 2003: 303.

7   I found only one positive comment about commercial gift lists within the Giving and Receiving Presents directive from correspondent A883 and this was a specific endorsement of John Lewis' rather than all such lists.

8   See Appendix 1.

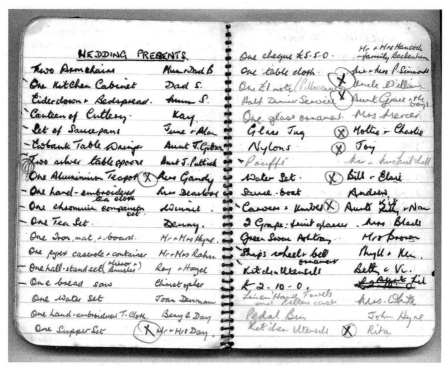

Figure 4.1   A list of wedding presents recorded in a 'notebook,' 1951 (S2662)

I intensely dislike wedding lists, even though I can see the point of them, especially these days when the couple have most likely furnished a home so don't want to duplicate items in their possession. I feel a bit insulted and intimidated by being told what to buy. Every list I've seen has contained maybe one item I could actually afford so I find it all very embarrassing (A2801).

For her, any kind of list creates social difficulties. Most disapproval, however, tends to fix upon one kind only, that organized through a retail outlet, the commercial list. After providing brief details of two marriages in 1948 and 1974 and apologizing for having 'no recollection of wedding gifts on either occasion', an engineer from Gloucester, concluded with:

One comment – the cold, calculating 'Wedding List' that nowadays arrives with an invitation from a distant relative I've not seen in years (and who is unlikely to acknowledge a gift anyway) makes me cross. – particularly when it takes the form of 'Our wedding list is at Marks and Spencers: you can see it at your local branch'. I regard it as a form of blackmail. Not only that, but it means the would-be recipient is too distant for us to have some idea of what they might like or for us to discuss it with them or their parents. Despite which, we do give wedding presents (L2669).

Figure 4.2   A list of wedding presents recorded in a 'wedding notebook,' 1962 (R2144)

A quite different account written by a clerical worker who married in 1969, which comprised six pages of detail and reflection, began:

> Let me say straight away that I do not like being told that a certain shop contains such and such china etc and that's the only sort they want buying. Hinting that is what you'd like would not offend me at all, but the choice at the end of the day would be mine. I don't like being made to feel that any other purchase would be unwelcome. Nevertheless I think having a present list is sensible and handy and very practical if someone is at a loss what to buy. But it shouldn't be shoved at people (H1703).

Domestic things are of much greater significance to this female correspondent, who described preparing to set up home as 'a very exciting time,' than to the engineer, a male correspondent. While their testimony is evidence of a gendered domesticity, of the way in which intimate lives and memories are shaped by different relationships to the material world,[9] their attitude to the publication of commercial lists is shared. The depth of feeling expressed by all three correspondents should not go unnoticed; lists provoked the kind of reactions usually associated with personal or political injustice: they caused hurt, anger and offence. It would be mistaken to regard such

---

9   Michael Pepler, *Family Matters: A History of Ideas about the Family since 1945* (Harlow: Pearson Education Limited, 2002) pp. 100–119.

responses as over-reactions to a minor alteration of conventional wedding practice. Distributing a list of desired objects reveals the usually undeclared relationship between economic position and social inclusion. Gift lists cite a minimum price for participation in a wedding. They also expose a social pretence: the existence of economic hierarchies is, of course, known but their operation in everyday life is often denied. Economic inequality is an accepted (even considered acceptable) fact of society as an abstract formation, but highlighting the differences of financial standing within local or 'knowable' communities that are usually avoided.[10] In preparation for calendric celebrations, such as birthdays or Christmas, who can afford to buy what is quietly negotiated in families and between friends so that when gifts are offered some appearance of fairness, if not material parity, is maintained. In contrast, wedding present lists register the economic differences within a community drawn together at a wedding; they enable wedding guests to position themselves and others according to the objects they can afford to give.

The problem with gift lists is that they specify too much (Figure 4.4 and 4.5). Although they do not tend to contain new knowledge about either givers or gifts, they break a consensus about revelation. They present information about both objects and people that is widely known but not publicized or defined precisely.

Most, if not all, wedding guests would be aware of the standard domestic object categories that make appropriate marriage gifts (utensils for use in the kitchen, ceramics for dining, textiles for bedroom and bathroom). But general knowledge held in common is not required when the desired gift is exactly specified. No longer invited just to give, the guest is prevented from drawing upon their experience of the material forms that are useful in a domestic context or their understanding of those that are desirable in their selection of an object as a gift (what works well in a home and what looks nice). Lists reduce the act of buying a gift to paying for it, denying the giver the more decisive act of selection and it is to this, in particular, that Mass-Observation writers object. Both female correspondents that I have already cited put it in exactly the same way: they do not like 'being told' what to buy and where to buy it (A2801, H1703). They understand the gift list as a means of exerting too much control over the act of giving and the engineer adds that when a list is issued negotiation over what would be an appropriate gift, a discussion 'with them or their parents,' does not take place (L2669). The coercive effect of listing is identified by a Staffordshire teacher:

> formal lists make people feel obliged to buy you something when quite honestly they may not want to or be able to afford to. Lists also inevitably make people spend more than they want or maybe can afford because they don't want to be seen as mean (W1813).

These recorded responses to wedding present lists demonstrate that people consume in ways they do not always choose. Significantly, there is articulate opposition to the practice of listing, a sense that Mass-Observation writers would like to resist

---

10 I have borrowed the term knowable from Raymond Williams, *The Country and the City* (London: Hogarth Press, 1985) pp. 165–181.

interference in their decisions about giving objects, but lists are accepted and used. The clerical worker clearly dislikes lists but believes they are 'sensible' for those who do not know what to give (H1703). The unemployed correspondent 'intimidated' by lists can 'see the point of them' (A2801) and the engineer considers he is being blackmailed 'Despite which' he concludes 'we do give wedding presents' (L2669).

Thus, reactions to gift lists also reveal the way in which people participate in cultural practice that they also wish to oppose. The disjunction between their opposition and their ability to act upon it provides an important insight into how cultural change occurs, how, in fact, it may be imposed. Historians have sometimes assumed that new cultural forms are resisted in preference for known traditions.[11] However, responses to the Giving and Receiving Presents directive suggests that people participate in new cultural practices despite disapproving of them and preferring past forms. Unwilling enactment of cultural practices enables change. Opposition is obscured by reluctant consent. Put simply, people do things they do not like.

Mass-Observation writing about gift lists and wedding presents can be read as nostalgic. Sources of social solidarity are understood to belong in the past, sustained by old ways of giving upon marriage that have been discontinued. There is a sense of regret, even loss, but this is tempered with a concern to make balanced assessments. They compare the moment in which they married with that in which they write, often evaluating the present as just different rather than inevitably worse. A secretary who also describes herself as a housewife states that 'When I was married in 1966 the idea of the very detailed wedding gift lists now considered acceptable to pass to those who wish to give the couple a gift, was not 'done.' But she also adds 'I do not necessarily mean that every couple marrying today is too specifically demanding when constructing their sometimes very elaborate wedding gift lists, its just the way times have changed' (D2585).

There is a consensus across all responses to the directive that change in wedding practices has occurred although that change is observed from different positions. There is not a unified account of the past. Mass-Observation writing does not present a consistent view of previous ways to give and receive wedding presents. That is, there are different memories and understandings of what constitutes past practices. For some, the high street store version of the wedding is not just a commercial adaptation of existing listing practice, any kind of systematic or formal list is new. A retired local government officer married in 1957 writes 'We did not have a formal wedding present list. I do not think people had such things in those days. It would have been considered bad taste' (H1543). A secretary who married the following year also recalls that lists were not used at this time. 'I did not have a formal list and I don't remember that anyone marrying in the 1950's/60's handed out a list as is normal today' (M1381). However, other correspondents who wed around the same time note that lists were used and, moreover, that they were expected to carry out marriage gift transactions in this way. 'Because it was the normal fashion in our social circle,' states a chartered surveyor who married in 1956, 'we did have a wedding list and we did earmark a department store in Manchester where it could be found' (B1509). An

---

11   Adrian Forty, *Objects of Desire* (London: Thames and Hudson, 1986) pp. 11–13.

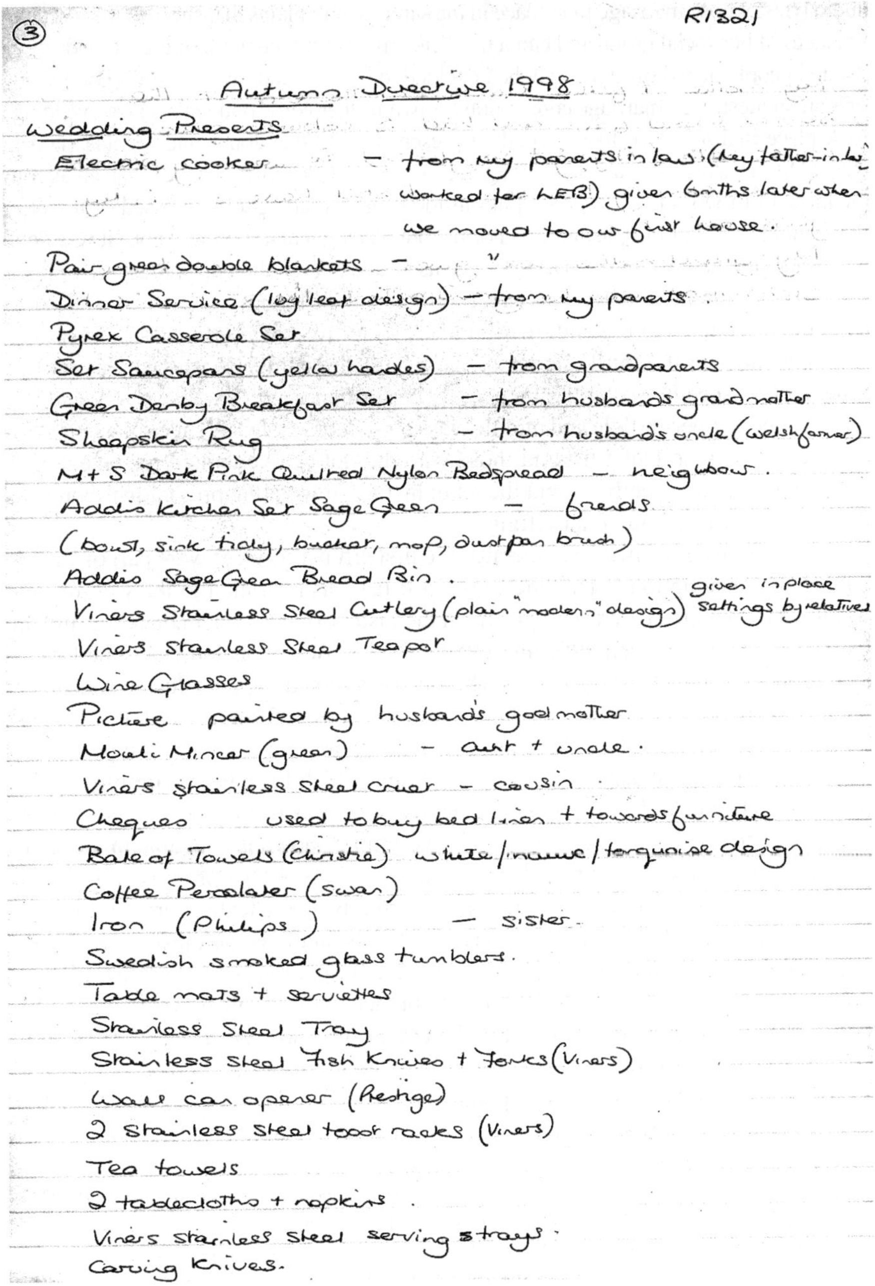

R1321

③

Autumn Directive 1998

Wedding Presents

Electric cooker — from my parents in law (they father-in-law worked for LEB) given 6mths later when we moved to our first house.

Pair green double blankets —

Dinner Service (ivy leaf design) — from my parents

Pyrex Casserole Set

Set Saucepans (yellow handles) — from grandparents

Green Denby Breakfast Set — from husbands grandmother

Sheepskin Rug — from husband's uncle (welsh farmer)

M+S Dark Pink Quilted Nylon Bedspread — neighbour.

Addis Kitchen Set Sage Green — friends.

(brush, sink tidy, bucket, mop, dustpan brush)

Addis Sage Green Bread Bin.

Viners Stainless Steel Cutlery (plain "modern" design) given in place settings by relatives

Viners Stainless Steel Teapot

Wine Glasses

Picture painted by husband's godmother

Mouli Mincer (green) — aunt + uncle.

Viners stainless steel cruet — cousin

Cheques used to buy bed linen + towards furniture

Bale of Towels (Christie) white/mauve/turquoise design

Coffee Percolater (swan)

Iron (Philips) — sister.

Swedish smoked glass tumblers.

Table mats + serviettes

Stainless Steel Tray

Stainless Steel Fish Knives + Forks (Viners)

Wall can opener (Prestige)

2 Stainless Steel toast racks (Viners)

Tea towels

2 tablecloths + napkins.

Viners stainless steel serving trays.

Carving Knives.

Figure 4.3   A list of wedding presents received in 1970 (R1321)

audio typist whose marriage took place in the same year explains that she also followed the practices of her social group and had a list. 'Like most of my contemporaries, I made out a list and people ticked off what they had decided to buy me and my husband' (B89). A list was an unquestioned marriage convention for two further correspondents whose weddings took place in 1965. 'We had a wedding present list at Peter Jones and a china shop in Regent Street' states one, a 'carer' living in Hampshire (C2078), while the other, an aircraft engineer from Dorset, writes, 'We put out the usual list and people crossed of the ones they would buy.' For him, listing was normal but placing it at a shop was not. 'It was done individually rather than through a store such as M and S as is often done today' (R1719).

These different recollections are a product of different experiences and so to state the obvious: making and distributing a list of marriage gifts was not a shared wedding ritual in the third quarter of the twentieth century. It was, at least at this time, a class-specific material practice; its performance was exclusive to weddings within upper, upper-middle and middle class communities. Differences of occupation between those who had a list and those who did not can be tentatively taken as an indication of class-specificity and the retail history of wedding present lists confirms the exclusivity of commercial gifting.[12]

These retail companies that operated the first gift list services were part of an elite culture of consumption.[13] That the use of gift list was restricted to the well-off and wealthy is illustrated by a brief episode in the history of consumer education and the Design Council. Between 1957 and 1959 a Brides' Book was lodged at the Design Centre showroom in the Haymarket. The Book was an attempt to educate consumers about the importance of design in domestic spaces informing wedding gift list making. Brides-to-be could draw up their lists from objects within 'the permanent display of about a thousand things for the home which have been carefully chosen for their high standard of design and performance.' It was not exactly a list service but a guide to good design in the shops. 'Everything shown is available in the shops and we can tell you the name of your nearest stockist.'[14] To promote the Brides' Book, the Council sought to create an opportunity for a feature article about an actual user. 'The deb, or at least society bride-to-be angle is the most obvious one.' They considered 'Sally Page, who has been a deb', but ran with 'Caroline Murray, not a deb, though with deb friends.' Their approach to the whole promotion had been informed by the understanding that: 'The use of the book has a 'class' rather than general appeal. The lower orders don't, I think, go in for brides' books.'[15]

Many Mass-Observation correspondents, especially the ones whose occupation positions them within a working class, assume that commercial lists are a recent

---

12 Since women's work in many cases still carries secondary status, it is more difficult, but not of course impossible, to read off class from female employment.

13 Erika D. Rappaport, *Shopping for Pleasure: Women in the Making of London's West End* (Princeton: Princeton University Press, 2000).

14 'Invitation,' The Design Centre Bride's Book Press Promotion and Direct Mailing 1956–7, file 1572/26 Design Council Archive, University of Brighton.

15 Memo to Mr. White from Miss Blow, 1.3.57, The Design Centre Brides Book Press Promotion and Direct Mailing 1956–7, file 1572/26 Design Council Archive, University of Brighton.

phenomenon and have no knowledge of their longer retail history. Those who may never have participated in weddings beyond their own communities of family and friends were not aware of different forms of giving and consequently remember their practices as the only form of that time. What is important about their assumption that lists were not widely used by anyone in the 1950s and 1960s is not that it is mistaken but that it is a sign of the separation and autonomy of class cultures in this period.

Those who married just a few years later, in the early 1970s, know about lists although they do not necessarily use them. Awareness of wedding practices that are not their own, registers a shift in class relationships, or at least in the kind of contact between classes. There is no sense, from the responses to the Giving and Receiving Presents directive, that at this moment the way many people wed dramatically altered but that the material practices of marriage associated with more wealthy social groups, the upper, upper-middle class and middle class, were becoming more visible to lower-middle and working class subjects. A number of correspondents relate that they did not participate in the forms that were new (or appeared new to them). 'I didn't have a list as I thought it presumtive' (R860) explains a hairdresser from Stockport whose marriage took place in 1971 and a Yorkshire book-keeper married two years later states: 'We didn't have a formal list as it was considered to be a little pretentious in those days' (S2581).

Their terms, pretentious and presumptive, indicate that their guests would not have expected to choose from a gift list and suggest that issuing one would have been regarded as ambitious and ostentatious. They describe both individual and general disapproval of the gift list, revealing how social frameworks limit the variations of material practice. Neither participate in a different way of receiving wedding presents despite the fact it could have enabled them to accumulate more objects for their married homes; they preferred to carry on the forms already practised in their communities. Their refusal to use a gift list to set themselves up above their family and friends implies that forms of cultural continuity and conformity (and perhaps even class solidarity) are created through the reproduction of existing consumption practices. Consumption is regulated in order that things remain the same. Emulation, the attempt to adopt the objects and acquire the status of those who represent the class 'above', is not driving consumption processes here. For these correspondents, it is, to all intents and purposes, prohibited.

One correspondent, a retired building worker from East London, ridicules emulation but believes it is why working class weddings have changed. He describes, in one dense sentence, how first wedding costumes and then gifts have mimicked 'high' society forms. Significantly, it is being asked to choose from a list that encourages him to reflect upon questions of class and consumption:

I HAVE BEEN TO LOTS OF FAMILY WEDDINGS AND BEEN GIVEN THE LIST TO CHOOSE FROM AND SOME THINGS ON THESE LISTS WERE REALLY BEYOND A JOKE, UNLESS WE WERE UPPER CLASS, WHICH IS WHAT THE ABSURD WEDDINGS OF TOP HAT AND TAILS TURNED OUT TO BE IN THE SIXTIES, APING A CLASS WE DESPISED (R450).

BRIDES

WEDDING LIST

FOR THE TABLE	Make	Design	Colour		Make	Design	Colour
Dinner service				**Cutlery**			
Dinner plates				Place settings			
Dessert plates				Coffee spoons			
Side plates				Teaspoons			
Tea plates				Serving spoons			
Cereal/dessert bowls				Steak knives			
Serving dishes				Butter knives			
Sauce boats				Fish knives and forks			
Soup bowls				Fish slice			
Soup tureen				Cake slice			
Other				Carving set			
Tea/coffee service				Ladles			
Teapot				Salad servers			
Milk jug				**Miscellaneous**			
Sugar bowl				Butter dish			
Teacups and saucers				Candlesticks			
Plates				Cheeseboard and knife			
Coffee pot				Egg cups			
Cream jug				Jam pot and spoon			
Coffee cups and saucers				Mugs			
Glassware				Napkin rings			
Goblets				Nutcrackers			
White wine glasses				Pepper and salt mills			
Claret glasses				Place mats/coasters			
Champagne flutes				Toast rack			
Tumblers				Trivet			
Brandy balloons				Other			
Sherry glasses				**Drinks accessories**			
Liqueur glasses				Bottle opener			
Water jug set				Ice bucket			
Decanters				Wine coasters			
Fruit bowl				Wine cooler			
Vases				Wine rack			
Other				Other			

LINEN	Make	Design	Colour		Make	Design	Colour
Bathmat				Napkins			
Bathrobe				Oven set			
Bath sheets				Pillowcases			
Bedspreads				Pillows			
Blankets				Sheets			
Duvet				Tablecloths			
Duvet cover				Table-mats			
Electric blanket				Tea-towels			
Facecloths				Throw/quilt			
Hand-towels				Valance			
Mattress cover				Other			

Figure 4.4   **'Wedding List,'**
Brides and Setting up Home **(Nov–Dec 1997)**

BRIDES
WEDDING LIST

KITCHEN	Make	Design	Colour		Make	Design	Colour
Baking tins				Knife sharpener			
Bread bin				Liquidiser			
Bread-board and knife				Measuring cups			
Broom				Microwave oven			
Cafetière				Mixer plus attachments			
Carving dish				Mixing bowls			
Casseroles s, m, l				Oven-to-table ware			
Coffee grinder				Pasta machine			
Coffee maker				Pastry board			
Colander				Pedal bin			
Corkscrew				Plate rack			
Deep fryer				Pressure cooker			
Double boiler				Ramekins			
Dustpan and brush				Rolling pin			
Electric can-opener				Salad bowl			
Electric carving knife				Sandwich toaster			
Electric kettle				Saucepans			
First-aid kit				Sieve			
Flan dish				Sink set			
Fondue set				Slow cooker			
Food processor				Soufflé dish			
Frying pans				Spice rack			
Garlic press				Steamer			
Grapefruit knife				Storage tins/jars			
Hotplate				Teamaker			
Iron				Toaster			
Ironing board				Trays			
Juicer				Vacuum cleaner			
Kitchen knives				Vacuum flask			
Kitchen scales				Vegetable rack			
Kitchen scissors				Whisk			
Kitchen tool set				Wooden spoons			
Knife holder				Wok			

GENERAL	Make	Design	Colour		Make	Design	Colour
Barbecue				Linen basket			
Baskets				Luggage			
Bathroom scales				Mirrors			
Books				Picnic basket			
Camcorder				Photo frames			
Coffee table				Radio			
Clocks				Rugs			
Electric drill				Stepladder			
Garden furniture				Stereo			
Garden tools				Telephone/answerphone			
Lamps				TV			
Lawnmower				Video			

Figure 4.5 **'Wedding List,**
Brides and Setting up Home **(Nov–Dec 1997)**

The mixture of anger and regret caused by forced participation in expensive weddings (being asked to select a gift from a list and feeling unable to refuse) expressed by other Mass-Observation correspondents is again set out here. But opposition to listing was not universal among Mass-Observation writers. Some seemed to have approached new ways of receiving gifts (or more precisely, ways which were new to them) with some optimism. Those who experimented with lists from the 1970s reveal their inexperience; they were not certain how they worked; some had to learn how to use them and others were not always successful. One correspondent who gave up research and teaching work upon her marriage in 1977 states: 'We did circulate a list – I got some ideas out of a wedding book I'd borrowed' (S1399). Another, whose wedding took place six years earlier in 1971, states 'I did compile a list which my sister-in-law photocopied and handed out which meant that no-one knew what had been crossed off and I got many duplicates' (D156). By the mid 1980s lists were more common and in the 1990s less remarkable, although correspondents married at this time carefully justify why they had a list, indicating that the practice was still not an unquestioned part of a wedding. For example, a television producer who wed in 1993 set out the circumstances that made her overcome her reluctance about having a list:

> We had been living away from home (parents) for several years before we met and then lived together and got a house a year before the wedding. This meant we'd already accumulated a lot of household items. Many relatives and friends asked us to do a wedding list. It felt greedy and we didn't want to be touting for gifts but they said it was normal nowadays and helped avoid getting three toasters (S2813).

The idea that making a wedding present list, composing and publicizing it, is 'normal' is one of the most persuasive arguments set out in bridal etiquette literature.

Bridal Magazines and the Commercial Gift List

Over the last few years there has been a proliferation of publications offering advice about how to get married. Glossy bridal magazines, which come out on a bi-monthly or quarterly basis, are a relatively recent phenomenon and are a crucial part of what is understood as the commercialization of the wedding.[16] Bridal magazines insist upon the use of commercial gift lists. This advice is shaped by the context in which it is offered and thus what I examine next is the form of the bridal magazine itself.

---

16 Weekend *Guardian* supplement columnist, Liz Jones, informed her readers that she bought her first bridal magazine in February 2002. Liz Jones, 'The Wedding Planner,' *Guardian*, 9 Feb 2002, weekend supplement: 63. *The Wedding Day* celebrated its 25th issue in Spring 2003 and marked just over three years of publication. However, Diana Leonard's late 1960s study of getting married refers readers to an issue of *Brides and Setting up Home*. Diana Leonard, *Sex and Generation: A Study of Courtship and Weddings* (London: Tavistock, 1980) p. 131, and this is by far the longest running of the current titles dating from 1964.

Their front covers draw upon women's magazine conventions: a colour photograph prominently featuring the head and shoulders of a smiling woman surrounded, and overlaid in places, with bold text (Figure 4.6).[17] The female figure is always a bride whose conventionally coloured but fashionably cut dress delivers the same message: the white wedding is a tradition that is not out-of-date. Despite the slightly shifting terms in their titles or sub-titles, the magazines are always addressed to the person who is going to wear the dress. Of the magazines' 300 or so pages, at least 100 are advertisements for bridal gowns. Positioned together in the first third of the magazine, with some always occupying the prime space between the cover and the contents page, the dominance of these advertisements within the magazines reflects the importance of the bride's clothing in wedding rituals. But every issue of every title also includes a small editorial introduction on each aspect of preparing and staging a wedding. Content is divided into fashion (the dress), beauty (on the bride's body shape, hair and make-up), planning (the tasks to be completed before and on the wedding day), home (sometimes called gifts) and honeymoon. These sections figure as the essential components of the complete wedding and correspond to the subject matter of lifestyle magazines: the adornment of bodies, the decoration of homes, the description of sites of adventure and escape. Indeed, some of the bridal magazines do call themselves Style Bibles.[18]

All titles are positioned together at the point of sale. They are found in the newsagents above, below or next to the women's magazines. They are sometimes juxtaposed between healthy living and cooking magazines, sometimes between the magazines devoted to parenting and those to personal grooming. The act of getting married, like other specific cultural practices, 'special interest' subjects according to retail classifications, has been subjected to an intensive styling and marketing process.

---

17 For an analysis of women's magazines see: Peter Corrigan, *The Sociology of Consumption* (London: Sage, 1997) pp. 81–95; Anna Gough-Yates, *Understanding Women's Magazines: Publishing, Markets and Readerships* (London: Routledge, 2003); Ellen McCracken, *Decoding Women's Magazines: From Mademoiselle to Ms* (Basingstoke: Macmillan, 1993); Janice Winship, *Inside Women's Magazines* (London: Pandora, 1987). In some cases bridal magazines are published by the same companies as women's magazines. Three of the bridal magazines are produced by big established publishing companies: *Brides and Setting up Home* is a Conde Nast title; *Wedding and Home* is an ipc magazine; *You and Your Wedding* is now part of the National Magazine Company Ltd. but initially it was independent, put out by You and Your Wedding Publications which also briefly published *Bride and Groom*. The newest title *Wedding Day* is put out by a small concern, Crimson Publishing Ltd. The magazines that are part of the larger companies are those that have survived the longest. *For the Bride*, published by XL Publications, discontinued between 1998 and 2003. Following McCracken, Sharon Boden argues that bridal magazines are intertextual and refer, in particular to women's magazines, Boden, p. 59.

18 *Bliss for Brides* calls itself 'The Original Bridal Style Bible' and *Wedding Day* is 'The Style Bible.'

Figure 4.6   Front cover of *You and Your Wedding*
(Nov–Dec 1997)

Periodicals solely devoted to getting married may be a relatively recent phenomenon but their magazine form is not. Existing magazine strategies have been applied to their specific subject. Bridal magazines have borrowed the graphic and journalistic forms of the mainstream glossies, including high finish photography and writing which follows the trends of popular women's magazine journalism. Bridal magazines occasionally carry articles on, for example, 'real life' or celebrity weddings. They seem new but are a remarkably stable cultural form. There is little variation. They stick to a basic format and repeat it. They have the same covers, same price, and same categories appear in the same order. Furthermore, their content is more or less the same between titles and issues. It is possible to be so repetitive because the reader is only expected to buy only one magazine once or twice at the most[19] but it is also the tendency of self-declared style manuals to be repetitive. Such texts are codes of conduct. Their purpose is to provide information about how to perform a particular cultural practice, how to dress or decorate a house in the most suitable style for 'today' or how to plan a marriage if you are a 'modern bride.' They offer such advice about the currently correct way to perform what they usually call 'your life' on the basis of knowing some new consensus about the appropriate forms for contemporary culture. At any one time style manuals will contain the same instructions about the same cultural practice and this is particularly the case with bridal magazines. Despite quite constant claims about demonstrating how your wedding (or your clothes or your life) can be personalized, style manuals are both prescriptive and conforming. Crucially, accounts of how to perform a cultural practice correctly are essentially descriptions of how to select specific types of objects that always concludes with information about where to purchase them. The best thing to do is the best thing to buy. Such advice, the inevitable outcome of an economy where most cultural forms are delivered to us through the market, is characteristic of the style manual form. Bridal magazines expose a close relationship between commerce and journalism typical of, although less overt in, other lifestyle glossies. Long runs of advertisements, uninterrupted even by page numbers, give the bridal magazine the appearance of a trade or retail catalogue, a form from which, at least in part, it derived.[20] Its glamorous images of models in bridal wear are organized into a useful listing of appropriate and available things. The positioning of adverts, ones for domestic objects surrounding an editorial introduction on the importance of making a gift list, for example, incorporates the advert into an information service about what to do when getting married. The inclusion of some bridal commodity alongside or directly before or after a feature is, of course, an endorsement of its appropriateness but such blatant promotion appears as useful consumer information. The editorial tone is always that of the friendly expert assessing the qualities of currently available items. However, all products and services are positively assessed, some things might be better than others at this or that moment, but nothing is actually bad. There is no critical distance between the magazine and the products it presents. Thus the adverts

---

19 *Wedding Day*, however, has a subscription price of £16.30 a year (for six issues).

20 *Bliss for Brides* initially included *Galleria*, a regional advertising magazine.

provide information and the journalism advertises and they are difficult to distinguish from each other although they do tend to deploy a different graphic formula.[21] Advertising images cover the entire page so that the reader is invited to look at a scene rather than at a page, whereas editorial interventions juxtapose text and image on a white background so the page can be seen (Figures 4.7 and 4.8). Also more text, organized into paragraphs, is evident. But text is also frequently used in advertising to make the advertised object appear as if it has an expert recommendation. Bridal magazines do not have a hard and fast rule of visual difference between their copy and that of their advertisers. It is all an act of promotion. The amount of journalism in bridal magazines, compared with glossies of a similar price, is very small and what little there is usually takes the form of reviewing current styles, shopping outlets and services. Reading about getting married reveals that it requires the acquisition of a detailed commercial knowledge. The appropriate enactment of a wedding (doing it right) means knowing what and how to consume. Consumption and conduct can no longer be distinguished. Bridal magazines commodify wedding rituals.

Advice about gifts and making lists occurs within the repeating format of every bridal magazine. The mix of adverts and editorial writing devoted to wedding presents sometimes arranged under the heading 'Home' or just 'Gifts' occurs in the magazines' final third. Advice about making lists is also always included in the wedding planner, which provides a model timetable for preparations for the whole wedding. The winter 1998 issue of *Bliss* noted that it should be done six or twelve months before the day, making it one of the first wedding tasks,[22] but usually readers are advised to 'make', 'prepare', 'plan' and 'organise' the wedding gift list three months before.[23] At this point, instructed the April/May 2003 issue of *Wedding and Home*, 'Post gift-list info and send thank-you letters when you receive presents.'[24]

Model gift lists have been also regularly included in the wedding planner section. Some were designed as pull-outs, printed on writing quality paper with boxes for the bride-to-be to tick or fill out. Thus the magazine's list would provide the actual form for her own. Even those model lists that were not easy-to-remove inserts could, of course, be ripped out or copied and used exactly (Figures 4.9 and 4.10). Every list, at the very least, could be used as a guide. They can help, as *Brides and Setting up Home* explains, to 'make your own list at home.'[25] 'Use our blueprint to draw up your own' *You and Your Wedding* insisted one year and the next the magazine

21 Paul Jobling and David Crowley, *Graphic Design: Reproduction and Representation since 1800* (Manchester: Manchester University Press, 1996) pp. 245–269.

22 *Bliss for Brides* Nov–Jan 1998: 21.

23 'Countdown to Your Big Day,' *For the Bride* Early Spring 1998: 19; 'Wedding Planner,' *Bliss for Brides* Nov–Jan 1998: 21; 'Wedding Guide,' *Brides and Setting up Home* Nov–Dec 1997: 81; 'The Big Countdown,' *Bride and Groom* Winter 1997–8: 48; *Wedding and Home* Feb–Mar 1998: 29.

24 'Wedding Planner,' *Wedding and Home* Apr–May 2003: 190.

25 'The Wedding Guide,' *Brides and Setting up Home* Mar–April 1998: 129

advised: 'use our list as a guideline.'[26] The model lists, like everything else in the bridal magazines are basically the same.[27] Content and layout vary only slightly. Some are longer than others (one of *Brides and Setting up Home* lists sets out over one hundred and fifty items while an issue of *Wedding and Home* includes a list of only fifty or so) but they are categorized in the same way. Objects are listed according to function and location. These are, of course, overlapping categories. Dining refers to the room or the activity of eating and objects classified as dining are often listed as 'Table' because that is where they would be put. Kitchen and Dining categories are usually listed first and second respectively and contain the most traditional wedding presents (knives, canteens of cutlery, dinner services) as well as old and new fashions in British cooking (fondue sets and pasta machines). Next, usually, are textiles for sleeping and washing, for the bedroom and bathroom, that are sometimes still called 'Linen' after the cupboard where they would have been kept. A 'General' section, comprised of objects of family leisure (camcorders, barbecues, computers) concludes the list.

Thus, the categories of the wedding present list correspond to the room and storage arrangements of the contemporary modern home. The list displays an everyday order but like other more professional and sophisticated classifying systems it performs the work of definition.[28] It defines what a home is for, describing its purpose as primarily a place for feeding and sleeping and when these activities, which are essential for what has been called the reproduction of labour are arranged, it becomes the site of leisure.[29] Not every object in a house is included on a list. Those associated with the routines of particular types of work completed or partially completed at home (for example, writing tools and technologies for 'doing the books') do not feature. Although the home is the site of paid work (and as I write these words I am sitting at a table working in a space created by clearing away the breakfast things) it is the idea of the home as a place of recovery and relaxation from work that is sustained by the wedding present list. The list also upholds the idea that the home is the site of shared living, if not 'family life.' Many of the gifts listed, from old-fashioned saucepans to the most up-to-date digital camera, will of course often only ever be used by one

---

26 'Wedding Planner,' *You and Your Wedding* Nov–Dec 1997: 59; 'The Wedding Organiser,' *You and Your Wedding* Mar–Apr 1998: 81.

27 The content of the model lists in *Bliss for Brides* and in *Brides and Setting up Home* is almost exactly the same.

28 Debate about how knowledge is created through the classification systems of institutions (academies and museums) has been generated by interpretations of Michel Foucault, *The Order of Things: the Archaeology of the Human Sciences* (London: Tavistock, 1970). See, for example, Eilean Hooper-Greenhill, *Museums and the Shaping of Knowledge* (London: Routledge, 1992) and Ludmilla Jordanova, 'Objects of Knowledge,' *The New Museology*, ed. Peter Vergo (London: Reaktion Books, 1989) pp. 22–40.

29 Hugh Mackay, 'Consuming Technologies at Home,' *Consumption and Everyday Life*, ed. Hugh Mackay (London: Sage, 1997) pp. 259–297; Roger Silverstone and E. Hirsch, *Consuming Technologies: Media and Information in Domestic Spaces* (London: Routledge, 1992).

Choosing your wedding list

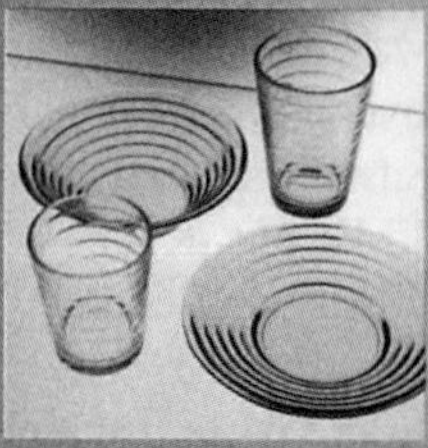

Choosing the gifts to put on your wedding list can be one of the most enjoyable bits of the whole wedding organisation palaver. It's one of the few situations in which you can forget about everyone else and just indulge yourself.

So make the most of it!

While it is great fun to choose presents you have always wanted and which someone else will pay for, some careful preparations will ensure that you get the most from this unique shopping experience and maybe even avoid those arguments about which goes on the list, the table football game or the espresso machine.

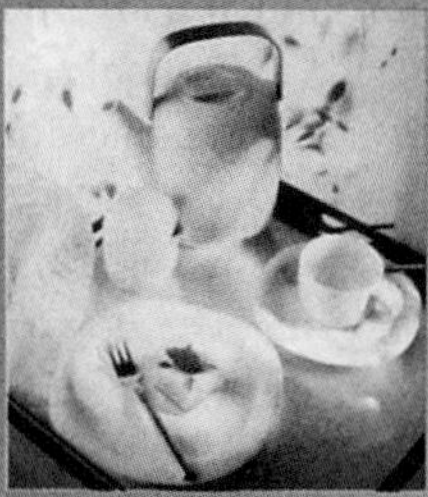

Because your list will go to all your friends and, probably, your parents' friends, it is also something of a 'style statement' for you as a couple. So it's worth making sure that the store you use and the gifts you select say the right things! We have asked Pepita Diamand-Levy to give us some tips on how to conjure up the most elegant, useful and interesting wedding list.

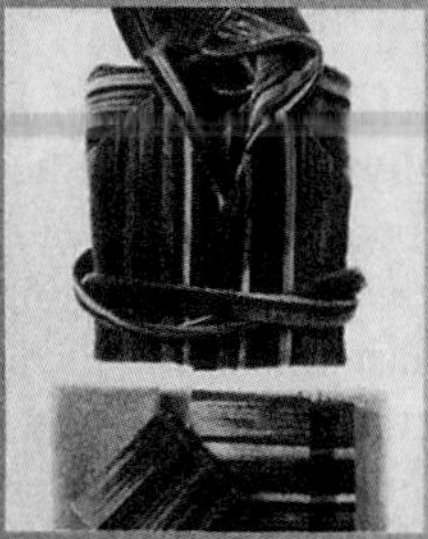

Pepita is Retail Director of Wrapit, a unique wedding list business, which combines a very personal service from its showrooms in London and Harrogate with a website which contains a 'virtual department store' featuring 100 departments and 13,000 possible gifts. So you can either have your hand held and be generally cosseted through the whole process or do it all yourself, online, from start to finish.

This combination has led Kodak Weddings, who provide wedding advice to more than 50,000 brides each year, to select Wrapit as the best gift list service in Britain in 2002.

For a copy of Wrapit's Wedding List Guide call 020 8875 8857 or visit www.wrapit.co.uk

Pepita's Top Wedding List Tips:

- The first thing to do is decide what style you are looking for - traditional or modern, budget or extravagant, detailed or plain, and apply this theme through all your selections.
- The best way to ensure an elegant list is to use a stylish wedding list service - one which features the sort of designers and styles which appeal to you. So look around. Some specialist wedding list shops (if you can find one in your area) will offer you a wider range than a department store.
- When it comes to choosing gifts for your list, be methodical and make a list of the things you really want. If you don't know where to begin, ask your wedding list service if they have a checklist for you to look at.
- The wedding list service you choose should provide discreet cards, which you can add to your invitations to let your guests know about your wedding list. Make sure you use them. Your guests will genuinely be pleased to have the guess-work removed.
- If you want to go for a new table-setting on your list, make sure your wedding list service gives you advice about what's "practical" as well as pretty. Ask questions like: Is that gold-rimmed china dishwasher safe? Will those oversize burgundy glasses even fit into your dishwasher?
- Don't despair if you feel that you already 'have everything'. Fine wines, pieces of art, coffee table books and even weekend breaks make perfect gifts that your friends will be happy to contribute towards. Just make sure that your guests can apply Gift Certificates towards your more expensive choices, Above All Enjoy!!!

Figure 4.7 A *Bliss for Brides* double page spread, left hand page showing an advertisement for wrapit.co.uk

Forget the doom and gloom merchants who drone on and on about planning weddings being time-consuming, expensive and stressful. It should be fun, so enjoy it! Our wedding planner has tons of tips to help your happy day run like clockwork...

the wedding planner

Select Your Style

So you've decided to commit to each other until death do you part and have announced the news to family and friends? All that's left is the small matter of making the whole thing legal and celebrating in style.

So how are you going to do it? Do you want a traditional white wedding in church or would you like a more laid-back affair; a ceremony in a hot air balloon, on a beach, or in a zoo, or perhaps a themed wedding?

While a civil ceremony in Britain opens up a huge choice of venues, you might want to consider tying the knot in an exotic foreign location. This option is becoming more and more popular, but requires some thought. While marrying on a beach or ski-slope can cost less than a white wedding at home with all the trimmings, it's unlikely that all your family and friends would be able to attend.But perhaps that's an advantage...

Your budget will help tame and frame your initial ideas, but the choice is yours – or at least it should be!

The Church Wedding

If you want a religious ceremony, your local place of worship is an obvious choice of venue. In some circumstances it may be possible to marry in another church, but don't bank on it, as many ministers will want evidence of a good reason for marrying in their parish if they've never seen you before. Banns (the publication of your intention to marry) are read out in church on three consecutive Sundays, and the wedding ceremony must take place within three months. If you're divorced or embarking on a marriage of mixed faiths, a full church marriage service may be difficult to arrange, so speak to the ministers involved as soon as possible.

The Register Office

Once you've both separately registered your intention to marry at your local register office, you can tie the knot in any office in England or Wales, as long as you live in either country. You need to apply for permission to marry, either by licence or certificate. To marry by licence you must give 21 days' notice, and one of you must be resident in the area for 15 days. The alternative, marriage by certificate, only requires one day's notice, and you both have to be resident for seven days. Both methods of notice are valid for three months.

Licensed Premises

Your local register office will be able to give you a list of premises licensed for the solemnisation of marriage which exist in your area. The Office for National Statistics (0151 471 4817 or www.statistics.gov.uk) can provide a list of all licensed buildings throughout the whole of the UK.

Figure 4.8 **The right hand page contains *Bliss for Brides* wedding planning advice, juxtaposing advert and editorial**

person and would ultimately or effectively end up belonging to an individual but such things are tools in collective practices: producing a family meal or filming a birthday party. Truly personal objects, like clothing, are never included on a gift list and the books that appear on them are those that could be read more than once by more than one person. As each model gift list is read and as each bride-to-be's list is written, the description of the home as shared space beyond work is disseminated and ideas about the proper way to live are perpetuated.

The list also, and maybe more obviously, defines the appropriate wedding gift. It legitimates requests for expensive objects and for quantities of them. It makes it acceptable to be specific. All lists include boxed spaces for their bride-to-be readers to enter their desired make and colour and there are spaces for design, shop and price on some. *For the Bride* argued in its Autumn 1997 issue that naming objects without citing the shop 'can cause problems unless you are specific. You could end up with towels of varying shades of green or kitchenware that doesn't quite make a set.'[30] The wedding present list is an attempt to control minutely the type of objects used to set up a home. The bridal magazines frequently assert the right of the bride-to-be to control the gift transactions and *Bliss'* headline 'Tell them what you want' is an example of this. Her right to control is legitimized through the need for complete collections, for having a set of things. A collection is a unified whole, a unity of connected things, objects that look alike or have a common function.[31] The concern, expressed as a need, for co-ordinated objects, full sets, matching colours is given as a reason for requiring a list and is, in fact, a rationale for creating collections. The most common argument for a list is that it prevents the bride from having to accept duplicates. All sources in this study, popular and commercial, identify the potential problem of receiving '3 toasters' or '27 deep-fat fryers.'[32] However, several extras are useful in a thrifty household economy since they can be kept for the day when the things in use wear out. They are only a problem for homemaking as a collecting practice. They are not required because they disturb the symmetry of the collection where everything has its place. The complete collection is a sign of perfection and the list projects the achievement of such perfection immediately upon marriage. It is an ideal representation of a home, unspoilt, untouched and waiting to be used.

Gift Giving: Traditional Necessities and Published Luxuries

Despite different and class-specific material practices, different ways of making lists and receiving gifts, only one form is held up as being traditional. 'Traditionally the

---

30 'Wedding Gift Services,' *For the Bride* Autumn 1997: 53.

31 Susan Stewart, *On Longing: Narratives of the Miniature, the Gigantic, the Souvenir, the Collection* (Durham: Duke University Press, 1993) pp. 151–169.

32 See, for example, Leah Maguire, 'Is Having a Wedding List just Greedy?' *Bella* 2 Nov 1999: 27. The problem of duplicates is far from new. Mrs C.W. Earle, *More Pot–Pourri from a Surrey Garden* (London, Smith, Elder, 1899) p. 143. I would like to thank Monica Brewis for this reference.

Mother of the Bride will co-ordinate the gifts and advise the guests' as is explained in *Bliss for Brides*.[33] This specific practice might be more accurately described as popular tradition that was, as I have tried to indicate, far from universally performed in the recent past. Many Mass-Observation writers did not follow this tradition. For some, it was not the way giving upon marriage was managed in their communities and others were prevented by, for example, post-war shortages or marrying in haste, from practising it. However, what is usually understood as 'the tradition' is contained within the responses to the Giving and Receiving Presents directive and is typified by one account in particular. A female correspondent from Aberystwyth who describes herself as a 'Genealogist and carer' begins:

> I was married in 1962 in a Welsh Wesleyan Methodist Chapel in North Wales. I had attended the chapel since I was twelve and my husband had gone there all his life so a lot of our presents were from chapel members who were not relations or close friends. It was a white wedding conducted in the Welsh language (quite an ordeal for me as I am not a Welsh speaker). We had three bridesmaids (all cousins of mine) and 60 guests. The guests were limited because the reception was in our house. As far as the gifts we received – my mother was a very organised lady and made lots of lists and the wedding present list I still have. We didn't have a formal list of what we wanted but my mother had a list of things she thought we needed so she could suggest things to people who asked. At that time although formal lists were becoming fashionable it was considered rather forward to have one. Most presents came before the wedding and were displayed on borrowed trestle tables in the week and on the day of the wedding. Each one was acknowledged by either my husband or myself with a hand written letter – indeed we did little else in the run up to the wedding when we met (P1009). [34]

Thus the type of list now regarded as traditional is that associated with the family wedding that takes place within a small community. When the bride is marrying within the community to which her family belongs, her mother would be an appropriate person to manage her list simply because she would be known to the wedding guests and could be approached by them in person. It is characteristic of this type of list that it is not published. There would be no need. It is therefore just a set of ideas about what is required for the establishment of a respectable home.

While the discussions between the bride's mother and the guests to her daughter's wedding might be dictated by what items have or have not yet been selected as gifts (what is or is not crossed off the unpublished list), there would be some exchange of ideas about what is an essential domestic object, whether one thing would be more useful than another, this thing more durable, more effective than that.[35] This form of listing is a way of transferring knowledge within a community and between one generation and another. Many of the listed objects are tools that would help the bride

---

33 Riley and Burns, p. 126.

34 This correspondent is also cited in Chapter 3 pp. 87–98, 100–1.

35 One other way of discussing wedding presents was described by a Mass-Observation correspondent, married in 1963: 'The list was available if anyone asked, several of my parents friends took us out to lunch and we chose our gift' (L1991).

acquire the skills of respectable housekeeping. The carer from Aberystwyth received, among other things, an electric kettle, an electric iron, a 'whiskette' hand-mixer, saucepans, tea-towels, butter-dish and companion set comprising a brush, poker and shovel. Even when the given objects are not exactly necessities, such as teapot mats and tray cloths, they still materialize ideas of good household management. For example, these fabrics protect wooden surfaces, increasing the durability of furniture and preserving them in a good condition for occasional moments of formal display. Thus individual objects and wedding presents as a collection embody housekeeping knowledge. They also ensure conformity to existing family practice as this Mass-Observation correspondent makes clear when she explains that her list comprised things her mother 'thought we needed' (P1009).

Although the list organized by the mother of the bride can be evoked as traditional in the way that post-war working class homes come to stand for a general idea of the past, the 'carer' who held such a list understood it to be traditional at the time. For her, the commercial list was a new development that she did not follow. Much like those other correspondents who described the commercial list as 'pretentious' and 'presumptive,' she knew that they would be neither appropriate nor welcomed in her community, 'too forward' in her words. Her reluctance to participate in practices that were out of step with expectations of her community is further evidence, if it were needed, that working class culture in the mid-twentieth century was not inevitably aspirational nor its consumption practices emulative.[36]

The form the gift list takes reveals a great deal about the wedding itself and the communities to which the marrying couple, and the bride in particular, belongs. Mass-Observation writers who had lists, therefore give quite detailed descriptions and are often concerned to explain that their list was not suitable for widespread distribution: it was not publishable. One correspondent who married in 1961 and another who wed in 1966 specify that their lists were hand-written (A883 and D2585). Yet another, a journalist from Durham states that theirs was 'just a list on a piece of paper, it wasn't lodged with a shop' (W633). While the types of gifts requested on a list (a wide-screen television in 2003 compared to a tablecloth in 1962) may seem obviously important, illustrative of the time, place and class of the wedding, the material form of the list itself is considered to be significant as is the way in which the list is announced.

Shops, stores and on-line companies that provide wedding list services advise the bride and groom to send a 'discreet' card informing guests where the list is held with the invitations. Many correspondents, however, explain that their list was 'only on request' or specify that it was not sent out with the invitations. Being asked to select a gift from a list at the same time as being invited to a wedding is the subject of comment and disapproval. An engineer called it 'blackmail' and a newspaper

---

36 For a review of work on consumption as a classed practice see Brian Longhurst and Mike Savage, 'Social Class, Consumption and the Influence of Bourdieu: Some Critical Issues,' *Consumption Matters: The Production and Experience of Consumpion*, ed. Stephen Edgell, Kevin Hetherington and Alan Warde (Oxford: Blackwell Publishers, 1996) pp. 274–301.

promotions manager explains that is 'not keen on' choosing from a list 'even less so when, on the two most recent occasions, the list has come in the same envelope as the wedding invitation itself' (D1602).

The published list is not, then, its accepted or traditional form. It makes the obligation between attending a wedding and buying a gift too explicit. Once again, the list specifies too much. It may be that it is necessary to publicize the details of a commercial list and inform guest where the list is held (rather than the mother of the bride sharing her ideas about what the marrying couple need) when the families of the bride and groom and the wider communities of guests are not close (either geographically or emotionally). Thus, the published list is simply indicative of weddings that occur within a spatially and socially separated society. More significant, perhaps, is that the published list is a way of announcing that the bride and groom already know what they want, they have decided how their home should be fitted up and organized. They do not ask their guests to use their knowledge of useful or desirable household objects nor allow them to make any connection between their domestic life and that of the bride and groom.

When critics of the lists call them 'impersonal' or 'clinical', and these terms occur with the Mass-Observation writing and other popular sources (C2654) they are identifying the way in which this kind of transaction fails to fulfil the understood purpose of the gift. Despite increasing commercialization and professionalization of giving upon marriage, the idea that the gift should be an intimate offering remains persuasive. Transferring an object from one person to another does not inevitably constitute giving a gift, for that the gift must become embodied. A gift exchange requires the giver to invest something of themselves in the gift. In contemporary capitalist culture, their investment usually takes the form of time spent thinking about the intended receiver as they consider what to buy. The commercial gift list saves their time but they end up contributing to someone's domestic collection without really giving them a gift.

The Bridal Magazines and Publication of the Gift List

It is evident from the comments of Mass-Observation Correspondents that, at the time they were made, in late 1998, while gift lists were being quite widely used, their use was also a matter for debate. For example, parts of the response to the Giving and Receiving Presents directive devoted to the analysis of gift lists were prefaced with announcements that the writer was about to voice an opinion in public: they began with 'one comment' (L2669) and 'let me say' (H1703). Indeed, the imposition of new practices of giving wedding presents was the subject of media attention, even regarded as a 'news' story that commanded some coverage in both popular and 'high-brow' media, in the closing months of the twentieth century and the early years of the twenty-first.[37] While the bridal

---

37 Maguire 27; 'All Wrapped Up: the 50 Best Wedding Presents' *The Independent* 13–19 May 2000 *The Information* supplement: 4–11; Michael Paterson and Laura Borg, 'The Newly Weds with Designs on Luxury,' *The Daily Telegraph* May 26 2000: 3.

magazines consistently recommended having a list, they too debated the appropriate methods of publication and distribution at this time.

Two ways of informing guests about the list are described: either the bride, her mother or another female relative holds the list, uses it to make suggestions, to relate what has been bought and what is most wanted from the remaining items, or it can be placed at a high street department store, specialist shop, showroom or sites online. Bridal magazines promote the latter, the commercial list. All such services work in basically the same way. Objects are chosen by the bride and groom, or just the bride, from a retail outlet and it holds a list of these selections. Apart from small independent shops that agreed to hold lists but do not specialize in the wedding present trade, selections are stored electronically. Wedding guests are informed that the list is held at a particular shop or is accessible via a particular web site by a card dropped in with their invitation to the wedding. As each guest purchases an item from the list it is withdrawn from sale so that no other guest can purchase it again. All transactions are recorded in order to produce an account of who bought which presents for the bride and groom. The guests do not have to visit the actual retail outlet where the bride and groom placed their list. If it is held by a high street department chain guests can buy presents at any branch but they do not have to leave their house. The gift can be selected and paid for over the phone. They may buy online. The giver does not have to see or handle the object that they give; they may hear a description or see an image and then agree to a price. Most shops and services deliver the gifts as a job lot after the honeymoon and many keep the list open for sometime after the wedding. Harrods keeps it open for one month, Marks & Spencer for three, the Conran Shop for six and David Mellor for a year. There are also financial inducements for taking up list services, cash rewards for holding it at a particular shop. Harrods gives the married couple between 3 per cent and 7.5 per cent of the total spent. The more you can get your guests to buy, the greater the bonus. Debenhams and John Lewis give 5 per cent of the total spent in vouchers. The expectation is that the vouchers or cash will be used in buying the un-bought gifts yourself. Marks & Spencer offers two years interest free credit on large (over £200) un-bought listed goods. The Conran Shop has a credit as well as a gift list where bought items can be exchanged for credit or anything else in the shop. So, for example, if a bride listed both cups and towels and a few of each were bought for her she could exchange one for the other to make a complete set. The opportunity to manage the list, to enlarge upon or alter it means that the recipient can overrule the decisions of the givers. Some lists ensure that the choice is entirely theirs. Credit lists that invite guests to pay a cash equivalent of an object with the marrying couple making their choices when they know how much they have to spend are operated by Selfridges, for example.

Specialist gift services began in elite retail areas of metropolitan centres in the early twentieth century. The General Trading Company based in Sloane Square, London, claims to have opened the first wedding list service in 1920.[38] It is very

38 'General Trading Company Wedding Services' (1998). Their 1998 catalogue also states that they are the ' 'grandfather' of wedding list services around the country (35).' They

likely that other central London shops with a similarly priced stock appealing to well-off, if not wealthy, customers also operated lists from around this time. This type of the retail practice, a gift service managed by shops whose selling point is their exclusivity, boomed in the late 1980s. The Wedding List Co. was established in 1987 'to provide' according to its founder, 'a service for couples looking for a very high quality and personal wedding list service.'[39] Its stock of supposedly elegant and always expensive objects of either traditional or contemporary design and its services, which include consultation with the bride and groom, management of the list and delivery of the presents, reproduce that of the elite metropolitan shop. Such specialist services have expanded and there are a dozen or more such companies including Lists Unlimited and The Wedding Shop, which began trading in 1990s, and The Wedding List and Present Company and confetti.co.uk established shortly after.

The most substantial expansion of commercial lists occurred in a different kind of retail space as a version of elite retail practices was reproduced at high street level and prices. Every major high street department store now has a registry (Debenhams, John Lewis, Marks & Spencer as well as Argos). Furthermore, it was as high street list services proliferated in the early 1990s that the bridal magazines devoted a significant amount of the small quota of editorial copy to gifts. Making a list was taken up as an 'issue' of wedding practice. The 1998 'Tell them what you want' *Bliss* article claims that it will 'untangle the wedding present dilemma' and 'explores the options open to you.' It begins with the formulaic rhetorical question of popular advice page journalism. 'Do you need the extra hassle of organising a gift list?' The answer will be no. The article positions the reader as an independent contemporary woman not interested in seeking out difficulty and open to new ideas. *Bliss* invites her to identify with 'the modern bride' who is 'opting for help from the experts.' And adds: 'Department stores and independent bridal agencies are playing a major role with nearly 60 per cent of couples now taking advantage of their services.' This is a warning to take up commercial lists or be left behind. And the rest of the piece is pitched as helpful hints on how to get the shop-held list right. It actually introduces a new code of wedding conduct:

> Choose the gifts together with your fiancé and do not let in-laws offer too much advice.... One way of making sure that you have everything is to look through each room in the house to fill in the gaps...do include a few of the more luxurious items.... Close family and friends will want to show their appreciation so do not feel guilty about asking for a gift that you really cherish and enjoy.... If you and your fiancé live together and already have a duvet and a toast rack, you may wish to replace you existing belongings with co-ordinated sets for a fresh outlook... most stores now have specially trained bridal advisors

---

provide 'the beautiful, the unusual, the classic' for their customers and described their stock in the following way: 'whilst the range of objects is wide and eclectic, they all share the common denominators of being stylish, well–made and timeless (3).' In a piece entitled, "A gift of an idea' in *Kodak Weddings* (a promotional magazine enclosed with *Wedding Day* Apr–May 2003) 'the idea' of placing a list at one shop is claimed to be 'about 100 years' old (12).

39 'The Wedding List Co. Check List' (1998).

	MAKE	DESIGN	COLOUR/SIZE		MAKE	DESIGN	COLOUR/SIZE
CHINA				RED WINE GLASSES			
DINNER PLATES				WHITE WINE GLASSES			
SIDE PLATES				CHAMPAGNE FLUTES			
DESSERT PLATES				SHERRY GLASSES			
CEREAL BOWLS				LIQUEUR GLASSES			
SOUP BOWLS				BRANDY BALLOONS			
SERVING DISHES				LARGE TUMBLERS			
SAUCE/GRAVY BOATS				SMALL TUMBLERS			
SOUP TUREEN				DECANTERS			
TEAPOT				WATER JUG			
MILK JUG				VASE			
TEACUPS & SAUCERS				FRUIT BOWL			
TEA PLATES				OTHER			
SUGAR BOWL				**MISCELLANEOUS TABLEWARE**			
COFFEE CUPS & SAUCERS				SALT & PEPPER MILLS/POTS			
COFFEE POT				TOAST RACK			
CREAM JUG				CHEESE BOARD & KNIFE			
BUTTERDISH				PLACE MATS			
OTHER				WINE COASTERS			
CUTLERY				CANDLESTICKS			
CANTEEN OF CUTLERY				SERVIETTE RINGS			
LARGE KNIVES & FORKS				EGG CUPS			
SMALL KNIVES & FORKS				MUGS			
SPOONS				OTHER			
SERVING SPOONS				**KITCHEN**			
STEAK KNIVES				BAKING TINS			
FISH KNIVES & FORKS				BREAD BIN			
CARVING SET				BREAD BOARD			
SALAD SERVERS				BREAD KNIFE			
FISH SLICE				CAKE STAND			
CAKE SLICE				CASSEROLE DISHES			
OTHER				CHOPPING BOARDS			
GLASSWARE				COFFEE GRINDER			
GOBLETS				COFFEE MAKER			
COCKTAIL GLASSES				DEEP FAT FRYER			

Figure 4.9   'Gift List,' *For the Bride*
              (Early Spring 1998)

	Make	Design	Colour/Size		Make	Design	Colour/Size
Dishwasher				Bedspreads			
Electric can opener				Towels			
Electric carving knife				Tea towels			
Electric knife sharpener				Tablecloths			
Electric toaster				Serviettes			
Fish kettle				Bathroom accessories			
Fondue set				Other			
Food processor				**LIVING ROOMS**			
Frying pans				Stereo			
Iron				TV			
Ironing board				Video recorder			
Kitchen knife set				Rugs			
Liquidiser				Stereo			
Microwave oven				Answering machine			
Mixing bowls				Coffee table			
Oven to tableware				Nest of tables			
Pasta making machine				Occassional tables			
Pedal bin				Carriage clock			
Pressure cooker				Mirrors			
Saucepans				Photograph frames			
Slow cooker				Lamps			
Spice rack				Light fittings			
Storage jars				Paintings/pictures			
Tumble dryer				Furniture			
Washing machine				Other			
Wok				**GENERAL**			
Other				Barbecue			
LINEN				Bathroom scales			
Sheets				Broom			
Pillows				Camcorder			
Pillowcases				Electric drill			
Duvet				Extending ladder			
Duvet cover				Garden furniture			
Valance				Garden tools			
Blankets				Greenhouse			

FOR THE **BRIDE** 85

Figure 4.10 'Gift List,'
            (Early Spring 1998)

to guide the couple through their options…. Many stores offer computerised systems with touch screen facilities and hand held scanners for guests to select their chosen gifts rapidly, with the minimum amount of fuss. To avoid duplications the wedding list is regularly updated.[40]

Thus the 'Tell them what you want' *Bliss* article illustrates what Sharon Boden has identified as the 'superbride' who project manages her own wedding as wish fulfilment.[41] It presents practical reasons for having a commercial list and attempts to dispose of any moral problems associated with issuing instructions to those already obliged to give about exactly what they should buy. Lists placed at shops are practical because they save time and effort; they are the easiest way to ensure the receipt of a complete gift collection. They are the best way of ensuring you have everything or can replace the things you no longer like. It should be noted that parental influence over object choices is rejected for a professional service. Readers are advised not to 'let in-laws offer too much advice' and reassured that 'most stores now have specially trained bridal advisors.' The substitution of family participation for market expertise is obscured by an insistence that the commercial list allows individual choice. Moreover, having it your own way is not inappropriately assertive. Indeed, according to *Bliss,* it is an act of virtue. There is a moral as well as practical argument for a commercial list. The bride's request for her most desired objects is actually unselfish because it brings benefits for those who have to give to her. Because they now know for certain what she wants, making her happy is guaranteed. It is all so easy.

The argument about the ease of commercial lists making them the most practical choice is exactly reproduced within all other bridal magazines. *Wedding and Home* simply states in its 1998 early Spring number that the 'easiest way to compile your list is to place it with a shop or department store.'[42] An issue of *You and Your Wedding* just a month later repeats 'the easiest option is to put your list with a department store who will handle all the administration either in person or over the phone.'[43] Ease is the theme of a thinly veiled promotional piece carried in the same magazine in the previous year. Entitled 'Will it work for you?' it presents the real speech of just married couples next to the store at which they placed their lists. They explain they chose particular commercial services because: 'We wanted as little hassle as possible', 'We thought…it would 'save a lot of hassle' or 'just for the ease of it.'[44] Bridal magazines also argue that lists help the guests as well as those getting married. A 'boon to harassed present buyers' states *For the Bride*.[45] Managing busy lives is, of course, a recurring theme of popular journalism aimed at working-age women. Although 'busy' initially appears as a problem, it always turns out to be a virtue, or at least an attribute of being modern and professional. It is a sign of success and women

40 Riley and Burns, pp. 126–7.
41 Boden, p. 60.
42 'Your Gift List,' *Wedding and Home* Feb–Mar 1998: 89.
43 'The Wedding Organiser,' *You and Your Wedding* Mar–Apr 1998:103
44 'Will it Work for You?' *You and Your Wedding*, Nov–Dec 1997:119.
45 'Wedding Gift Services,' *For the Bride* Autumn 1997: 53.

are dissuaded from reducing their work loads, encouraged to continue their lives at a rapid pace by seeking new technologies of assistance, labour-saving services. As long as the help is professional, a contemporary identity is maintained. As *You and Your Wedding* expressed it: 'Putting together a list – let alone managing it – can be very time consuming so you might want to think about a specialist gift list company to relieve some of the stress.'[46]

The practicality of placing a list at a shop or online service seems so sensible that it overrides any moral dilemmas that might be associated with requesting objects. Furthermore, the aesthetics of completeness is so unquestioned it appears as justifiable need, most effectively realized by the commercial list. However, the issue of asking for expensive things rather than just having reasonable desires fulfilled poses a greater difficulty and is discussed at (slightly) greater length. Despite its assertive headline, the 1998 'Tell them' *Bliss* article, is cautious and reassuring about including expensive objects on a list: 'do include' a few 'more luxurious items' and 'don't feel guilty.' A 1997 review of contemporary gifts, labelled 'trendy' or 'funky', published in *You and Your Wedding* joked about asking for highly priced individual items. 'When can you afford a toilet brush that costs £40?' Alongside an image of a Merdolino cactus shaped brush, the answer followed: 'When you put it on your wedding list!'[47] With fake carelessness, *You and Your Wedding* registered some unease about requests for designer objects, things whose expensive styling transformed them into luxuries. By the twenty-first century, confidence about requesting expensive objects has increased and styling the home has become the purpose of the list. A change of tone is evident in both *You and Your Wedding* and *Bliss*. One argues that lists can be used 'to upgrade what you already have'[48] and the other suggests that: 'If you are the couple that has everything, why not go for gold and ask wedding guests to contribute to a hefty size gift such as the new Sony Wega 42 inch plasma TV?[49]

Encouraging brides to ask for luxury objects as marriage gifts is, in part, an extension of the idea that the wedding is the brides' day.[50] She should have what she wants, down to the last detail. The right to have it, whatever it may be, is also one of the most powerful languages of the market employed to sell disposable luxuries such as chocolate or ice cream. Adverts for these commodities repeat mantra-like phrases such as 'you deserve luxury' or 'treat yourself.'[51] These kinds of statements are used to expand the consumer base for designer objects where quality is discernible in

46 'In Search of the Perfect Wedding List,' *You and Your Wedding* Mar–Apr 2003: 298.

47 'Homes Dossier,' *You and Your Wedding* Nov–Dec 1997: 117.

48 'In Search of the Perfect Wedding List,' *You and Your Wedding* Mar–Apr 2003:298.

49 'Interiors News,' *Bliss for Brides* Feb–Mar 2003:170.

50 The idea of the wedding as the bride's day seems strongest in North America. Chrys Ingraham, *White Weddings: Romancing Heterosexuality in Popular Culture* (London: Routledge, 1999); Cele Otnes and Elizabeth Pleck, *Cinderella Dreams: The Allure of the Lavish Wedding* (Berkeley: University of California Press, 2003).

51 The advertising address to a subject as an individual is considered in Kathy Myers, 'Towards a Theory of Consumption. Tu: a Cosmetic Case Study,' *BLOCK* 7 (1982): 48–59.

small differences: ice-cream that has a slightly stronger vanilla taste, or in the case of wedding presents, a very shiny saucepan that when held feels somewhat heavier than others, or dining cutlery with forms that are more elongated than usual, or cotton sheets that are just that bit thicker. The notion that it is acceptable just this once to indulge yourself with something special is premised upon a hierarchy of objects and of the people who can always afford the most expensive and those who can only occasionally acquire them. Some consumers usually buy cheap stuff while others always have better things. Getting hold of a highly priced commodity that presents those small signs of better quality asserts equal personal value through the market as a momentary exception to the routine rule of inequality. Or in the assertive language of the contemporary market: you too are special enough for that expensive commodity. Thus one of the functions of wedding presents, according to bridal magazines in the twenty-first century, is to validate the bride as an individual. 'Choosing the gifts to put on your wedding list', *Bliss* argues is 'one of the few situations in which you can forget about everyone else and indulge yourself.'[52] For *Wedding and Home*, an ambitious list is the proper expression of the bride herself. 'BRIDGE THE DISTANCE BETWEEN THE SO-SO STYLE OF WHAT YOU ALREADY OWN AND THE FABULOUSLY INDULGENT GIFT LIST ITEMS YOU REALLY DESERVE.'[53]

Claiming the right to have expensive things alters the nature of giving upon marriage. The gift list, at least the kind advocated by the bridal magazines, *asserts* the value of the individual whereas giving without a formal request to do so *confers* value. A detailed list demonstrates that the bride already knows exactly what she is worth; the cited objects function only as monetary measurements of individual esteem. Whereas a gift transaction that appears to be initiated by the giver rather than the receiver, one that begins with an offer rather than a request, endows an object with a social significance that is not necessarily related to its market price. The act of offering anything is an act of inclusion. An offering, and I am referring to both the act and the object, recognizes an individual recipient within a social relationship, it acknowledges them and their place and, at best, approves of them.

Giving and receiving is rarely, if ever, an equal exchange but it is one where obligations are negotiated if not shared. Being grateful for objects that another has decided you should have can be uncomfortable but it is a sociable feeling. Just as to give is to offer an individual a place in a society, to incorporate them into an economic and affective community, to accept a gift is to agree to belong to it. To identify who should give before they give, which is what happens as a list is distributed, makes the act of giving almost redundant and certainly much less meaningful. The community to which the bride belongs has already been determined by who has the list. An object is required to complete the gift transaction although with such a reduced function, it becomes a form as empty as the hastily written or efficiently word-processed letter of thanks exchanged in return. Each time a bride considers having a gift list, she is

52 'Choosing Your Wedding List,' *Bliss for Brides* Feb–Mar 2003:190.
53 'The Luxury Gap,' *Wedding and Home* Apr–May 2003: 213.

deliberating between realising the right to have expensive objects and fulfilling the obligations to accept that which is offered; her choice is made between the isolating freedoms of the market and the regulatory ties of community life.

Increasingly, the bridal magazines deliberate upon the array of choices within the market and that between the market and making your own list is discussed less and less. Thus the debate about how to make a list and what it is for has been resolved, at least for the readership of the bridal magazines. The discussion has moved onto which gift list is the most suitable and the question of whether the bride should distribute one at all is no longer addressed. But the gift list debate was always phoney. The promotional editorial policy of the bridal magazines ensured that every title was little more than the vehicle for the booming gift list industry. Their arguments about the sense and acceptability of commercial lists derive directly from retail publicity and follow their lead. The shifting justifications for having a list, from their usefulness to their ability to realize desires, traced through the bridal magazines at the turn of the twenty-first century, is evident in the gift list industry's own promotional literature. In the late 1990s, for example, Heals described its operation of a gift list as a 'practical service' that 'helps you avoid duplications and ensures that you receive the gifts you really want.'[54] Selfridges make the same claim. Using their Bridal and Gift Registry 'avoids any duplications and ensures that the gifts chosen are those preferred by the list-holder.'[55] By the early years of the twenty-first century pleasure has overtaken practicality as the main reason for a commercial list. Argos announces in its Wedding Gift Service Pack that: 'We think you'll have a lot of fun looking through our catalogue.'[56] Wish fulfilment is the purpose of wrapit. 'We hope,' reads the preface to the guide to its on-line service, 'you will choose wrapit to create the wedding list of your dreams,' concluding with 'We look forward to helping you make this dream come true.'[57]

Making and distributing a list that specified exactly the objects desired as wedding gifts is now a widespread practice and the bridal magazines played a crucial supporting role in making this material practice acceptable. Significantly, their dissemination of information about lists was a function of their promotion of the wedding industries rather than any attempt to engage with their readership or address their actual desires. Commercial development has effected a change in material practices and the meanings that material forms acquired through those practices. Exchange relationships have been altered. With the publication of a gift list, the gift becomes a sign of an individual's own assessment of their value and its ability to express relationships between people, to negotiate value, is superseded.

---

54 'Heal's Wedding Gift Service' (1998).
55 'Selfridges' Bridal and Gift Registry' (1998)
56 'Wedding Gift Service Pack,' Argos (2003).
57 'the wrapit Guide to Your Wedding List' (2003).

Chapter 5

Methods: Mass-Observation

'As most good researchers know, it is not unusual to make up the methods as you go along' (Jim McGuigan, 1997)[1]

Introduction

The analysis of domestic consumption does not belong to any one academic practice or theoretical perspective. Studies of homes and social relationships of domestic exchange are undertaken within a variety of disciplines, including anthropology, sociology, cultural studies and some of the varieties of history, cultural history, design history and history of architecture, in particular. Those researching domestic consumption may belong to any one of these disciplines but also locate their work within the fields of gender studies or studies in material culture and are united by theoretical perspectives rather than disciplinary practice. Such diversity has stalled discussions upon the reflections upon methods and methodology in domestic consumption, and indeed consumption more generally. Indeed, I would even argue that there is some reticence about methodology as an issue. A collegiate culture of polite respect for any method has developed in studies of consumption. Certainly, proponents of gender and of material culture as fields of inquiry have made eloquent cases for the importance cases for their subject of study. For a number of years feminists have argued that investigating the gendered formations will produced an account and analysis of the whole of society because it exposes the systems of difference upon which society is based.[2] Daniel Miller, in particular, has argued for the 'continued importance of material forms' and that material culture is and should remain 'eclectic in its methods.'[3] These quite fiercely held positions about the two

---

1   Jim McGuigan, 'Introduction,' *Cultural Methodologies* ed. Jim McGuigan (London: Sage, 1997) p. 2.

2   Joan Kelly, *Women, History and Theory: The Essays of Joan Kelly* (Chicago: University of Chicago Press, 1984) pp. 1–18 and pp. 51–64.

3   Daniel Miller, 'Why Some Things Matter' *Material Cultures: Why Some Things Matter*, ed. Daniel Miller (London: UCL Press, 1998) pp. 3 and 19. For eclecticism of method in consumption studies see, for example, Alan Warde, 'Afterword: The Future of the Sociology of Consumption,' *Consumption Matters: The Production and Experience of Consumption*, ed. Stephen Edgell, Kevin Etherington and Alan Warde (Oxford: Blackwell Publishers/The Sociological Review, 1996) p. 307 and the range of method within *The Politics of Domestic Consumption,* ed. Stevi Jackson and Shaun Moores, (London: Prentice Hall and Harvester Wheatsheaf, 1995)

fields that contributed greatly to the analysis of consumption are about focus not method. Such respect for different methodologies is productive allowing us all to get on with our studies in our own way, to do the work without having to stand on our principles, defend our way of working and I would certainly not advocate a battle of the disciplines nor do I seek to reopen a epistemological discussion about qualitative versus quantitative studies. However, a series of debates about such practical matters as the merits of small scale or large scale studies the extent to which such studies are absolutely unique or widely representative, or the effect of particular practices of interpretation upon whatever information has been collected would help assess both individual collective scholarship. It would help us reflect on what we can claim to know about the exchange and meaning of things in our lives. One effect of a pluralist, relaxed, live and let live approach to method has been the lack of attention paid to the 'sources' of information. Who exactly are the subjects of our study? Which people? From what places? For example, Peter Lunt and Sonia Livingstone's *Mass Consumption and Personal Identity* (1992), is based on information gathered via questions and interviews from 279 people that were described in their introduction as 'predominately lower middle/upper working class.'[4] Most, they state in their Appendix, were 'living in and around Oxford.'[5] The social and geographic location of their 'respondents' does not necessarily make any of their insightful conclusions about how consumption decisions are entwined with a discourse of morality or ideas about social position less valid but more specific. As they point out, their research is 'not simply generalizable to people living in different socioeconomic conditions.'[6]

Fuller accounts of the subjects we expose to scrutiny, or just some more detail of the people whose practices we study, would deepen our understanding of the ways in which material cultures are shared or specific. There are distinctions and similarities between a British and a Scandinavian home or between a British and a North American wedding. Greater attention to studied constituencies would allow us to see the meanings held in common or how material culture might be used to defend difference. The purpose of this chapter is to examine the methods and sources employed in the study of domesticity and domestic material culture in order to make some assessment of the academic field to which this book, *The Wedding Present* belongs. I discuss a selection of studies of domestic material culture whose conclusions have in some way shaped this book but whose methods to a greater or lesser extent are quite different from my own. Thus this chapter nudges my book towards a conclusion. I also, importantly, reflect upon my method and sources. Although there is always a tendency to justify or even defend work that you have spent years doing, I hope to open up to question my practices of collection and interpretation of accounts of the materiality of everyday domestic life and thereby

---

4   Peter Lunt and Sonia Livingstone, *Mass Consumption and Personal Identity* (Buckingham: Open University Press, 1992) p. 4.
5   Lunt and Livingstone, p. 173.
6   Lunt and Livingstone, p. 4.

contribute to a greater awareness about the extent or the limits of our understanding of the domestic experience.

What follows is a discussion of qualitative interviewing, sociological survey techniques, case studies and ethnography. My review of method begins with a series of works that interrogate the practices of marriage and establishing a married household that have most concerned me. They are not devoted to marriage gifts but explore the wedding ritual and the meanings of marriage. None of these are famous or frequently cited and so are set out in some detail in order to guide the reader through their assertions and arguments as well as discussing the basis upon which such statements are made. Before I begin, I feel I should apologize for the workmanlike nature of this chapter: it places in the main text of a book details of the nitty-gritty side of research that are usually relegated to appendices or footnotes in order to foreground questions of method.

Method and Sources: Studying Weddings and Marriage

In 1980, Diana Leonard published a study, *Sex and Generation*, which she had began 12 years earlier. In it, she provides a meticulously detailed account of the processes of getting married, the 'life-cycle phases of adult children living at home, courtship, and setting up a new household.'[7] But it is not marriage itself that interests her; she studied the 'semi-public events, such as engagements and weddings' as a 'window' through which she could see into the private domain of the family and its perpetually unequal relationships.[8]

Leonard locates *Sex and Generation* as a sociological study and I want to consider Leonard's method investigating marriage in relation two more recent studies, that are also part of a broadly defined sociological field, which focus upon the wedding itself and its material forms. Sharon Boden's *Consumerism, Romance and the Wedding Experience* (2003) seeks to 'understand the wedding as an expanding, commercial phenomenon'[9] while Cele Otnes and Tina Lowrey explores the bride's and the groom's relationship to types of wedding artifacts, identifying gendered differences

---

7   Diana Leonard, *Sex and Generation: A Study of Courtship and Weddings* (London: Tavistock, 1980) p. 256.

8   The term 'window' is taken from a longer phrase 'opening a window onto opaque urban social processes' from R. Frankenburg, 'British Community Studies: Problems of Synthesis,' *The Social Anthropology of Complex Societies*, ed. Michael Banton, (London: Tavistock, 1966).

9   Sharon Boden, *Consumerism, Romance and the Wedding Experience* (Basingstoke: Palgrave, 2003) p. 20. Another important study of contemporary marriages that I do not have space to discuss but should be at least noted here is Penny Mansfield and Jean Collard, *The Beginning of the Rest of Your Life: A Portrait of Newly-Wed Marriage* (London: Macmillan, 1988).

and differences between those that are sacred and those profane.[10] Thus all three studies have a separate object of focus and could be considered complimentary investigations whose conclusions in no way contradict each other. One of Leonard's conclusions (with which, to some extent, my work concurs) is that the practices of getting married are part of a culture of conformity. She states:

> Very, very few people set out to have a consciously different wedding format or make an active gesture of alternative values, which suggests that, in regard to marriage at least, Britain is an extremely cohesive society, with shared values and aspirations across the social strata.[11]

Boden's most important insight relates to how the wedding is imagined and lived out; how differences between fantasy and reality are negotiated through consumer culture.[12] Lowrey and Otnes argue that a greater number of wedding artifacts are more sacred to brides than to grooms confirming the general pattern of gendered 'participation' in 'consumption rituals.'[13] But before using these studies to build an entirely plausible picture of British and North American marriages as a widely shared culture of gender difference that is now also a consumerist dream, an examination of methods these studies employ and the sources they depended upon, ought to prevent us from making all too easy assumptions about western patterns of married life.

Diana Leonard's fieldwork was undertaken in Swansea, South Wales, between November 1968 and March 1969. 'I sought to produce an ethnographic account' she states and, as a 'young, recently married woman'[14] living in the town, described herself as a 'participant observer' that made 'lengthy contact with more than fifty couples around the time of their marriage.' It was 'a haphazard sample' gathered by enquiries made to vicars, ministers, priests and registrars that she characterized as 'fairly homogenous, mostly geographical non-mobile, lower-middle and upper-working class group.'[15] Boden undertook 'qualitative interviews' with 15 couples 'both before and after their own 'big day.'[16] The interviews, semi-structured around 14 leading questions with selected prompts, took place between November 1999 and November 2000. Her informants all lived in the Midlands. She used similar strategies to Leonard in the creation of her sample, contacting vicars and registry

---

10 Otnes and Lowrey's research discussed here is published in two articles: Cele Otnes and Tina M. Lowrey, 'Til Debt Do Us Part: The Selection and Meaning of Artifacts in the American Wedding,' *Advances in Consumer Research* 20 (1993) pp. 325–329 and Tina M. Lowrey and Cele Otnes, 'Construction of a Meaningful Wedding: Differences in the Priorities of Brides and Grooms,' *Gender Issues and Consumer Behaviour*, ed. J.A. Costa (Thousand Oaks: Sage, 1994) pp. 164–183.

11 Leonard, p. 256.

12 Boden, p. 156.

13 Otnes and Lowrey, 'Til Debt Do Us Part' p. 329; Lowrey, and Otnes, 'Construction of a Meaningful Wedding' p. 181.

14 Leonard, pp. 3–4

15 Leonard, pp. 29–30.

16 Boden, p. 20.

offices, but she also advertised in local newspapers, used wedding websites and drew upon 'kinship and friendship networks.' Of her sample, she notes that she 'recruited a reasonable sample of people having commercialized weddings' but was unable to represent the ethnic diversity of the location of her study as 'only white British-born people responded to my invitation to participate in research.' A further important 'bias' that she identified in her research is that while the age of the brides ranged form 20–51 years none were marrying for the second time. It was only first-time brides that Boden noted were 'feeling more excited about the day and wanting to talk about it.'[17] Research produced by Lowrey and Otnes drew upon a sample similar in size to Boden's and they also used the qualitative interview as one of their methods. In the summer months of 1991 in a 'Midwestern city' with a population of 100,000, they established focus groups to discuss 'the ritual artifacts that brides and grooms deem most important in planning their weddings.' They recruited 19 brides and 14 grooms with ages ranging between early 20s and mid-30s through advertisements placed in newspapers and bridal shops. The sample included 'undergraduate and graduate students from the local university and working adults not associated with the university.'[18] They were paid $25. From this group of 33 informants, nine brides participated in 'a more in-depth study of the wedding as consumption ritual.' Otnes and Lowrey explain:

> Brides were paid £40 for participating in two in-depth interviews and allowing the researcher to accompany them on two wedding related shopping trips…. Interviews were structured to examine four aspects of the wedding ritual: artifacts, ritual scripts, performance roles and the ritual audience…. Interviews included scripted questions and carefully scheduled prompts…. Informants chose the sites for all shopping trips. These included: bridal shops, florists, caterers, fabric stores and other speciality shops. Researchers typically spent 1–11/2 hours with informants on each trip. Using interviews and shopping trips allowed us to create a "thick description" of our informant's experiences.[19]

Just setting out of these methods highlight some key differences. There is the question of the sample size. While Boden's was the smallest sample (15 couples or thirty people), it is not significantly different from the 33 people (19 brides and 14 grooms) recruited by Otnes and Lowrey. Moreover, she uses her study to test a theory, 'to offer an empirically grounded exploration of Campbell's Romantic ethic,'[20] the idea that consumption is fuelled by a never fulfilled desire whereas that completed by Otnes and Lowrey is understood as indicative of consumption patterns on the occasion of

---

17 Boden, pp. 160–1.

18 Lowrey and Otnes, 'Construction of a Meaningful Wedding' p. 167.

19 Otnes and Lowrey, 'Til Debt Do Us Part' p. 325.

20 Boden, p. 20. Colin Campbell developed the theory that consumption was shaped by a 'Romantic ethic'. Colin Campbell, *The Romantic Ethic and The Spirit of Modern Consumerism* (Oxford: Blackwell, 1987). I would suggest that his notion of a 'Romantic ethic' refers to a culture of individualism rather than emotion and ideas of love, but this is a side issue given the matter being addressed in this here: the methodological principle of testing theory through empirical research.

'the American wedding.'[21] It is usual to argue that a larger sample is needed for a study to claim to be representative than to question a theoretical proposal. However, the validity of both studies is staked on the type of interviews and not the number of people interviewed, on their quality not quantity. I have described the method employed by Boden and Otnes and Lowrey as qualitative. Boden is very clear on this point. As well as 'qualitative interviews' that were also 'informal' and 'semi-structured', the overall research design is 'a qualitative orientated one.'[22] Qualitative interviews refer to the level of detail in the information collected (for example, Otnes and Lowrey report that 'focus groups and in-depth interactions yielded over 500 pages of text'[23]) and its type, its subjective nature. Otnes and Lowrey wanted to know how brides and grooms felt about the different kinds of objects employed in the wedding rituals and Boden explains that she 'wanted couples to feel able to relate to me their wedding fantasies and desires as well as any fears and frustrations they might have.'[24]

There is, I think, a danger of simply swapping quantity for quality particularly if we question, as we ought, the common sense assumption (that underpins journalist as well as academic interviewing) that the lengthy or relaxed interview that probes for emotional responses inevitably reveals real feelings, the truth behind outward behaviour. These kinds of verbal exchanges can allow the interviewee space and time to present an interior self to an outsider, to compose their feelings into carefully structured narratives. Indeed, unguarded remarks and awkward silences may be just as telling as any confession, which is always staged to some extent.

Thick Description

The display of detail and apparent depth of qualitative interviews are often optimistically considered to be 'thick description' or a contribution to it. Otnes and Lowrey claim this as the status of their research since it combined interviews with shopping trips.[25] They have clearly undertaken intensive forms of fieldwork but thick description, as it is defined in Clifford Geertz's influential 1973 essay of the same name, is an ethnographic way of working.[26] To do justice to Geertz's use of the term it cannot be loosely applied to all qualitative, subjective or small scale studies. Indeed, he outlines what he sees as the best type of ethnographic investigation: 'long-term, mainly (though not exclusively qualitative) highly participative, and

---

21 Otnes and Lowrey, 'Til Debt Do Us Part' p. 329.

22 Boden, p. 160.

23 Otnes and Lowrey, 'Til Debt Do Us Part' p. 325.

24 Boden, p. 160.

25 Otnes and Lowrey, 'Til Debt Do Us Part' p. 325.

26 Clifford Geertz, *The Interpretation of Cultures,* 1973 (London: Fontana, 1993) pp. 3–30. The full title of the essay is 'Thick Description: Towards an Interpretative Theory of Culture.'

almost obsessively fine-comb study in confined contexts.'[27] Of the three studies of marriage that I have discussed here, it is Leonard's slow burning Swansea research undertaken when she was a newly wed living in the town that is closest to Geertz's thick description. It was also, we should note, the largest study.

I am tempted, as you can see, to use thick description as a standard of measurement of method but it is not, in the way it is introduced by Geertz, reducible to method. Thick description is 'a kind of intellectual effort.'[28] Although his essay is frequently cited in debates about methodology,[29] it is actually addressed to an epistemological concern, to the question of what it is possible to know about another culture. We can guess. 'Cultural analysis is (or should be)', he argues, 'guessing at meanings, assessing the guesses, and drawing explanatory conclusions from the better guesses.'[30] Interpretation, or more precisely 'constructing a reading,'[31] is advocated against the false promise of totalizing knowledge delivered through high theory. For Geertz, ethnography has to be a practice of reading because culture is 'semiotic'; it is, as he famously put it, 'the webs of significance' that man 'himself has spun.'[32] Thus thick description is interpretation. I would say that much stronger distinctions need to be made between an interpretative study and a qualitative one. For example, to read an interview, regardless of its subjective content, as a truth is not interpretative. It should be recognized that all description, thick or thin, is a translation, a text created out of the different positions that the researcher and informant occupy. Thick ones are produced from lengthy but specific studies, 'exceedingly extended acquaintances with extremely small matters.'[33]

Geertz's entire essay can be read as a declaration that specific cultures may be just that and as warning against claims to generalize about them. It has provided the impetus and justification for small, interpretative studies that are engaged in a search for specific meanings rather than large-scale patterns. Small scale studies have been adopted by all the disciplines involved in the analysis of consumption, including sociology that has been the home of quantitative analysis, the survey. Surveys could be regarded as the anti-thesis of thick description because they aim to make generalizations possible.

---

27 Geertz, p. 23.

28 Geertz, p. 6.

29 Graham Murdock, 'Thin Descriptions: Questions of Method in Cultural Analysis,' *Cultural Methodologies*, ed. Jim McGuigan (London: Sage, 1997) pp. 178–192.

30 Geertz, p. 20.

31 Geertz, p. 18.

32 Geertz, p. 5.

33 Geertz, p. 21.

Surveys and Quantitative Analysis

Although one of the most influential texts on consumption, Pierre Bourdieu's *Distinction* (1984), is based on a large-scale survey of 1,217 people,[34] surveys as tools of analysis are not fashionable. Such large-scale surveys are rarely initiated by academics and there few equivalents to the scale of information gathering about cultural forms that Bourdieu has directed. Furthermore, he and his teams of researchers translated the findings of his surveys into statistics; *Distinction* is a work of quantitative analysis. Bourdieu's method is not entirely quantitative, of course, but some of the most important and most cited moments in the text, such as manual and clerical workers preference for the Blue Danube or their lack of competence when talking about art, occur when statistical evidence is compiled.[35] Key insights into the class politics of taste, the persistence of cultural regularities, or what could be called consumption patterns, derive from statistical mappings of preferences. But it is Bourdieu's conclusions and the models of culture that he generated that have been so profoundly influential and not his methods. When studies based on surveys are published they tend to be widely cited despite the unfashionability of surveys as a method. This method, therefore, has an important place in the historiography of consumption and continues to be used as authority for a range of statements about human-object relations. Not all surveys are the same. Here I want to look at three very different survey methodologies that underpinned the research for Susan Pearce's *Collecting in Contemporary Practice* (1998), Mihaly Csikszentmihalyi and Eugene Rochberg-Halton's *The Meaning of Things* (1981) and David Cheal's *The Gift Economy* (1988).

Although Pearce's *Collecting in Contemporary Practice* (1988) is the most recent of the texts that I shall discuss here, it employs the most conventional survey method. The method evoked by the word survey is in fact only one survey type, used in the research for this book. *Collecting in Contemporary Practice* (1998) is based on a postal questionnaire sent out to a large randomly selected sample of individual adults. The Contemporary Collecting in Britain Survey was sent out between July and August 1993 to 1,500 addresses extracted from the electoral registers and 836 'usable' forms were returned a respectable reply rate of 57 per cent. Information provided on the returned forms was categorized then translated into statistics and displayed as graphs. 'Each question on the questionnaire was cross-tabulated against all of the demographic variables to yield a run of bar charts showing comparative percentages.'[36]

A focus of Pearce's research, of which The Contemporary Collecting in Britain Survey is an important part, has been the uncovering of collecting practices characteristic of everyday life: who collects which kinds of objects and how and why

---

34 Pierre Bourdieu, *Distinction: A Social Critique of the Judgement of Taste*, 1979, (London: Routledge, 1989).

35 Bourdieu, pp. 17 and 90.

36 Susan M. Pearce, *Collecting in Contemporary Practice* (London: Sage, 1998) 191.

they do so. The site of such collecting activity is the home and Pearce's interest in this 'major social and individual phenomenon'[37] is a particular way of envisioning some of the practices I have tended to call domestic. Surveying, especially a postal survey designed to be self-explanatory, easily filled in with information ready to be grouped into categories and so, for the most part comprising boxes to be ticked[38] is a very particular way of investigating domestic arrangements; it is a search for typicality or frequencies, a drawing of individual experience into a pattern. It answers questions about how often women collect textiles or men catalogue collections of old watches. The Contemporary Collecting in Britain Survey provided statistical authority for observable cultural formations. Its numerical force enables Pearce to confirm the existence of gendered domestic material culture:

> It is immediately apparent that the great bulk of collecting is carried out within, rather than in any defiance or subversion of, traditional patterns of gender image: women collect soft, pretty, display-worthy things, and men collect metal goods with which things can be done. There is no evidence here of widespread dissatisfaction with traditional, even stereotyped, gender roles. On the contrary, people seem very happy to collect well-established gender styles without any sense of strain, and this in spite of the fact that such an essentially private habit could be an excellent vehicle for rebellion or diversity. [39]

These kinds of general arguments can be made because the survey is understood to be representative. It aimed 'to achieve a representative sample of the whole of the adult British population'[40] and could claim to do so, according to Pearce because there was a large enough randomly selected group who completed the postal questionnaire in confidence with little external pressure or interference.

The representativeness of the survey that underpinned Csikszentmihalyi and Rochberg-Halton's book, *The Meaning of Things* (1981) was based on the opposite principle: deliberate and careful selection not random procedure. Csikszentmihalyi and Rochberg-Halton set out to discover the symbolic nature of everyday domesticity in modern capitalist culture and appropriately enough basing their efforts on a 'major

---

37 Pearce, 1998, p. 1. See also Susan M. Pearce, *On Collecting: An Investigation into Collecting in the European Tradition* (London: Routledge, 1995).

38 There were also questions 'which called for a written reply' notes Pearce, *Collecting in Contemporary Practice* p. 18. A small number of the 836 random sample, 27 in all, also agreed to a telephone interview (189–190) and a further 201 collectors who had been involved in the People's Shows (18–19) completed the survey. These additional sources of information were not integrated into the statistical analysis but drawn upon in the discursive sections of the book.

39 Pearce, *Collecting in Contemporary Practice*, p. 135. Because the collecting Pearce is investigating takes place within homes it is unlikely, I think, to subvert the gendering of material forms. To do so would be un-home like, against the orderings of objects through which we know a home.

40 Pearce, *Collecting in Contemporary Practice*, p. 186.

metropolitan area' of 'contemporary urbanised America.'[41] Underlying their study was a search for the survival of meaningfulness in an alienated world. It was rewarded. 'Despite the fact that so many objects are mass-produced today, it is still possible to achieve some unique expression by careful selection and combination of items.'[42] Their optimism about the potential individuality of standardized domestic commodities is less cited than their conclusions about domesticity itself. They famously state that 'a home is much more than a shelter; it is a word in which a person can create a material environment that embodies what he or she considers significant.' [43]

That consumption, including domestic consumption, is an expression of individuality is no longer controversial (although disputed by some studies, including this one, which emphasize that consumption is not necessarily individualistic). Back in 1981, or rather 1977 when their research was conducted, Csikszentmihalyi and Rochberg-Halton wanted to make a case that people could create personal meanings with their possessions and this, a generalization about the human condition at the end of the twentieth century, required a particular type of survey. They needed to create a representative sample to study and therefore selected, with some rigour, who could participate. They chose two neighbouring areas of Chicago, Rogers Park and Evanston because 'both have a long tradition of social, ethnic and economic diversity' and within these areas they sought out a 'socioeconomically stratified sample of three-generation families' using 'census tract information concerning income' and canvassing door-to-door and by telephone. This process produced a sample of 82 families and a total of 315 people, of which 174 were female and 141 male.[44] The strength of the sample was its intergenerational character[45] but even according to their own account, it was a middle class study. The economic character of the sample had an ethnic dimension; it was 67 per cent 'white', 30 per cent 'black' with 3 per cent belonging to 'other' categories. Csikszentmihalyi and Rochberg-Halton state:

> Of the whites, 66 per cent received an upper-middle class socioeconomic rating, and the remaining 34 per cent were placed in the lower-middle class whereas only 22 per cent of the blacks were in the upper-middle class and 79 per cent in were in the lower-middle class.[46]

---

41 Mihaly Csikszentmihalyi and Eugene Rochberg-Halton, *The Meaning of Things: Domestic Symbols and the Self* (Cambridge: Cambridge University Press, 1981) p. x. 'We wanted to examine,' they state here, 'the role of objects in people's definition of who they are, of who they have been, and who they wish to become.'

42 Csikszentmihalyi and Rochberg-Halton, p. 94.

43 Csikszentmihalyi and Rochberg-Halton, p. 123.

44 Csikszentmihalyi and Rochberg-Halton, pp. 250–1.

45 The sample was composed of fairly equal numbers of grandparents and children, 77 and 79 respectively. Children were defined as sons and daughters between the ages of 8 and 30 living in family homes. Not surprisingly since the middle generation are most often the householder, the largest numbers of respondents were parents, 82 mothers and 68 fathers. Csikszentmihalyi and Rochberg-Halton, p. 251.

46 Their class definitions were based on occupation and education of the 'middle-generation' father. Csikszentmihalyi and Rochberg-Halton, p. 251.

These middle-class people from north Chicago were interviewed in their own homes, 'where we could see and discuss the things that were part of their everyday lives.' The key question on their pre-determined interview schedule was: 'What are the things in your home which are special for you?'[47] Csikszentmihalyi and Rochberg-Halton state that their method was 'basically ethnographic', defining this as:

> to describe as precisely and completely as possible the phenomena to be studied, using the language and the conceptual categories of the respondents themselves. It was to be a descriptive study.... Classifications of objects and meanings were to be derived from their responses.[48]

Collecting information from people within specific locations, examining how they rank their possessions, using their terms as tools of analysis, arguing that theory should be developed from practice are all ethnographic manoeuvres. But their interviews produced data for statistical analysis. A list of 1,694 objects with 7,875 significations was created and divided into 10 classes and 37 categories of meaning.[49] Their respondents do have a place in the text that their interviews generated and extracts from the interviews are cited at different points but the overriding tendency of *The Meaning of Things* is to reduce description, their ethnography, to numerical signs. This a little bit like saying that qualitative research has been transformed into quantitative analysis. For example, one of the 'most cherished objects in the home' categories is 'plates' which covered dishes, china, cups, mugs and pewter trays. Plates, Csikszentmihalyi and Rochberg-Halton report, are mentioned as special by 15 per cent of their respondents.[50] This bare statistic is misleading for a number of reasons. It is a rather artificial grouping of objects that mixes media (ceramic and pewter) and rank (cups and mugs) that other studies of domesticity have indicated are regarded very differently. At best, then, the 15 per cent is an average of differential values of the many different objects that can be drawn into the category of plates and at worst it hides more than it reveals. 15 per cent is a measurement of personal significance in an unequally shared domestic space although such figures are used, ultimately, to re-describe that space, to suggest the meanings of the home as a whole. Respondents were asked to identify which objects were special to them. Thus high scoring objects are quite likely to be the common denominators across all the generations that occupied the home and not necessarily those things most significant to those who were responsible for the arrangement of domestic space: wives and mothers. More important than these criticisms, which can be levelled at any attempt to categorize, is that flat statistical figures tell very little about content of the relationships to objects. It is the narrative detail of the initial interviews cited by Csikszentmihalyi and Rochberg-Halton that are more revealing in this respect.

---

47 Csikszentmihalyi and Rochberg-Halton, pp. x and 257.
48 Csikszentmihalyi and Rochberg-Halton, p. x.
49 Csikszentmihalyi and Rochberg-Halton, p. 268.
50 Csikszentmihalyi and Rochberg-Halton, p. 82.

Like that of Csikszentmihalyi and Rochberg-Halton, David Cheal's work affirms the continuing significance of the domestic domain in a modern world; he studies gift transactions in contemporary capitalist societies. This shared focus aside, Cheal's *The Gift Economy* (1988) differs from Csikszentmihalyi and Rochberg-Halton's *The Meaning of Things* (1981) in a number of important respects, not least because his work is directed at the exchange rather than ownership of objects and at relationships of exchange within the domestic domain, or what he would call the moral economy, rather than the identity of individual participants. Cheal argues that gift transactions are 'used in the ritual construction of small social worlds.'[51] Cheal's survey method differs significantly also.

The Gift Economy is based on a research project entitled the Winnipeg Ritual Cycle Study wherein 80 adults (52 women and 28 men) were interviewed between November 1982 and February 1983. They were asked to recount all gifts that they had given and received during 1982 and 'a number of discursive questions about gift giving' were put in order to 'elicit the interviewees interpretations of their gift practices.' Details of gift transactions were entered onto a colour coded system while answers to the 'discursive questions' were taped and transcribed with field notes and 'were treated as qualitative materials from which a deeper understanding of the individual cases could be obtained.'[52] A further study of 'valuable Christmas gifts and wedding gifts' based on a 'random sample of 573 adult members of the population of Winnipeg' was used as 'a check on the validity' of the Winnipeg Ritual Cycle Study.[53]

While Cheal's work clearly lies within sociology survey methodology frameworks, he makes no claims about the representative nature of his study, indeed quite the reverse. With an 'intensive' study such as the Winnipeg Ritual Cycle 'it is not possible to count on having a representative sample of the population of a large urban center such as Winnipeg'. And he adds, 'That disadvantage, from the statistical point of view, can be turned into an advantage from certain theoretical points of view.'[54] Instead of using a simple standard of representativeness (finding enough people who belong to different types of communities so that the sample becomes like the population from which it is taken and the survey is an analogy of the society being studied), he uses a technique of purposive sampling, a comparative method that allows for the development of theoretical 'propositions', which can

51 David Cheal, *The Gift Economy* (London: Routledge, 1988) p. 16. He also goes on to argue that the gift economy is '*a system of redundant transactions within a moral economy, which makes possible the extended reproduction of social relations,*' p. 19 (original emphasis). A key similarity between Cheal's work and that of Csikszentmihalyi and Rochberg-Halton is their engagement with symbolic interactionism. See comments in Aafke Komter, 'Introduction,' *The Gift: An Interdisciplinary Perspective*, ed. Aafke Komter (Amsterdam: Amsterdam University Press) p. 6.

52 Cheal, pp. 29–31.

53 Cheal, p. 26. Another discrete piece of research informed Cheal's analysis, the Hotel Chateau Study, which comprised interviews with 18 newlyweds in 1981.

54 Cheal, p. 26.

be tested within the research, rather than 'representative' statements. Purposive sampling 'involves identifying *comparison groups* whose similarities and difference seem likely to generate theoretically useful insights.'[55]

Thus Cheal's method of purposive sampling resembles that of the case study, at least as defined by J. Clyde Mitchell. Case studies are not, or should not be according to Mitchell, compilations of "'apt illustrations.'" Their strengths are not the identification of representative cultural forms but the principles that operate within them and may operate in other cases.[56] Case studies enable provisional theoretical propositions to be made. Indeed, the implication of case study methodology is that all theory is provisional. It is as a case study in this strict sense that I introduced Mass-Observation.

Ethnographies

Clifford Geertz remarked that ethnography is what anthropologists do.[57] It has also become the method of choice for those working in cultural studies as well as some sociologists and design historians.[58] However, for anthropologists, ethnography is the sum of practices, often labelled participant observation, that are undertaken during a prolonged period of fieldwork whereas in other disciplines ethnography is often reduced to interviews with people. More attention needs to be paid to the dynamics of interviewing, to differences between qualitative and ethnographic interviewing. Asking numerous people the same questions from an interview schedule is quite distinct from 'conversations' within an ethnography that may raise questions that shape further conversations.[59] The problem with attempts 'to stretch the definition of ethnography to cover almost any attempt to collect extended accounts of people's

---

55 Cheal, pp. 26–7. Within the Winnipeg Ritual Cycle study the comparison groups were Anglo-Canadians and Ukrainian Canadians.

56 J. Clyde Mitchell, 'Case Studies,' *Ethnographic Research: A Guide to General Conduct*, ed. R. F. Ellen, (London: Academic Press, 1984) p. 238.

57 Geertz, p. 5.

58 Judith Attfield, 'Moving Home: Changing Attitudes to Residence and Identity,' *The Journal of Architecture* 7 (2002) pp. 249 and 261; Judith Attfield, *Wild Things: The Material Culture of Everyday Life* (Oxford: Berg, 2000) pp. 256–261; Richard Johnson, Deborah Chambers, Parvati Raghuram, Estella Tincknell, The *Practice of Cultural Studies* (London: Sage, 2004) pp. 205–224.

59 A. P. Cohen, 'Informants,' *Ethnographic Research: A Guide to General Conduct*, ed. R. F. Ellen, (London: Academic Press, 1984) pp. 225–229. I would also argue that oral history interviewing is distinct from both qualitative research and ethnography. Despite its potential oral history has been rarely used in the analysis of domesticity. An important exception is Judy Attfield, 'Inside Pram Town: a Case Study of Harlow House Interiors, 1951–1961' *View from the Interior: Feminism. Women and Design,* eds Judy Attfield and Pat Kirkham (London: The Women's Press, 1989) pp. 215–238. See also the introduction to this essay in *The Politics of Domestic Consumption,* eds. Stevi Jackson and Shaun Moores, (London: Prentice Hall and Harvester Wheatsheaf, 1995) p. 290.

beliefs,' as Graham Murdock argues, is the absence of 'a rounded account of the ways that people's utterances, expressions and self-presentations are shaped and altered by the multiple social contexts they have to navigate in the course of their daily lives.'[60]

Here I want to briefly identify the characteristics of an anthropologist's ethnography, an extended social encounter combining observations of and discussions with people. Daniel Miller's writings, always directed at raising the profile of studies in material culture have also without doubt, but much less deliberately, contributed to the popularity of ethnography as a method of investigating contemporary consumption. He carried out, with Alison Clarke, one of the most influential ethnographies of consumption practices, or as Clarke puts it, 'the provisioning of households in north London.'[61] Their study developed a number of ideas, or more precisely theoretical propositions, about consumption and its place in everyday life that have been incorporated into the analysis of consumption that extends some way beyond north London. A notion of a house as a process, the idea consumption as appropriation and an understanding of shopping as an act of sacrifice that routinely stages the historical contradictions of oppression and power derived from this ethnography.[62]

Neither Miller nor Clarke make great play about how they studied the north London Street they called Jay Road, but given the importance of this work as a source for theory, it is worth considering their methods. Their research took place in a 'confined context,'[63] a specific location but with characteristics from which it might be possible to generalize from. Miller states:

> The street where the ethnography took place was chosen partly because it lacked any outstanding features. One side is mainly occupied by council estates. Although clearly working class, they are not the most impoverished of such estates. Most of the other side is owner occupied, but although more likely to be middle class it is not especially wealthy. There are many people in the area who were born in places other than Britain, but there is no single alternative place of origin that is conspicuous. In short, the street is typical of north London in being cosmopolitan but manifestly ordinary.[64]

Clarke identifies the different housing types within their 'ethnographic site' indicating the way in it could potentially include a wide spectrum of home-making strategies. It consisted of:

---

60 Murdock, p. 184.

61 Alison J. Clarke, 'The Aesthetics of Social Aspiration,' *Home Possessions: Material Culture Behind Closed Doors*, ed. Daniel Miller (Oxford: Berg, 2001) p. 25.

62 Clarke 2001, pp. 23–45; Daniel Miller, 'Appropriating the State on the Council Estate,' *Man* 23 (1988) pp. 353–372; Daniel Miller, *A Theory of Shopping* (Cambridge: Polity Press, 1998) Clarke 2001, pp. 23–45. See also Alison J. Clarke, 'Window Shopping at Home: Classifieds, Catalogues and New Consumer Skills,' *Material Cultures: Why Some Things Matter*, ed. Daniel Miller (London: UCL Press, 1998) pp. 73–99.

63 Geertz, p. 23.

64 Daniel Miller, 'Possessions,' *Home Possessions: Material Culture Behind Closed Doors*, ed. Daniel Miller (Oxford: Berg, 2001) p. 113.

a cross-section of housing: 1960s blocks of council (State owned) flats and maisonettes; semi-detached 1930s homes; Edwardian rented and small-owner occupied maisonettes as well as larger Victorian family houses occupied predominately by middle-class families on adjoining streets.[65]

They worked with 76 households over three years in the late 1980s observing and asking about their 'formal' and 'informal' provisioning practices. Clarke states 'initial stages of the ethnography...combined preliminary interviews and participant observation.'[66] Further interviews and participation in specific shopping practices followed. For Miller, there is a productive tension between observing and interviewing. There are differences between what people say they do and what they actually do[67] that has implications for ethnographies that rely upon only one of these methods. He also notes that interviewing and observations that made up the Jay Road ethnographic fieldwork were supplemented by forms of storytelling:

> one of our techniques (which we undertook together), was to ask people stories about how objects in the living room and kitchen were obtained and came to be in the place they now occupy. This provided us with narratives not only of how people came to own these goods but the subsequent issues over how these goods should be consumed in the longer term.[68]

The authority of ethnography is not only established through its mix of information gathering techniques deployed over a long period but also its specificity. Representativeness is not sought after as it is with a survey. Claims to know about consumption or whatever else is being studied are based on the saturation of detail relating to just one case. The question that arises is not is it representative, but can the same cultural formations be seen to occur in another place? Does it confirm or suggest the re-evaluation of ways of thinking about or theorizing cultural practices, such as consumption? Are there principles or theoretical propositions that apply elsewhere? Each ethnography calls for another to be conducted. One approach to ethnographic practice is that it is impossible, or at the very least flawed, to generalize from any study but each can contribute to a comparative project that will ultimately enable us to see the broad sweeps of culture, such as the shared and unique, collective and particular forms of consumption and domesticity.[69] However, for this comparative project to really develop, it requires those involved in the analysis of domestic consumption of contemporary societies to pay close and critical attention to the work of others, to the method as well as the content of the studies within their field.

---

65 Clarke, 'The Aesthetics of Social Aspiration' p.26.

66 Clarke, 'The Aesthetics of Social Aspiration' p. 25. Clarke defines formal provisioning as shopping at retail outlets and informal as a slighter wider range of activities: non-market transactions, second-hand and catalogue shopping.

67 Miller, *A Theory of Shopping* (Cambridge: Polity Press, 1998) pp. 65–72.

68 Miller, 'Possessions' p. 113.

69 Daniel Miller, 'Introduction,' *Home Possessions: Material Culture Behind Closed Doors*, ed. Daniel Miller (Oxford: Berg, 2001) p. 2.

In the ordinary way of lining up alongside one interpretation and rejecting another, scholars are of course contributing to a comparative project. For example, Marianne Gullestad's notion of the home as a 'cultural symbol' that is 'highly gendered and highly *shared*'[70] as well as her positioning of home decoration in a culture of conformity grounded in an ethnography of urban working class families in Bergen has been applied in other European contexts.[71] But she argues anyway that ethnography can have immediate relevance beyond its confined context or as she puts its 'defined physical locations.'[72] She states:

> I want to create a systematic argument for the idea that such partcultural practices may contain information about cultural processes in a wider region, be it Norway, Scandinavia, the Nordic countries of northern Europe.[73]

Home decoration, as she defines it, is a 'partcultural' practice. Continuing her larger argument about the relevance of a specific study, she adds:

> I do not see this as a question of "generalisation" of qualitative analysis. Such phrasing of the problem very quickly leads to questions of sampling and boundaries which make anthropologists look like bad survey sociologists. I would rather like to rephrase the problem as one of "range", "extent", "era and area of relative power" of our interpretations. I would argue that we sometimes have to dare to stretch our observations to produce attempts at synthesis, knowing full well that these are provisional and partial constructions. Synthesizing interpretations have to be based on extensive evidence, but they cannot be completely documented. Such attempts at synthesis can then be checked with further observations and interpretations.[74]

Her confidence about how far her interpretations might reach are related the scope of her ethnography, to her gathering of 'extensive evidence.' Her understanding of the function of strategies of home making she calls home decoration in the maintenance of social identities set out in *The Art of Social Relations* (1992) is based on 'long-term fieldwork' on two separate occasions with urban working class families in Bergen as well as the analysis of written autobiographies from 'all over Norway'. Thus you could say that she drew upon a smaller and larger ethnographic sites and was able to see what concepts travelled between them.[75]

---

70 Marianne Gullestad, *The Art of Social Relations: Essays on Culture, Social Action, and Everyday Life in Modern Norway* (Oslo: Scandinavian University Press, 1992) p. 64.

71 Daniel Miller, 'Consumption and its Consequences,' *Consumption and Everyday Life*, ed. Hugh Mackay (London: Sage Publications, 1997) pp. 51–52.

72 Gullestad, p. 26.

73 Gullestad, p. 20.

74 Gullestad, p. 27.

75 Gullestad, p. 64. Her work with 'young working-class mothers' was initially published in Marianne Gullestad, *Kitchen-table Society* (Oslo: Universitetsforlaget, 1984) p. 49. She carried out two years of fieldwork with 15 women that began in 1979.

Examining the methods and sources of any study tends to lead us towards making statements about the limits of its explanatory force, asserting its cultural specificity and saying, in usually quite sophisticated ways, that it only happens like that over there. We should guard against undermining the efforts of scholars working in fields other than our own, whose methods have integrity within their disciplines, but this should be tempered with the acknowledgement that, in general, we claim to know too much. For instance, as I reflect upon the studies that have informed my own, outlined within this chapter, it becomes impossible not to notice that whilst they have been conducted in a variety of locations (Oxford, South Wales, Chicago, Winnipeg, North London and Norway to name a few) most of the people studied are urban waged or salaried workers, the lower middle or working classes.[76] I have realized that I know little about consumption practices of the very poor, the very rich or those living in rural areas. My involvement in the Mass-Observation Contemporary Project and interest in 'ordinary peoples'' writing explains but does not, of course, excuse this absence. Acknowledging the limitations or specificity of a body of work is humbling but also critically constructive. Above all, it shows where new work and more work are needed.

Mass-Observation

Diary writing and other forms of autobiography have a reasonably secure place in ethnographic methodologies. It would not be at all difficult to make a convincing argument that the Mass-Observation Archive, which comprises boxes of writing from people who call themselves 'ordinary' that offer their experiences and views of aspects of everyday life and reflections upon how national and international events are played out in everyday life, is ethnographic. I do not want to make this claim just yet, if at all. Before I position, categorize, or label Mass-Observation writing, I want to discuss its usefulness, or otherwise, as a source for understanding domestic exchange relationships and examine my own method. In other words, I will try to practice what I have preached.

The status of Mass-Observation as ethnography proper and therefore as an appropriate source for the study of domesticity, consumption or everyday life is ambiguous. In its early inter-war days, it had some very eminent anthropological critics, no less than Bronislaw Malinowski and Raymond Firth. The founders of Mass-Observation, Charles Madge, Tom Harrisson and Humphrey Jennings sought the approval of the community of professional anthropologists to which they to greater

---

76 One exception to this is Suzanne Reimer and Deborah Leslie, 'Identity, Consumption and the Home,' *Home Cultures*, 1.2 (2004) p. 190, study home furnishings based on interviews of manufacturers, retailers, designers, magazine editors and consumers that were 'middle-class to upper middle-class urban dwellers.' The study that most forcefully demonstrates the limited 'range' and 'extent' (Gullestad, *The Art of Social Relations*, p. 27) of this one is Pnina Werbner, *The Migration Process: Capital, Gifts and Offerings among British Pakistanis* (Oxford: Berg, 2002).

and lesser extents belonged, but they did not wholeheartedly receive it. Malinowski wrote a 'relatively complimentary' introduction to the first Mass-Observation publication, *First Year's Work* (1938). However he believed that its founders placed false hopes in the creation of an objective record instead of developing an objective analysis. Mass-Observers could not represent the facts of British society and like other subjects of ethnography relayed 'stories and myths' that then required anthropological analysis.[77] Importantly, this is not criticism of Mass-Observation material but of the attitude of the founders towards it. Firth's concerns also relate to the lack of methodological rigour in the conduct of Mass-Observation investigations and the dissemination of their results. He thought Mass-Observation writing was impressionistic and the status of the paid Mass-Observers, those sent out to observe and interview British people returning their findings for collation, interpretation and publication by Harrisson, Madge or Jennings, troubled Firth.[78] They were neither nor anthropologists nor their informants but somewhere in between, not quite the subjects of study or those that carried it out.

The Contemporary Mass-Observation Project, of which the Giving and Receiving Presents directive is a small part, may be viewed as redressing the problems of the early Mass-Observation material and placing new work on a surer academic footing by only drawing upon one of its early methods: the panel of writers. They are the informants, their writings are read by researchers and thus the appropriate critical distance is established. Although this account of the re-launch of Mass-Observation in the 1980s is rather neat it does not take into account the disciplinary shifts within which its contemporary work should be located. The Mass-Observation Archive can now be regarded as a much more viable ethnography for two closely related reasons. Firstly, objectivity has been recognized as an unfulfilled promise of science that assumes hovering somewhere is a neutral space to which the researcher could remove himself or herself from the context that he or she inhabits or studies. Secondly, the interpretative role of 'informants' has been embraced. Acts of communication with anthropologists, or anyone else, are mediations of subjectivity, performances of identity. A re-evaluation of signs of subjectivity in academic practice as the only source material of social life that we have has invested Mass-Observation with newfound authority.

If the problem of subjectivity of Mass-Observation writings has been resolved, or at least not regarded as a obstacle to the truths of culture by researchers who have rejected scientific authority as the trappings of grandeur, as the emperor's new clothes, there remains an issue about representativeness. Dorothy Sheridan has been very clear about the ways in which Mass-Observation material is not representative. 'The people who write for Mass-Observation live throughout the United Kingdom,

---

77 Dorothy Sheridan, Brain Street, David Bloome, *Writing Ourselves. Mass-Observation and Literacy Practices* (New Jersey: Hampton Press, 2000) p. 86. They are citing from Bronislaw Malinowski, 'A Nation-wide Intelligence Service' *The First Year's Work*, Charles Madge and Tom Harrisson (London: Lindsay Drummond, 1938) p. 98.

78 Sheridan, Street and Bloome, pp. 88–93

although primarily in England,' she states and around the time the Giving and Receiving Presents directive was sent out 'the majority of correspondents are over 45 years of age and 70 per cent of them are women.' Thus, Mass-Observation writing, as Sheridan plainly points out, derives 'from a statistically unrepresentative sample of the population.'[79] A self-selecting group could not be otherwise. The value of Mass-Observation is not predicated on being a small scale version of the British population, on being a kind of microcosm or analogy; it is, as I have noted already, a case study. Case studies are not small surveys; they are descriptions of specific practices located in particular times and spaces or enacted by particular groups of people. The contribution a case study makes to scholarship can be its specificity alone, the understanding of just that moment, that place, those people. Its relevance may also be that an understanding of one social or cultural formation can generate ways of thinking about similar phenomena in other contexts. Case studies should not be pressed into a projection of their findings onto other people or places but used to develop theoretical propositions. Instead of regarding the replies to the Giving and Receiving Presents directive as a terrible survey sample, which extends the inherent bias of Mass-Observation because it contains too much writing from older women who married in the third quarter of the twentieth century, this is its strength as a case study. It is a rich source relating to the subjects at the centre of gift giving relationships.

A case study does need to be located. Given the disparateness of Mass-Observation correspondents, it is important to consider how this important principle of case study methodology applies. We could call Mass-Observation a British case study because it involves people throughout Britain, from the conurbations along the south coast of England, to small communities in North Wales and large provincial cities such as Liverpool and beyond. But what connects them is not necessarily their national identity, an idea of Britishness that may or may not be held in common: their shared practice is writing. Mass-Observation, as it is currently configured, is an 'ordinary people's' writing project. Dorothy Sheridan with Brian Street and David Bloome have paid close attention to conditions in which Mass-Observation correspondents write, situating the material that I and other researchers have spent years poring over. As I hope I emphasized enough in my introduction to this book, my interpretation of Mass-Observation material has been shaped by their understanding of writing as a 'literary practice,' as a social act. Sheridan, Street and Bloome are particularly concerned to resist the reduction of writing to its socially legitimate form, the published text. They state:

> As people conduct their daily business, whether at home, at work, at school, or elsewhere, they use written language to get things done, to communicate with others, to establish and maintain social relationships, to enact rituals, to create meaning. [80]

---

79 Dorothy Sheridan, '"Damned Anecdotes and Dangerous Confabulations": Mass-Observation as Life History,' *Mass-Observation Archive Occasional Paper*, No. 7 (Brighton: University of Sussex Library, 1996) p. 2; Sheridan, Street and Bloome, p. 13.

80 Sheridan, Street and Bloome, p. 3.

The Mass-Observation Archive is one of the very few sites where a record is kept of writing that is a part of an ordinary or everyday world. It is important to remember that Mass-Observation writers are as committed to this project of recording everyday life as it is lived by 'ordinary people' as the Mass-Observation archivists and researchers, if not more so. They cannot, therefore, be regarded as passive informants, but as interpreters of their own lives. Mass-Observation material avoids easy academic categorization; it is 'part history project, part anthropology, part auto/biography, part social commentary'[81] because it began in an everyday world where all these things are tangled up together. Mass-Observation is housed in a University setting but is not written according to its rules of dividing up knowledge into different disciplinary practices.

However, I cannot really avoid calling the Contemporary Mass-Observation Project, including the Giving and Receiving Presents directive, an ethnographic project because it lines up so well with Geertz's account of the inevitability of ethnography as 'constructing a reading.'[82] My reading of the meanings of material culture of married domesticity began by examining a reading produced, that is, written, by someone else. But reading writing is not what is usually meant by doing an ethnography, regardless of the place of autobiographies within the ethnographic tradition.[83] There are, of course, important and obvious differences between reading the responses to an open-ended questionnaire and talking to someone face-to-face. The researcher in the Mass-Observation Archive does not see the Mass-Observation writer is not able to identify them through their age, their dress, the colour of their skin, their accent. They may some advantages to reading over interviewing in that it prevents the all too easy social positioning of people. Without a visual confrontation, it is more difficult to assume knowledge of a writer's identity and perhaps frees the Mass-Observation researcher of some of their prejudices about who an 'ordinary person' might be and what that person might think and say. However, first impressions are not restricted face-to-face encounters. The Mass-Observation writers are met through the materiality of their writing. They are seen in the wobbly script of an elderly person on note paper, the capitals used by someone who wrote little for a living, the mistake free typing of a woman who worked as a secretary all her life, the rapid writing of a busy mother. While it is not possible to reproduce the material form of the writing of many Mass-Observation writers in a book like this, I have attempted to cite enough of their words to provide a modified version of the encounter that occurs when reading Mass-Observation material first hand.

Before a researcher looks at a piece of Mass-Observation writing, he or she would know that it written by a man or a woman as the directive replies are

---

81 Sheridan, Street and Bloome, p. 12.

82 Geertz, p. 18.

83 A comparing between my work and that of Sarah Pink makes clear some of the differences between writing as ethnography and physically 'stepping into the intimate context of the domestic world.' Sarah Pink, *Home Truths: Gender, Objects and Everyday Life* (Oxford: Berg, 2004) p. 1.

archived according to gender; placed in different boxes if sent in by male or female correspondents. This is the only social classification that is used in the archiving practice of Mass-Observation writing; material is grouped by directive and sorted according to the number given to each correspondent to preserve their anonymity. Census type information about each correspondent (occupation, place of residence, date of birth and marital status) is listed but separately from the boxed directive responses while Mass-Observation correspondents are encouraged to provide their own abbreviated autobiography on the opening page of the writing that they return to the Archive. For example, one male correspondent gives quite a bit of detail on the top of his first page, he states 'Age 44 Civil Servant/Artist married two children – girls aged 12/17 Lives in small village E Sussex. Works in east London' (J2187) whereas most follow this shorter format: 'female 39 separated Shetland single parent' (C411). Such information is usefully suggestive but does not fix the identity of the Mass-Observation writers and I have adopted this way of introducing them in my text, always giving their occupation and location but usually privileging (for obvious reasons) the date of their marriage or marriages over other information such as their age. I have avoided terms such as housewife or retired person that quickly conjure up a stereotype unless they are quite explicitly used as a self-description. Similarly, I have not tended to label Mass-Observation correspondents working class or middle class but allowed such social identities to be revealed through their own writing.

Although the encounter with Mass-Observation correspondent is not interpersonal, you neither see them nor know their name, it is nevertheless intimate. When I first began reading Mass-Observation writing I was rather overwhelmed and, I must admit, unsettled, by the way in which the details of material existence brought me such close proximity to other people's lives. There were the unused white towels that a husband found at the back of the airing cupboard after his wife had died, a mother's china carefully preserved for more than a lifetime, a worn out electric iron, a wooden spoon with a burnt handle, the clothes airer that became a pirates ladder and all that Pyrex. It is even possible to suggest that testimonies generated by the solitary and anonymous act of writing can be more intimate than that produced by an interview where the person being interviewed may seek to engage or deflect the interviewer, to please them or guard against them.

My strategy of reading Mass-Observation writing attempted to draw out the meaning of each response as an individual text, interpreting the many small and significant details of everyday domestic life that each piece of writing contained. I also sought to identify similarities and differences across the Giving and Receiving Presents directive as a whole. The recurring themes, such as the opposition but acceptance of the commercialization of giving practices, the preservation of ceramic objects, the hierarchical ordering of domestic material culture gave this book its shape. Shared domestic practices were expressed through the use of the same or very similar language, of which the phrase 'still in use' is the best example. However, since what began to emerge from my reading of Mass-Observation writing was an argument about how the material relationship of married households were part of conformist culture of consumption, when a correspondent represented a different kind of domestic life I paid particular attention to their text.

Significant differences, such as the wholesale rejection of gift-giving practices in the establishment of a home, were only really evident in the writings of single people and long-term cohabitees. It must be emphasized that *The Wedding Present* is an analysis of the material practices of the married household. This is the dominant domestic forms but not by any means the only way to set up home. I want to give the last word to those who have attempted to establish an alternative. Over the page in my conclusion, is an all too brief account of cohabitation and home-making, an important study in domestic material culture in its own right but also useful here because it throws the specific practices of married domesticity into sharper relief.

Chapter 6

Afterword: Unmarried Households

'It is very difficult for people to cobble together their own lives, making up their own rules as they go along, and continually figuring out how everything is supposed to work'
(Patricia Morgan, 2000).[1]

Cohabitation and Marriage: Equal or Different?

The forms of domesticity described in *The Wedding Present* are specific to married households. For example, a hierarchical domestic material culture that allots one of the highest places to wedding presents, preserving these objects as embodiments of family relationships or even as potential inheritances is not, of course, reproduced in homes that do not contain any such gifts. This is not to say that preservation does not occur in other domestic contexts, underpinning the arrangements of homes and securing the survival of objects that have, one way or another, become entwined with the past of that household. The instances of objects outlasting one marriage to become a fixture within another suggest that practices of preservation are not necessarily tied to one version of family life. But I have not presented enough evidence here to make this case. The home as a storehouse can only be taken as a provisional statement about domesticity in general, a way of thinking about it, which could, of course, be proved to be inappropriate, unhelpful or just wrong in contexts other than the married family home.

However, cultures of marriage and cohabitation are not isolated from each other. Another example of from *The Wedding Present* illustrates this. The awkward social dynamics that follow from a bride and groom placing their list at a high street bridal registry are played out between those getting married and their guests. But the effect of material practices are not only limited to those that directly perform them. Now that the gift list has become so closely bound up with the wedding, especially the proper or the big do, cohabiting couples may choose not to get married in order to avoid making a list or participating what one Mass-Observation correspondent called the 'Wedding Present syndrome' (B2728, 1998).

As I have noted before, the 1998 Giving and Receiving Presents directive was addressed primarily to married people but unmarried correspondents were also encouraged to reply. Those that did provided insights into the differences and similarities between giving, receiving and using of objects, between the forms of

---

1 Patricia Morgan, *Marriage-Lite: the Rise of Cohabitation and its Consequences* (London: Institute for the Study of Civil Society, 2000) p. 54.

consumption (if that term is still relevant) associated with married, cohabiting and single households. Their replies generated further questions that it seemed important to ask. At the beginning of July 2003 I re-contacted 14 correspondents who had registered 'a lack of involvement in conventional ways of getting married.'[2] I wrote to one correspondent, a geography teacher from northeast England, whose initial response to questions about weddings was: '*Ughh!*' He explained his reaction:

> As a gay man, these are hardly my favourite occasions – all those people coming together to celebrate 'coupledom.' I have never been married myself (not even an alternative one) and I suppose the closest I've have been to receiving some kind of 'wedding list' was when I moved out of home into my first flat and an aunt bought me some pans – still in use! (A2464, 1998)

Some of his account points to a shared practice of giving and keeping. The aunt may very well have given saucepans as a house-warming present in order to register her approval of her nephew and his single domestic life. Such useful domestic tools, an acceptable gift for a single man as well as a quite conventional marriage gift, allowed her to fulfil the obligation of an older generation to give to a younger one and do so without a wedding. The geography teacher seemed surprised he still has them. He expresses some pride in the durable object although it could also be argued that he hangs on to them for the same reasons that wedding presents are preserved: they represent connections within family, they embody family relationships. But this begs the question of whether the gifts given when people move into a new home, often called moving-in as well as house-warming presents, which are received by married and unmarried alike, really are the equivalents of wedding presents. If he had been leaving home to set up a married household perhaps his aunt would have given him china. Pans are objects of lesser status and significance.

In my follow-up letter to single and unmarried Mass-Observation correspondents I explained that 'I would very much like to find out more about the ways that you, your family and friends have set up home without getting married or have adapted the usual wedding arrangements' and asked:

> How, in your experience, are 'long-term' relationships celebrated and endorsed without marriage? Are gifts presented? If so, what kind of things and by whom? What types of wedding have you attended or participated in? Traditional? Or completely unconventional? Were gifts part of any of these weddings?[3]

The geography teacher replied to this letter, remembering his past remarks about coupledom. 'How things change over the years!' he opened. 'Since 1998 I have been in a 'long term' gay relationship for over three years.' He was not living with his partner but speculated about gift-gifting should that ever happen:

---

2   See Appendix 4. I sent out 14 letters and had five replies. These single or cohabiting correspondents were contacted at the same time as I approached recently married correspondents in order to find out more about how attitudes to wedding presents may change. See Appendix 3.

3   See Appendix 4.

If my partner and I were to set up house together (a possibility…?) I don't think that my family would respond in the 'present giving for the relationship' sense, but we might get a house-warming gift. My family and his father have accepted 'us,' although 'nothing is said.' I do get a Christmas present from his father – this is quite an acceptance – and my family will buy Christmas and Birthday presents for my partner. We do not send Christmas cards from the two of us – we probably would if we lived together. Only my other gay friends would send a Christmas card to both of us and even then I think the envelope would simply be addressed to me (A2464, 2003).

In this scenario, a house-warming gift is a substitute for a wedding present but is not its equivalent. It seems less charged with meaning and therefore an easier gift for parents, who have tacitly rather than openly acknowledged their son's gay relationship, to give. Because house-warming presents are not necessarily for a couple or jointly received by them, their approving effect is diluted. It follows the form of other gift giving practices between the geography teacher, his partner and their families. He describes the exchange of Christmas and birthday presents as signs of 'acceptance' but also indicates that such gifts are given to him or to his partner as individuals. There can be a staged ambiguity giving to unmarried partners, heterosexual as well as gay; a gift to an individual may only recognize the partner as a friend and therefore deny the sexual significance of the relationship. The act of giving and the content of the gift may not specify whether it is intended for a family friend or family member. For the geography teacher, a lack of recognition for relationships other than married ones is demonstrated by the exchange of cards that mark the occasion of a wedding. 'I don't usually bother with sending my parents or my sister a Wedding Anniversary card, although I know they exchange them. I suppose that this is another way in which I feel outside the situation.' His family practices seem part of a wider material and symbolic inequality between married and unmarried relationships that he has observed:

I have only been to traditional weddings…. I have obviously provided a 'traditional' gift for such occasions and have fortunately never been invited to a wedding that has provided an exorbitantly priced wedding list. This would really stick in my craw as I don't think that many of these friends would attend an 'alternative service' for my partner and I – and certainly not with a 'wedding list'! I'm not sure I would want it either! So I suppose that the lack of formalisation of gay relationships leaves them a bit 'out in the cold'. If the latest Government legislation is passed allowing more gay financial rights as long as a civil service is carried out, then perhaps there will be a change here. At the moment I think that gay people do not want to be seen as 'aping' straight relationships…. Two of my female friends are 'out of the loop' as well. One is expecting her second child to the same partner and they simply co-habit. No weddings and anniversaries in the mix here. I also feel that I relate to her as an individual rather than as part of a couple, but I suppose that is the way that I have come to expect to be treated myself…I think my reactions to weddings and anniversaries have remained mainly the same over the years – I don't feel I can fully participate and share in them. Until society changes even more and positively encourages the diversity of all relationships without the requirement of some religious mystique, then I think there will always be some couples existing outside the expected social norm. Of course, there will always be couples deliberately doing this to underline their difference, but would we want to shower them with gifts to recognise this? (A2464, 2003)

As is clear in his reply to the 2003 follow-up letter, he wrote it before the Civil Partnership legislation, enabling what has been dubbed gay marriage with 'almost the same legal rights as those enjoyed by straight married couples'[4] had been passed. The practices of gift giving upon civil partnerships, the extent to which forms of giving upon marriage are adopted, adapted or rejected, will be important to study, especially for those interested in contemporary domestic material culture. However, the geography teacher already anticipates the role that gifts may play in asserting that a civil partnership as the same as marriage. Continued absence would certainly be a sign of continued difference.

In her 1998 Giving and Receiving Presents response, a library assistant based in Dudley in the West Midlands wrote:

> I've never been married so received no presents. It's a pity there's no similar scheme for people setting up home together. 26 years ago when my partner and I moved in together we received the occasional gift from friends or relatives but that was more a 'new house' present. The amount of goods that newly-married couples ask for (and get) amazes me – we 'non-marrieds' definitely lose out in this respect! (T2543, 1998)

Since she does not announce her sexuality, we assume (correctly in this case) that she is discussing cohabitation based on a heterosexual relationship. But she, like the gay Mass-Observation writer, makes the same comparison and distinction between house-warming and wedding presents; the former are fewer in number and they have less material and symbolic weight. They do not seem able, as she explains in her reply to the 2003 follow-up letter, to convey approval for cohabitation in the way that a wedding present simultaneously endorses a marriage and a married home:

> When we first moved in together, it was with the disapproval from our parents, and thought by them to be shocking and scandalous situation, certainly not an event to be celebrated by the giving of presents. The only time I can recall receiving gifts was when we bought our first flat together after renting for about 10 years – we were give a few items for the home as presents, but more to mark our move to a new place than our partnership (T2543, 2003).

The West Midlands library assistant understands why she received no gifts when she began cohabiting in what must have been 1972; she did not seek approval and so the absence of the signs of it is not her main complaint. This is the accumulation of gifts by marrying couples, a process to which she has contributed to without reciprocation. 'We have often joked that having set up home together without being married, we have missed out on all the usual goodies that other couples receive,' she remarks. Attending weddings highlights an unequal gift relationship between cohabitees and

---

4   David Ward, 'Couples Together for 40 Years – or just Two Months – Sign Up to Tie the Knot,' *Guardian* 6 Dec 2005: 6.

those that marry. 'Gifts in abundance for the happy couple, and my partner and I moan about the money we've spent over the years, without receiving any prezzies in return!' The mix of irritation, resignation and humour in these statements makes it difficult to read her attitude but she is clearly asserting that reciprocation should be the rule of the gift and therefore arguing for material equivalence between marriage and cohabitation. The geography teachers makes a similar point; he participates in the rituals of validation of other people's relationship without expecting that such an act, including the giving of a gift, will be reciprocated.[5] But he also reflects upon the possibility of the equal social, even public, acknowledgement for gay relationships without their difference being subsumed by the material culture of marriage.

Is it possible, then to get married, or more precisely, to achieve marital status, without receiving marriage gifts? In the introduction to this book, I noted that of the weddings reported within the Giving and Receiving Present directive very few took place without a gift exchange, suggesting that weddings, just as the marriages that they announce, must be understood as inextricably social and material affairs. There were just two exceptions. A twice-married Suffolk housewife stated that 'I got no presents because both marriages were not approved by any sets of parents' (W1835, 1998). One further case is found in the replies to the 2003 follow-up letter. A London local government officer, who described herself as 'single but with male partner and children' at the time of the Giving and Receiving Presents directive, got married (B2728, 1998). In 1998, she distanced herself from marrying types. 'Because of my age and the attitudes of my peer group, I have been to remarkably few weddings,' she claimed. Her own wedding in the early twenty-first century shunned all ceremony and was almost conducted without involving any family members at all:

> We did it for purely practical reasons to do with pensions, security and children and did our utmost to avoid the trappings of the traditional wedding security of traditional wedding ceremony. Our approach involved using the very unromantic local registry office, telling no one apart from our three children and the two witnesses and the banning (no pun intended!) all additional extras such as photos, hen parties, presents, etc. We disagreed about telling the children. My partner didn't think it was necessary but I felt that because it required a change to their birth certificates it did concern them and it would be better to tell them in a matter of fact way than let them find out later on and think we had concealed our marriage from them (B2728, 2003).

It seems that her and her partner wanted to be married without getting married, or rather to continue cohabiting with the legal reassurances of a marriage. Since she and partner sought neither material or symbolic equivalence to marriage, indeed,

---

5   Aafke Komter's comments upon the gift exchanges as simultaneously empowering and disempowering, inclusive and exclusive, their sociability defining and limiting a network, are interesting in this respect. Aafke Komter, 'The Social and Psychological Significance of Gift Giving in the Netherlands,' *The Gift: an Interdisciplinary Perspective* Ed. Aafke Komter (Amsterdam; Amsterdam University Press) p. 118.

wanted to preserve their cohabitation in all but its 'common law' aspect, no gifts was a requirement of their wedding.

Compared to the 254 responses to the Giving and Receiving Present directive, the few details of gift-giving and long-term relationships outside marriages that I have presented here do not amount to a case study nor approach a thick description. They are merely suggestive and, in the traditions of concluding comments, indicative of further work that must be done. The testimony I have been able cite here does, albeit in quite different ways, indicate the power of the marriage gift to confer approval and to evoke a traditionally dominant version of the family household: respectable, large, long lasting and matriarchal. Indeed, the prohibition of wedding presents at non-traditional weddings demonstrates the difficulty of appropriating gift giving for alternative forms of domestic life. But a much more focussed and thorough investigation of gift giving practices for and in single and cohabiting households could, for example, identify more precisely the status of a gift for a new home. It could also ask whether, once an unmarried household is established, gifts sustain a domesticity of a different order. Is there a material culture of cohabitation distinct from that of marriage, dependent upon domestic practices unlike those of preservation and hierarchical organization that have been described in this book? Again I do not have enough detail to begin to answer this question but only open up a line of inquiry. So, to quote from the Giving and Receiving Presents directive for the final time. The Mass-Observation correspondent from the West Midlands, library assistant and long-term cohabitee contrasted her home with that of a newly wed:

> Our possessions are a motley collection of what we each owned when we teamed up, odd unmatching crockery and cutlery, books, pictures and ornaments. No smart matching china dinner-services for us! Most of our stuff now is what we've bought together since but much still remains form our original collections (T2543, 1998).

Despite her complaints about material inequities of cohabitation, she displays a sense of pride in a domestic culture of making do. This is another form of the practice of preservation. Furthermore, regardless of her lasting commitment to cohabitation in opposition to marriage, she honours the wedding presents that belonged to her mother:

> Many items still in constant use in the household today were originally wedding presents to my parents in 1933. The quality of goods over 65 years ago was obviously exceptional – things were made to last, unlike the 'instant obsolescence' of today. My everyday cutlery (knives + forks, in 2 sizes, desert spoons + tablespoons in stainless steel, the knives with bone handles) was a wedding present to my mother by a rather well-to-do sister in law. I remember mother telling me how she went to 'the top shop' in Birmingham to choose the best available and they've certainly proved their worth! I also have cut-glass from my parents' wedding presents, including a large bowl which is used for the Christmas sherry trifle. These things aren't kept in any special place in the house but live in the kitchen cupboards together with other households utensils + are used every day (T2543, 1998).

After writing a book about married domesticity, many of its material forms and practices are represented here, woven into an account of cohabitation: kept objects, durable and fragile objects, both highly valued but used differently, as well as things reserved for special occasions, wedding presents that have become a maternal inheritance, objects that embody familial relationships and tell family narratives. The cutlery contains a story of a mother's once in a lifetime visit to the best shop. However, the cohabiting household, as revealed through this small piece of Mass-Observation writing, is more disorderly. Objects kept for special occasions are jumbled up in the kitchen cupboards with all the everyday things. There does not seem to be a clear separation between the sacred and the profane. Cohabitation may be similar to married domesticity because it has adopted some of its housekeeping practices, but is much more messy, materially and socially, and its meanings are consequently less secure.

Bibliography

Adorno, Theodor. *Minima Moralia*. 1951. London: Verso, 1997.

Aldridge, Alan. *Consumption*. Cambridge: Polity Press, 2003.

Appadurai, Ajun. Ed. *The Social Life of Things: Commodities in Cultural Perspective*. Cambridge: Cambridge University Press, 1986.

Ashplant, T. G., Graham Dawson, and Michael Roper. 'The Politics of War Memory and Commemoration: Contexts, Structures, Dynamics.' *Commemorating War: The Politics of Memory*. Ed. T. G. Ashplant, Graham Dawson and Michael Roper. London: Routledge, 2000, pp. 3–85.

Atterbury, Paul, and Louise Irvine. *The Doulton Story*. London: Victoria and Albert Museum, 1979.

Attfield, Judith. 'Moving Home: Changing Attitudes to Residence and Identity.' *Journal of Architecture* 7 (2002) pp. 249–262.

Attfield, Judy. *Wild Things: The Material Culture of Everyday Life*. Oxford: Berg, 2000.

Attfield, Judith. 'Inside Pram Town: a Case Study of Harlow House Interiors, 1951–1961.' *View from the Interior: Feminism: Women and Design*. Ed. Judy Attfield and Pat Kirkham. London: The Women's Press, 1989, pp. 215–238.

Baker, John C. 'James A. Jobling & Co. Ltd., Subsequently Corning Ltd., Manufacturer of PYREX Brand Glassware.' *Pyrex: Sixty Years of Design*. Tyne and Wear County Council Museums, 1983, pp. 6–11.

Barrell, John. 'Visualising the Division of Labour: William Pyne's 'Microcosm."' *The Arts, Literature and Society*. Ed. Arthur Marwick. London: Routledge, 1990, pp. 95–132.

Beck, Ulrich, Anthony Giddens, and Scott Lash. *Reflexive Modernization*. Cambridge: Cambridge University Press, 1994.

Belk, Russell W., Melanie Wallendorf, and John F. Sherry. 'The Sacred and the Profane in Consumer Behaviour: Theodicy on the Odyssey.' *Journal of Consumer Research* 6 (June 1989) pp. 1–38.

Belk, Russell W. *Collecting in a Consumer Society*. London: Routledge, 1995.

Belk, Russell W., Melanie Wallendorf, and John F. Sherry. 'The Sacred and Profane in Consumer Behaviour: Theodicy on the Odyssey.' *Journal of Consumer Research* 16 (1989) pp. 1–38.

Benedict Anderson. *Imagined Communities: Reflections on the Origins and Spread of Nationalism*. London: Verso, 1983.

Berg, Maxine. 'New Commodities, Luxuries and their Consumers in Eighteenth-century England.' *Consumers and Luxury: Consumer Culture and Europe 1650–*

1850. Ed. Maxine Berg and Helen Clifford. Manchester: Manchester University Press, 1999, pp. 63–85.

Black, Lawrence. *The Political Culture of the Left in Affluent Britain, 1951–64: Old Labour, New Britain?* Basingstoke: Palgrave, 2003.

Boden, Sharon. *Consumerism, Romance and the Wedding Experience.* Basingstoke: Palgrave, 2003.

Bourdieu, Pierre. *Distinction: A Social Critique of the Judgement of Taste.* 1979. London: Routledge, 1989.

Breward, Christopher. *The Hidden Consumer: Masculinities, Fashion and City 1860–1914.* Manchester: Manchester University Press, 1999.

Brewer, John, and Roy Porter, eds. *Consumption and the World of Goods.* London: Routledge, 1994.

Brewis, Monica. "The Garden that I Love': Middle Class Identity, Gender and the English Domestic Garden, 1880–1914,' unpublished Ph.D thesis. University of Brighton, 2004.

Buchli, Victor, Alison Clarke and Dell Upton. 'Editorial.' *Home Cultures* 1.1 (2004) pp. 1–3.

Burman, Sandra. *Fit Work for Women.* London: Croom Helm, 1979.

Campbell, Colin. *The Romantic Ethic and the Spirit of Modern Consumerism.* Oxford: Blackwell, 1987.

Carrier, James G. *Gifts and Commodities: Exchange and Western Capitalism since 1700.* London: Routledge, 1995.

Chaney, David. *Cultural Change and Everyday Life.* Basingstoke: Palgrave, 2002.

Cheal, David. *The Gift Economy.* London: Routledge, 1988.

Cieraad, Irene, ed. *At Home: An Anthropology of Domestic Space.* New York: Syracuse University Press, 1999.

Clarke, Alison J. 'The Aesthetics of Social Aspiration.' *Home Possessions: Material Culture Behind Closed Doors.* Ed. Daniel Miller. Oxford: Berg, 2000, pp. 23–46.

Clarke, Alison J. 'Window Shopping at Home: Classifieds, Catalogues and New Consumer Skills.' *Material Cultures: Why Some Things Matter.* Ed. Daniel Miller London: UCL Press, 1998, pp. 73–99.

Clarke, Alison J. *Tupperware: The Promise of Plastic in 1950s America.* Washington: Smithsonian Institution Press, 1999.

Clifford, James. *The Predicament of Culture: Twentieth Century Ethnography, Literature, and Art.* Cambridge, MA : Harvard University Press, 1988.

Cohen, A. P. 'Informants.' *Ethnographic Research: A Guide to General Conduct.* Ed. R. F. Ellen, London: Academic Press, 1984, pp. 225–229.

Corrigan, Peter. 'Gender and the Gift: The Case of the Family Clothing Economy.' *Sociology* 23.4 (1989) pp. 513–34.

Corrigan, Peter. *The Sociology of Consumption.* London: Sage, 1997.

Csikszentmihalyi, Mihaly, and Eugene Rochberg-Halton. *The Meaning of Things: Domestic Symbols and the Self.* Cambridge: Cambridge University Press, 1981.

Davidoff Leonore and Catherine Hall. *Family Fortunes: Men and Women of the English Middle Class 1780–1850*. Revised ed. London: Hutchinson, 2002.

Davidoff, Leonore, et al. *The Family Story: Blood, Contract and Intimacy 1830–1960*. London: Longman, 1999.

Davidoff, Leonore. 'Class and Gender in Victorian England.' *Sex and Class in Women's History*, Ed. Judith L. Newton, Mary P. Ryan and Judith Walkowitz. London: Routledge and Kegan Paul, 1983, pp. 17–71.

Davidoff, Leonore. 'The Rationalisation of Housework.' *Dependence and Exploitation in Work and Marriage*. Ed. Diane Leone Barker and Shelia Allen. London: Longman, 1976, pp. 143–148.

Davidoff, Leonore. *Worlds Between: Historical Perspectives on Gender and Class* Cambridge: Polity, 1995.

Delphy, Christine. *Close to Home: A Materialist Analysis of Women's Oppression*. London: Hutchinson, 1984.

Dilnot, Clive. 'The Gift.' *Design Issues* IX. 2 (1993) pp. 51–63.

Douglas, Mary, and Baron Isherwood. *The World of Goods: Towards an Anthropology of Consumption*. London: Allen Lane, 1979.

Duncan, Carol. *Civilizing Rituals: Inside Public Art Museums*. London: Routledge, 1995.

Earle, Mrs. C. W. *More Pot-Pourri from a Surrey Garden*. London, Smith, Elder, 1899.

Longhurst, Brian, and Mike Savage. 'Social Class, Consumption and the Influence of Bourdieu: Some Critical Issues.' *Consumption Matters: The Production and Experience of Consumpion*. Ed. Stephen Edgell, Kevin Hetherington and Alan Warde. Oxford: Blackwell, 1996, pp. 274–301.

Edwards, Elizabeth. 'Photography as Objects of Evidence.' *Material Memories*. Ed. Marius Kwint, Chris Breward and Jeremy Aynsley. Oxford: Berg, 1999, pp. 221–236.

Ermisch, John, and Marco Francesconi. *Cohabitation in Great Britain: Not for Long, but Here to Stay*. Colchester: Institute for Social and Economic Research, University of Essex, 1998.

Evans, Stuart. 'PYREX Glassware, a Commentary on Sixty Years of Design.' *Pyrex: Sixty Years of Design*. Tyne and Wear County Council Museums, 1983. 21–40.

Eyles, Desmond. *Royal Doulton 1815–1965: The Rise and Expansion of the Royal Doulton Potteries*. London: Hutchinson, 1965.

Fine, Ben, and Ellen Leopold. *The World of Consumption*. London: Routledge, 1993.

Slater, Don. *Consumer Culture and Modernity*. Cambridge: Polity Press, 1997.

Forty, Adrian. *Objects of Desire*. London: Thames and Hudson, 1986.

Foucault, Michel. *The Order of Things: The Archaeology of the Human Sciences*. London: Tavistock, 1970.

Frankenburg, R. 'British Community Studies: Problems of Synthesis.' *The Social Anthropology of Complex Societies*. Ed. M. Banton. London: Tavistock, 1966.

Geertz, Clifford. *The Interpretation of Cultures*, 1973. London: Fontana, 1993.

Gell, Alfred. 'Vogel's Net: Traps as Artworks and Artworks as Traps.' *Journal of Material Culture* 1.1 (1996) pp. 15–38.

Gillis, John. R. *For Better, For Worse: British Marriages, 1600 to the Present.* Oxford: Oxford University Press, 1985.

Godbout, Jacques T., with Alain Caille. *The World of the Gift.* Montreal: McGill-Queens Univeristy Press, 1998.

Godlier, Maurice. *The Enigma of the Gift.* Cambridge: Polity Press, 1999.

Goffman, Erving. *The Presentation of Self in Everyday Life.* London: Penguin, 1990.

Gough-Yates, Anna. *Understanding Women's Magazines: Publishing, Markets and Readerships.* London: Routledge, 2003.

Gregory, C. A. *Gifts and Commodities.* London: Academic Press, 1982.

Gullestad, Marianne. *Kitchen-table Society.* Oslo: Universitetsforlaget, 1984.

Gullestad, Marianne. *The Art of Social Relations: Essays on Culture, Social Action and Everyday Life in Modern Norway.* Oslo: Scandinavian University Press, 1992.

Gunn, Simon. 'The Middle Class, Modernity and the Provincial City: Manchester c1840–1880.' *Gender, Civic Culture and Consumerism.* Ed. Alan Kidd and David Nicholls. Manchester: Manchester University Press, 1999, pp. 112–127.

Hall, Catherine. *White, Male and Middle-class.* Cambridge: Polity Press, 1992.

Hebdige, Dick. *Hiding in the Light: On Images and Things.* London: Routledge, 1988.

Highmore, Ben. *Everyday Life and Cultural Theory: An Introduction.* London: Routledge, 2002.

Hooper-Greenhill, Eilean, *Museums and the Shaping of Knowledge.* London: Routledge, 1992.

Ingraham, Chrys. *White Weddings: Romancing Heterosexuality in Popular Culture* London: Routledge, 1999.

Jackson Stevi, and Shaun Moores, eds. *The Politics of Domestic Consumption: Critical Readings.* London: Harvester Wheatsheaf 1995.

Jobling, Paul, and David Crowley. *Graphic Design: Reproduction and Representation since 1800.* Manchester: Manchester University Press, 1996.

Johnson, Richard and Deborah Chambers, Parvati Raghuram, Estella Tincknell. *The Practice of Cultural Studies.* London: Sage, 2004.

Jordanova, Ludmilla, 'Objects of Knowledge.' *The New Museology.* Ed. Peter Vergo. London: Reaktion Books, 1989, pp. 22–40.

Kelly, Joan. *Women, History and Theory: The Essays of Joan Kelly.* Chicago: University of Chicago Press, 1984.

Kiernan, Kathleen E., and Valerie Estaugh. *Cohabitation: Extra-marital Childbearing and Social Policy.* London: Family Policy Studies Centre, 1993.

Kitchen, Juliet. 'Interiors: Nineteenth-century Essays on the 'Masculine' and 'Feminine' Room.' *The Gendered Object.* Ed. Pat Kirkham. Manchester: Manchester University Press, 1996, pp. 12–29.

Knell, Simon, ed. *Museums and the Future of Collecting*. Aldershot: Ashgate, 1999.

Komter, Aafke. 'Hidden Power in Marriage.' *Self and Society*. Ed. Ann Branaman. Malden, MA: Blackwell, 2001, pp. 359–380.

Komter, Aafke. 'Women, Gifts and Power.' *The Gift: An Interdisciplinary Perspective*. Ed. Aafke Komter. Amsterdam: Amsterdam University Press, 1996, pp. 119–131.

Kopytoff, Igor. 'The Cultural Biography of Things: Commoditization as Process.' *The Social Life of Things: Commodities in Cultural Perspective*. Ed. Arun Appadurai. Cambridge: Cambridge University Press, 1986, pp. 64–91.

Kwint, Marius. 'Introduction.' *Material Memories*. Ed. Marius Kwint, Chris Breward and Jeremy Aynsley. Oxford: Berg, 1999, pp. 1–16.

Barker, Diana Leonard, and Sheila Allen. eds. *Dependence and Exploitation in Work and Marriage*. London: Longman, 1976.

Leonard, Diana. *Sex and Generation: A Study of Courtship and Weddings*. London: Tavistock, 1980.

Lewis, Jane, *Women in Britain since 1945: Women, Family, Work and the State in the Post-War Years*. Oxford: Blackwell, 1992.

Lowrey, Tina M. and Cele Otnes. 'Construction of a Meaningful Wedding: Differences in the Priorities of Brides and Grooms.' *Gender Issues and Consumer Behaviour*. Ed. J. A. Costa. Thousand Oaks: Sage, 1994, pp. 164–183.

Lunt, Peter, and Sonia Livingstone. *Mass Consumption and Personal Identity*. Buckingham: Open University Press, 1992.

Lury, Celia. *Consumer Culture*. London: Polity Press, 1996.

Mackay, Hugh. 'Consuming Technologies at Home.' *Consumption and Everyday Life*. Ed. Hugh Mackay. London: Sage, 1997, pp. 259–308.

Mankowitz, Wolf. *Wedgwood*. London: Spring Books, 1966.

Mansfield, Penny, and Jean Collard. *The Beginning of the Rest of Your Life: A Portrait of Newly-wed Marriage*. Basingstoke: Macmillan, 1988.

Mauss, Marcel. *The Gift: The Form and Reason for Exchange in Archaic Societies*. 1925. London: Routledge, 1990.

McCracken, Ellen. *Decoding Women's Magazines: From Mademoiselle to Ms*. Basingstoke: Macmillan, 1993.

McCracken, Grant. *Culture and Consumption: New Approaches to the Symbolic Character of Consumer Goods and Activities*. Bloomington: Indiana University Press, 1988.

McGarth, Mary Ann, and Basil Englis. 'Intergenerational Gift Giving in Subcultural Wedding Celebrations: The Ritual as Cash Cow.' *Gift Giving: A Research Anthology*. Ed. Cele Otnes and Richard F. Beltramini. Bowling Green State University Popular Press, 1996, pp. 123–141.

McGuigan, Jim, ed. *Cultural Methodologies*. London: Sage 1997.

McKendrick Neil. 'Commercialisation and the Economy.' *The Birth of a Consumer Society: The Commercialisation of Eighteenth-Century England*. Neil McKendrick, John Brewer, and J.H. Plumb. London: Hutchinson, 1983.

McRae, Susan. *Cohabiting Mothers: Changing Marriage and Motherhood?* London: Policy Studies Institute, 1993.

Miller, Daniel. 'Appropriating the State on the Council Estate.' *Man* 23 (1988) pp. 353–372.

Miller, Daniel. *A Theory of Shopping.* Cambridge: Polity Press, 1998.

Miller, Daniel. 'Appropriating the State on the Council Estate.' *Man* 23 (1988) pp. 352–72.

Miller, Daniel. 'Consumption and its Consequences.' *Consumption and Everyday Life.* Ed. Hugh Mackay. London: Sage Publications, 1997, pp. 14–63.

Miller, Daniel. 'Consumption as the Vanguard of History.' *Acknowledging Consumption.* Ed. Daniel Miller. London: Routledge, 1995, pp. 1–57.

Miller, Daniel. 'Possessions.' *Home Possessions. Material Culture behind Closed Doors.* Ed. Daniel Miller. Oxford: Berg, 2001, pp. 1–14.

Miller, Daniel. 'Why Some Things Matter.' *Material Culture: Why Some Things Matter.* Ed. Daniel Miller. London: UC L Press, 1998, pp. 3–21.

Mitchell, Clyde J. 'Case Studies.' *Ethnographic Research: A Guide to General Conduct.* Ed. R. Ellen. London: Academic Press, 1984, pp. 237–241.

Morgan, Patricia. *Farewell to the Family? Public Policy and Family Breakdown in Britain and the USA.* London: The IEA Health and Welfare Unit, 1995.

Morgan, Patricia. *Marriage-Lite: The Rise of Cohabitation and its Consequences.* London: Institute for the Study of Civil Society, 2000.

Murdock, Graham. 'Thin Descriptions: Questions of Method in Cultural Analysis.' *Cultural Methodologies.* Ed. Jim McGuigan. London: Sage, 1997, pp. 178–192.

Myers, Kathy. 'Towards a Theory of Consumption. Tu: a Cosmetic Case Study.' *BLOCK* 7 (1982) pp. 48–59.

Nippert-Eng, C. E. *Home and Work.* Chicago: Chicago University Press, 1995.

Osteen, Mark, ed. *The Question of the Gift: Essays across Disciplines.* London: Routledge, 2002.

Otes, Cele, and Elizabeth Pleck, *Cinderella Dreams: the Allure of the Lavish Wedding.*Berkeley: University of California Press, 2003.

Otnes, Cele, and Tina M. Lowrey. 'Til Debt Do Us Part: the Selection and Meaning of Artifacts in the American Wedding.' *Advances in Consumer Research* 20 (1993) pp. 325–329.

Pahl, R. E., ed. *On Work: Historical, Comparative and Theoretical Approaches.* Oxford, Blackwell, 1988.

Papenek, Victor J. *Design for the Real World: Human Ecology and Social Change* St Albans: Paladin, 1974.

Parry, Jonathan, and Maurice Bloch. 'Introduction: Money and the Morality of Exchange.' *Money and the Morality of the Exchange.* Ed. Jonathan Parry and Maurice Bloch. Cambridge: Cambridge University Press, 1989, pp. 1–32.

Pearce, Susan M. *Collecting in Contemporary Practice.* London: Sage, 1998.

Pearce, Susan M. *Museums, Objects and Collections.* Leicester: Leicester University Press, 1992.

Pearce, Susan M. *On Collecting: An Investigation into collecting in the European Tradition*. London: Routledge, 1995.

Peplar, Michael. *Family Matters: A History of Ideas about the Family since 1945*. Harlow: Pearson Education Limited, 2002.

Pink, Sarah. *Home Truths: Gender, Objects and Everyday Life*. Oxford: Berg, 2004.

David Pocock 'Introduction.' *Movable Feasts*. Ed. A. Palmer, Oxford: Oxford University Press, 1984, pp. xi–xxxiv.

Pringle, Rosemary. 'Women and Consumer Capitalism.' *Defining Women: Social Institutions and Gender Divisions*. Ed. Linda McDowell and Rosemary Pringle. Cambridge: Polity Press, 1992, pp. 148–152.

Putnam, Tim, and Charles Newton, eds. *Household Choices*. Futures Publications and Middlesex Polytechnic, 1990.

Rappaport, Erika. *Shopping for Pleasure: Women in the Making of London's West End*. Princeton: Princeton University Press, 2000.

Reilly, Robin. *Wedgwood: The New Illustrated Dictionary*. Woodbridge: Suffolk: Antique Collectors' Club, 1995.

Reimer, Suzanne, and Deborah Leslie. 'Identity, Consumption and the Home.' *Home Cultures* 1.2 (2004) p. 192

Richards, Sarah. *Eighteenth-century Ceramics: Products for a Civilised Society*. Manchester: Manchester University Press, 1999.

Rook, Dennis W. 'The Ritual Dimension of Consumer Behaviour.' *Journal of Consumer Research* 12 (December 1985) pp. 251–264.

Rose, Sonya O. ''Gender at Work': Sex, Class and Industrial Capitalism.' *History Workshop Journal* 21 (Spring 1986) pp. 113–131.

Scanlon, Jennifer, ed. *The Gender and Consumer Culture Reader*. New York: New York University, 2000.

Schofield, John, William Gray Johnston, and Colleen. M. Beck. 'Introduction: Materiel Culture in the Modern World.' *Materiel Culture: The Archaeology of Twentieth-century Conflict*. Eds. John Schofield, William Gray Johnston and Colleen. M. Beck. London: Routledge, 2002, pp. 1–8

Scott, Gill. *Feminism and the Politics of Working Women: The Women's Co-operative Guild, 1880s to the Second World War*. London: UCL Press, 1998.

Shaw, Cindy and Stuart Evans, 'Technical History.' *Pyrex: Sixty Years of Design*. Tyne and Wear County Council Museums, 1983, pp. 13–20.

Sheridan, Dorothy, Brian Street, and David Bloome. *Writing Ourselves: Mass Observation and Literacy Practices*. New Jersey: Hampton Press, 2000.

Sheridan, Dorothy. '"Damned Anecdotes and Dangerous Confabulations": Mass-Observation as Life History,' *Mass-Observation Archive Occasional Paper*, No. 7. Brighton: University of Sussex Library, 1996.

Silverstone, Roger, and E. Hirsch. *Consuming Technologies: Media and Information in Domestic Spaces*. London: Routledge, 1992.

Smart, Carol, and Pippa Stevens, *Cohabitation Breakdown*. London: Family Policy Studies Centre for the Joseph Rowntree Foundation, 2000.

Smith, Adam. *Wealth of Nations I–III*, 1776. London: Penguin Books, 1986.

Stephen Edgell, Kevin Etherington, and Alan Warde, eds. *Consumption Matters: The Production and Experience of Consumption*. Oxford: Blackwell/The Sociological Review, 1996.

Stewart, Susan. *On Longing: Narratives of the Miniature, the Gigantic, the Souvenir, the Collection*. Durham: Duke University Press, 1993.

Stoke-on-Trent Museum and Art Gallery. The *Legacy of Henry Doulton: 120 Years of Royal Doulton in Burslem, 1877–1997*. Stoke-on-Trent: Stoke-on-Trent Museum and Art Gallery, 1997.

Stone, Lawrence. *Road to Divorce: England 1530–1987*. Oxford: Oxford University Press, 1990.

Strathern, Marilyn. *The Gender of the Gift: Problems with Women and Problems with Society in Melanesia*. Berkeley: University of California, 1988.

Swales, Valerie M. 'Making Yourself at Home: A Study in Discourse.' *Household Choices*. Ed. Tim Putnam and Charles Newton. Futures Publications and Middlesex Polytechnic, 1990, pp. 103–118.

Thompson, F. M. L., ed. *The Rise of Suburbia*. Leicester: Leicester University Press, 1982.

Veblen, Thorstein. *The Theory of the Leisure Class*. 1989. New York: Dover Publications, 1994.

Vincentelli, Moira. *Women and Ceramics: Gendered Vessels*. Manchester: Manchester University Press, 2000.

Weatherill, Lorna. *Consumer Behaviour and Material Culture in Britain 1660–1760*. 1988. London: Routledge, 1996.

Weiner, Annette, *Inalienable Possessions: The Paradox of Keeping-While-Giving*. Berkeley: University of California Press, 1992.

Werbner, Pnina. *The Migration Process: Capital, Gifts and Offerings among British Pakistanis*. Oxford: Berg, 2002

Williams, Raymond. *The Country and the City*. London: Hogarth Press, 1985.

Winship, Janice. *Inside Women's Magazines*. London: Pandora, 1987.

Appendices

3. Wedding presents

Most of this section applies to people who have got married. However, if you are unmarried, please do feel free to comment on the questions in relation to the experiences of your friends and relatives.

YOUR WEDDING PRESENTS
Please start by giving the year of your wedding, and if you have been married more than once, please give answers for each separate occasion.
Please also briefly describe the kind of wedding you had, whether it was religious or civil. If religious, it would help to have some background about your faith, and any traditions which affected present-giving.

You might find it helps to do a sort of list. We realise it may be a long time ago, so anything you can remember would be helpful.

What gifts did you receive? Please be as detailed as possible - if you can recall not only the items, but also the make and design of objects, that would be appreciated.
Who gave you gifts? Close family? Friends? Employers? Colleagues?
When did you receive them? At the wedding, before or after?
Did you have a formal list? How was it organised?
Which gifts have you kept? When are they used and where do you keep them?
What memories do they hold for you?

Were you ever given gifts of money? Or second-hand things, like furniture?

Did you collect things for your married household? Did you have a 'bottom-drawer'? And what things did you buy for you new home? Were these things different from your gifts?

FAMILY WEDDING PRESENTS
Do you keep any of parents' wedding presents? Or wedding presents given to other members of your family? When are they used and where are they kept?

Appendix 1

PART II: OBJECTS ABOUT THE HOUSE

(Please start your answer on a SEPARATE sheet)

When future generations try to understand how we lived in our homes they will have a
great many images to help them, both the glossy images of advertising and family
snaps. But neither of these sources will tell much about what we think and feel
about the objects we've gathered round us and how those feelings have changed over
time.

Some objects, clearly, have   aesthetic value and others have a sentimental value for
a special reason. But we are also thinking of the things which have 'stood the test
of time', because they've served us well or given continuing pleasure. And you may
fondly remember things you had, reluctantly, to discard for some reason. We would
like you to tell us about the things of which you are most fond, and why. Include
examples of those which have lasted well, or which you now miss, even if they don't
have a special sentimental importance, remember not to overlook objects just because
they are either very large or very small. On the other hand, we all have made
purchases which we later came to regret, even though they seemed all right at the
time. Some objects around the house may not have lasted well, or don't look the same
in today's light. Please tell us about these things as well, and why your feelings
about them have changed.

A list of half a dozen objects of each sort, with your feelings about them, will
leave a fine record for tomorrow's historians. But if you would like to add
reflections on other 'favourites' and 'follies', that's also welcome.

Please try to give <u>detailed descriptions</u> of unusual objects.

David Pocock

Appendix 2

Faculty of Arts and Architecture

University of Brighton

l.purbrick@bton.ac.uk
01273 230295/6

School of Historical
and Critical Studies

1st July 2003

Giving and Receiving Presents Directive Autumn 1998

Dear Mass-Observation correspondent

10 -11 Pavilion Parade
Brighton BN2 1RA
Telephone 01273 600900
Fax 01273 681935

I am hoping that you will remember writing a response to the Giving and Receiving Presents Directive sent out in autumn 1998. I am the researcher, now based at the University of Brighton, who co-wrote the section on Wedding Presents. I am working on a book about the significance of objects in domestic life. Much of it is devoted to the analysis of those things formally given and received upon marriage but I am also concerned to represent non-traditional as well as traditional ways of formalising and celebrating a partnership.

I found your response to the 1998 Giving and Receiving Presents Directive very helpful because you registered a lack of involvement in conventional ways of getting married. I would very much like to find out more about the ways you, your family or friends have set up home without getting married or have adapted the usual wedding arrangements. Would you mind responding to the following questions? Your reply would be treated with the same confidentiality and respect as a formal directive.

How, in your experience, are 'long-term' relationships celebrated and endorsed without marriage? Are gifts presented? If so, what kind of things and by whom?

What types of wedding have you attended or participated in? Traditional? Or completely unconventional? Were gifts part of any of these weddings?

Could you send your response to the Archive? I am sure you know the address but in case it is not to hand it is:
The Mass Observation Archive
The Library
FREEPOST
BR2112
The University of Sussex
Brighton
BN1 1ZX

You are very welcome to write or talk directly to me, especially if you would like to find out more about my research and how I have used the Mass-Observation Archive in my work.

I am very grateful for your time and will look forward to hearing from you.
Yours

Appendix 3

Faculty of Arts and Architecture

University of Brighton

School of Historical
and Critical Studies

l.purbrick@bton.ac.uk
01273 643085/6

10th July 2003

10 -11 Pavilion Parade

Giving and Receiving Presents Directive Autumn 1998   Brighton BN2 1RA

Telephone 01273 600900

Dear Mass-Observation correspondent   Fax 01273 681935

I am hoping that you will remember writing a response to the Giving and Receiving Presents directive sent out in autumn 1998. I am the researcher, now based at the University of Brighton, who co-wrote the section on Wedding Presents. I am working on a book that explores how people created their homes when they married and how they have subsequently used, preserved or disposed of their wedding presents. The working title of the book is *The Wedding Present.*

I found your response to the 1998 Giving and Receiving Presents Directive very helpful and would very much like to find out what has happened to your wedding presents since then. Would you mind responding to the following questions? Your reply would be treated with the same confidentiality and respect as a formal directive.

Have your feelings changed about any of the gifts you received when you married in [date of wedding]*? And, why?*

Which gifts, if any, are still used or displayed? Have any been broken, lost, given or thrown away?

Do you still like all of them? Some? None?

Could you send your response to the Archive? I am sure you know the address but in case it is not to hand it is:
The Mass Observation Archive
The Library
FREEPOST
BR2112
The University of Sussex
Brighton
BN1 1ZX

You are very welcome to write or talk directly to me, especially if you would like to find out more about my research and how I have used the Mass-Observation Archive in my work.

I am very grateful for your time and will look forward to hearing from you.

Yours

Appendix 4

Index